GETTING A LIFE

GETTING A LIFE

The Social Worlds of Geek Culture

BENJAMIN WOO

McGill-Queen's University Press

Montreal & Kingston · London · Chicago

© McGill-Queen's University Press 2018

ISBN 978-0-7735-5284-5 (cloth)
ISBN 978-0-7735-5295-1 (ePDF)
ISBN 978-0-7735-5296-8 (ePUB)

Legal deposit first quarter 2018
Bibliothèque nationale du Québec

Printed in Canada on acid-free paper that is 100% ancient forest free
(100% post-consumer recycled), processed chlorine free

This book has been published with the help of a grant from the Canadian Federation
for the Humanities and Social Sciences, through the Awards to Scholarly Publications
Program, using funds provided by the Social Sciences and Humanities Research
Council of Canada.

We acknowledge the support of the Canada Council for the Arts, which last year
invested $153 million to bring the arts to Canadians throughout the country. Nous
remercions le Conseil des arts du Canada de son soutien. L'an dernier, le Conseil a
investi 153 millions de dollars pour mettre de l'art dans la vie des Canadiennes et des
Canadiens de tout le pays.

Library and Archives Canada Cataloguing in Publication

Woo, Benjamin, author
     Getting a life : the social worlds of Geek culture / Benjamin Woo.

     Includes bibliographical references and index.
     Issued in print and electronic formats.
     ISBN 978-0-7735-5284-5 (cloth). – ISBN 978-0-7735-5295-1 (ePDF). –
     ISBN 978-0-7735-5296-8 (ePUB)

     1. Subculture. 2. Fans (Persons). 3. Individuality. 4. Mass media
and culture. 5. Popular culture. I. Title.

HM646.W66 2018   306'.1   C2017-906099-6
                                                        C2017-906100-3

This book was set by True to Type in 10.5/13 Sabon

Contents

Acknowledgments vii

Introduction: "What Is a Nerd?" 3

1 Talk Nerdy to Me: The Meaning of Geek Culture 29

2 Taking Geek Culture Seriously: A Practice-Theoretic
Account 49

3 Values and Virtues: What Is Best in Life? 67

4 Careers: Boldly Going On 89

5 Making Communities from Mass Culture 108

6 Institutions: Building Worlds between Production
and Consumption 131

7 The Limits of Participation 152

8 The Geek, the Bad, and the Ugly 172

Conclusion 191

Appendix: Participant Profiles 203

Notes 231

References 237

Index 257

Acknowledgments

I've been living with this book, in various forms, for quite some time now, and it has left a trail of people who need to be thanked criss-crossing the country.

I once again offer my greatest and sincerest thanks to the many people who agreed to speak with me, at length, about their lives. This book could not possibly exist without your generosity, and it wouldn't be what it is without your warmth, wit, and insight. Having smart, articulate interviewees makes it look easy. Thank you.

At Simon Fraser University, I am grateful to the faculty who enabled and supervised the original research on which the book is based, notably Gary McCarron, Shane Gunster, and Stuart R. Poyntz; to the Social Sciences and Humanities Research Council for funding the project through the doctoral fellowships program; and to the friends and colleagues who kept me on track – and helped me find it again whenever I went astray. I want to extend particular thanks to Danielle Deveau, Sara Grimes, Dylan Mulvin, Siobhàn Quinn, Jamie Rennie, and Rebecca Scott Yoshizawa.

My first attempts at revising the manuscript into publishable form were undertaken while I was a SSHRC postdoctoral fellow at the University of Calgary, and I owe an inestimable debt to Bart Beaty for making that opportunity possible, as well as to Rebecca Sullivan, Christian Bök, my fellow postdoc Paul Huebener, and the graduate student community in the Department of English for welcoming me with such hospitality.

The final push came during my first years on faculty in the Communication and Media Studies program at Carleton University, and I was given the opportunity to return to some of the ideas in this book in the context of a graduate seminar I taught there in the winter of 2015.

I feel very lucky to have landed in this department and am privileged to have truly outstanding, supportive colleagues. I offer my thanks to the writing group that applauded the feathers in my cap and commiserated with my black eyes during the last rounds of revisions: Aubrey Anable, Laura Banducci, Rena Bivens, Amrita Hari, Christian Holz, Laura Horak, Irena Knezevic, Tracey Lauriault, Merlyna Lim, and Megan Rivers-Moore. Responsibility for any errors remain, of course, mine alone.

My editor at McGill-Queen's University Press, Jonathan Crago, has been a steadfast supporter of this book. I am deeply appreciative of his work guiding me through the publication process. I want to further express my thanks to the rest of the team at MQUP who helped make it a reality. The book is much stronger for the application of copyeditor Kathryn Simpson's proverbial red pen.

Some of this research has been previously published in somewhat different forms: a précis of the book's argument was published under the title "Nerds, Geeks, Gamers, and Fans: Doing Subculture on the Edge of the Mainstream" in the edited collection *The Borders of Subculture: Resistance and the Mainstream* (Woo 2015); an earlier version of chapter 6 appeared as "Alpha Nerds: Cultural Intermediaries in a Subcultural Scene" in *The European Journal of Cultural Studies* (Woo 2012a); and sections of chapters 3 and 7 were adapted into "Understanding Understandings of Comics: Reading and Collecting as Media-Oriented Practices" in *Participations* (Woo 2012b) and "A Pragmatics of Things: Materiality and Constraint in Fan Practices" for *Transformative Works and Cultures* (Woo 2014), respectively.

Finally, I'd like to thank my parents, Daniel W.K. Woo and Ruth Woo, for raising this nerdy kid, and – above all others – Laurena Nash for putting up with the bad puns, opaque references, and the comics and action figures for all these years. <3 <3 <3

GETTING A LIFE

"What Is a Nerd?"

This book is about someone you probably know. It might be about you. It's about the people we sometimes call "geeks" and "nerds."

While many have struggled to articulate an explicit definition of these terms, we all know one when we see them. Characters like Louis Tully, Napoleon Dynamite and Andy Sitzer, Steve Urkel, George Michael Bluth and Sheldon Cooper, Walter Mitty, Hermione Granger and Oscar Wao can, each in their own special way, be recognized as geeks and nerds. This capacity extends to people we encounter in real life, whether they are frequenting the game and comic store in our local mall, camping out for the premiere of a big new sci-fi blockbuster, standing awkwardly at the margins of a party, or reading quietly by themselves. Indeed, geeks have become such ubiquitous stock characters, in fiction and in fact, that it may be difficult to remember that we didn't always have them with us.

That's not to say there haven't always been quiet, introspective people who are intensely engaged by things that most people don't care about, but that we didn't always use these labels to describe them. This nomenclature is actually a relatively recent addition to our repertoire of social types. Far from a naturally occurring, universally identifiable character, people had to be taught what a nerd was. In a 1979 letter to the editor of Toronto's *Globe and Mail*, for instance, Louise Duncan of Markham, Ontario, wrote to complain about the paper's use of unfamiliar slang terms, asking: "What is a nerd?" The emergence of a new (or newly popular) piece of vocabulary can offer a clue to changing understandings of social reality. Language is, among other things, a collective practice of sense-making: "A good way of ascertaining real social types is to make use of the natural instincts of the public or the media, i.e., to look for special nicknames attached to certain groups. For example, consider the role of a new term like 'nerd' in the social construction of the reality of this type" (Almog 1998, under "A Few Practical 'Tips' for Social Type Analysis"). These "natural instincts" can be traced by searching large corpora of texts, such as the LexisNexis Academic Major World Publications and Google Books databases. Simply counting how often words appear will not give us the whole picture. It is blind to context and subject to false positives. Nonetheless, these searches point to a dramatically expanding discursive space between 1975 and 2008 (the last available year in the Google Books n-gram viewer). As figure 1 suggests, the discourse really takes off around 1984–85, following the introduction of Nerds candy and more importantly, for my purposes, the theatrical release of *Revenge of the Nerds*, which remains a touchstone for the popular stereotype of the nerd or geek. It received a further boost with the 1987 Broadway debut of *The Nerd*, starring Robert Joy in the eponymous role and Mark Hamill of *Star Wars* fame. This new way of talking about an old phenomenon did not go unremarked upon. For example, Martin and Koda give "star billing" to the Jock and the Nerd among the dozen "male identities" they profile because "they are roles that have arisen to new respectability in the present day" – that is, 1989 (7). Although "nerd" is the more popular term at first, "geek" eventually overtakes it around 2000. By the first decade of the twenty-first century, journalists, critics, and other writers were producing much more material for and about people they thought of and explicitly called "geeks" and "nerds."

The etymology of "geek" can be traced to the nineteenth century, perhaps coming into English via the Low German *geck*, when "gawk," "geek," "gowk," and "gowky" meant "a fool," "person uncultivated," or "a dupe" according to a nineteenth-century dictionary of Yorkshire dialect. In the early twentieth century, it also referred to a carnival performer who bit the heads off live chickens or performed some other grotesque spectacle. Thus, "freak" and "geek" were basically interchangeable, and neither referred to ordinary teenagers like those in the similarly titled television series. It is only later that "geek" develops its more specific meaning of "an overly diligent, unsociable student" ("geek, *n.*" 2012). These two definitions compete with one another into the 1980s, though the former also feeds into the latter – there remains, for instance, an echo of the freak show about MIT's "Ugliest Man on Campus" contest, as described by Sherry Turkle. During the contest, which raised money for charity, "the students who think of themselves as most ugly parade around the main corridors of the Institute, wearing placards that announce their candidacy. They flaunt their pimples, their pasty

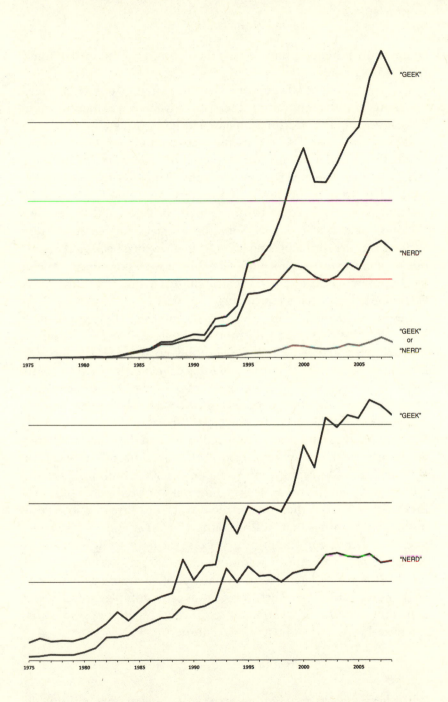

Figure 1   Triumph of the nerds? Hits for records containing "nerd" and "geek" in LexisNexis Major World Publications (above) and Google Books (below) databases, 1975–2008. Data series are stacked to show overall growth in discourse concerning nerds and geeks in the press and in books.

complexions, their knobby knees, their thin, undeveloped bodies" (Turkle 1984, 196).

The origins of "nerd" are somewhat more mysterious. It has been used in its familiar sense since at least 1951 when it was mentioned in a *Newsweek* article as Detroit slang for a "drip" or "square" – though Dr Seuss had used "nerd" as a nonsense word in his *If I Ran the Zoo* the year before. In an instalment of his *New York Times Magazine* column, "On Language," devoted to collegiate slang, William Safire (1980) speculated that "its origin is probably in a 40's variation of 'nuts' – as in 'nerts to you' – and a 'nert' became a 'nerd', probably influenced by a rhyming scatological word."[1] Some have suggested that its current spelling is a corruption of "knurd," or "drunk" spelled backwards, while others note the resemblance to "snerd," as in Mortimer Snerd, one of the dummies in Edgar Bergen's ventriloquist act. But none of these folk etymologies is especially convincing.

Despite their distinct histories, the meanings of these words have largely converged. As Randall Munroe humorously suggests in one of his *xkcd* comic strips (fig. 2), there's nothing geekier – or, if you prefer, nerdier – than caring about the nuances of meaning between them. Dictionaries today define them in basically identical terms, and they share the same basic contradiction at their core: on the one hand, nerds and geeks are highly accomplished at technical or scientific pursuits that they practice with uncommon dedication; on the other hand, they are foolish, inept, clumsy, unattractive, offensive, boringly conventional, worthless, and insignificant. Somehow, they are both brilliant and dull. To put it another way, geeks – however knowledgeable or skilful they may be within the areas of their expertise – are not so accomplished in the things that "really" count. The *Oxford English Dictionary* gives the latter definitions priority because the more straightforwardly pejorative uses are earlier and more common ("geek, *n.*" 2012; "nerd, *n.*" 2012). It is only later that potentially positive meanings have been layered on top of them. These words point to a complex social object that is the product of a particular set of conceptual oppositions that emerged during the mid-twentieth century.

DEARTH OF THE COOL

Whatever else geeks may be, they aren't *cool* – at least not anything like what that word has conventionally meant. Indeed, the increasing popularity of cultural goods and styles associated with nerds and geeks has

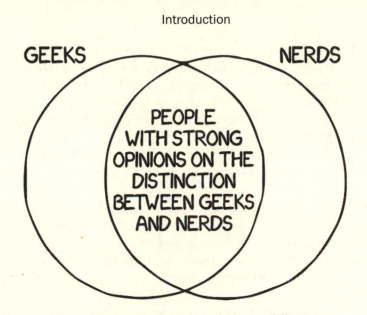

Figure 2   Who *really* cares? "Geeks and Nerds" by Randall Munroe
(https://xkcd.com/747/). Redrawn by the author.

required coinages like "geek chic" (first attributed to a 1991 article in
The Face; "geek, *n.*" 2012) in order to register their paradoxical position
with respect to existing canons of taste and status. Coolness is perhaps
the defining ideal of American popular culture, at least since the post-
war rise of youth culture (Danesi 1994), and the American formulation
of cool has become a globally recognizable phenomenon thanks to the
United States' potent culture industries.

Many writers have identified African or African-American roots to
the genealogy of cool (Mailer 1959; Majors and Billson 1992; Pountain
and Robins 2000; Leland 2004). As Majors and Billson describe, performances of cool masculinity are a way for African-American men to
cope with the frustrated ambitions, humiliations, and real physical dan-
gers produced by personal and structural racism: "Presenting to the
world an emotionless, fearless, and aloof front counters the low sense
of inner control, lack of inner strength, absence of stability, damaged
pride, shattered confidence, and fragile social competence that come
from living on the edge of society. [...] Black males have learned to use
posing and posturing to communicate power, toughness, detachment,
and style – self" (1992, 8). The modern, mainstream ideals of coolness
sold to us by the culture industries are the product of a long history of
white appropriations of black cultural forms and styles, including of

the mode of self-presentation Majors and Billson call the "cool pose." American examples from jazz to hip-hop are perhaps most familiar, although Hebdige (1979) noted a similar relationship between black and white youth in Britain.

This dynamic is still at work today. Examining language use in a multiracial high school, for example, Mary Bucholtz (1999a, 1999b, 2001, 2009) found that most white students regularly borrowed elements of black culture. This appropriation could be fraught, as white students were penalized if their peers believed they "want to be black" (1999b, 445), but references to hip-hop and limited uses of slang and pronunciations copied from African American Vernacular English were necessary components of mainstream adolescent coolness. However, one group of students, a clique Bucholtz (1999a) describes as a "community of nerd girls," studiously avoided them. Instead, they spoke what Bucholtz terms "superstandard English," which "contrasts linguistically with Standard English in its greater use of 'supercorrect' linguistic variables: lexical formality, carefully articulated phonological forms, and prescriptively standard grammar" (2001, 88). Although they were not all in fact Caucasian, the way they used the English language marked them racially, disrupting the usual ideological work of masking whiteness as the implicit norm. Hence, musician Brian Eno's tendentious definition of a nerd as "a human being without enough Africa in him or her" (Kelly 1995); in this formulation, "Africa" is only coolness, a trait to which anyone can lay legitimate claim. Or at least anyone but nerds. Indeed, one way to understand the popular figure of the nerd or geek is as a Bizarro version of the masculine ideal of cool. Popular media depict geeks as in every respect the inverse of the "cool pose":

- *Where cool is rebellious, geekiness is conformist.* Pountain and Robins (2000, 12) argue that coolness is, first and foremost, a "mode of individualism," an embodied, aestheticized expression of individuality in a mass society. It thus bears a patina of resistance, though this is usually a matter of style rather than substance. Geeks and nerds, however, are tainted by conformity. In childhood and adolescence, they may be the goody two-shoes who excel in the sanctioned competitions constituted by adults – such as those for grades, for example – but never quite grasp the culture of the schoolyard. As obsessive fans and collectors, nerds are too engaged with media. Jensen (1992) argues that representations of fans tend to demonize them, either as obsessive loners or as hysterical crowds. In part, then, geekiness appears as a pathology of liberal individualism.

- *Where cool is emotionally restrained, geekiness is irrepressible.* The imperative "be cool" means to control the expression of one's emotions. Geeks and nerds, by contrast, are often characterized by their unbounded enthusiasm in general and for a distinctive set of interests – comic books, gaming, science and technology, certain texts or genres such as sci-fi and fantasy – in particular. These activities are pursued in a characteristically fastidious or fanatical way to the detriment of a "healthy" or "well-rounded" life. To "geek out" is, proverbially, to lose all sense of one's surroundings in fannish rapture. Among fellow enthusiasts, this is all well and good, but in mixed company it is a serious *faux pas*, a failure to play it cool.
- *Where cool is physical and practical, geekiness is intellectual and theoretical.* The distinction between the cool and the nerdy rehearses traditional dualisms between body and mind, action and thought, hands and head. In portrayals based in schools and colleges, nerds are contrasted with attractive and athletic students, the proverbial jocks and cheerleaders. This is not to say that the cool kids are stupid – indeed, "hip" refers to a kind of knowing (Leland 2004) – but that coolness demands a practical cunning, an ability to know the right thing to say or do at the right time. It involves "knowing how," not "knowing that" (Ryle 2009). Nerds know many things but lack the knack for getting along in everyday life, which is what is truly valued in high school and beyond.
- And, finally, *where cool is manly and confidently sexual, geekiness is immature and inept.* Based on his clinical practice, Anderegg (2007, 35) argues that, before it means anything else, "nerd" means "babyish." Again, this involves a sense of conforming to (adults') expectations and rules. This connotation of juvenility is strengthened by the enduring link between geek identity and a prolonged, serious interest in children's media culture. Many children show enthusiasm for superheroes, sci-fi, and games, but nerds make this media culture grow up with them. The framing of nerdiness as childish also implies an infantile or inept sexuality. The media's stereotypical geek is not necessarily asexual; rather, he does not know how to effectively pursue the objects of unrequited lust. His affections remain secret or, perhaps worse, are well known and laughable.

In sum, stereotypes of geeks and nerds describe a particular performance of the self that bundles together negative attributes that might otherwise accrue around white men – particularly when compared with the African-American men from whom they crib their dominant expressions of masculinity. Thus, we can perhaps see geekiness as it is constructed in popular media as the remainder purged from hegemonic masculinity. Christine Quail (2011, 461) notes that "the nerd moniker has historically been used as a way of distinguishing, and discrediting, a particular expression of nonhegemonic masculinity and favouring the more hegemonic, consumer-viable contrast." Represented as white men who are too white and not masculine enough, these caricatures provide cover for the racialized and gendered economy of cultural appropriations that funds pop culture cool (Eglash 2002). If, as Norman Mailer (1959) would have it, the hipster is the "white negro," then the nerd is his bad conscience, a nagging reminder of the unbearable whiteness at the core of his being.

To borrow a phrase from the sociologist Pierre Bourdieu, geeks and nerds are discursively constructed as a dominated fraction of society's dominant group. The reality is, of course, more complex. While the image chosen to represent geeks and nerds in the media is almost invariably a straight white man, women and people of colour have long been part of the subculture (Eglash 2002; Stanfill 2011; Busse 2013). This is, to me, the clearest indication that the geek as social type does a kind of discursive work for mainstream consumers of these representations. Like shadows on the wall of Plato's cave, they are taken by many as real – and are subsequently *taken up* in complex ways: adapted, negotiated, challenged, and celebrated, in both sincere and ironic modes.

THE TRIUMPH OF GEEK CULTURE

In September 2014, the *New York Times' Learning Network*, a collection of lesson plans and activities based on *Times* articles, invited students to discuss the following questions:

- Are you a nerd or a geek?
- Has our society fully embraced geek culture? Can someone now declare, without shame or embarrassment, 'I am a nerd'? Is being a nerd or a geek something to be proud of?
- Is it cool to be a nerd or a geek in *your* school? Or, is being good at science, or the high scorer on the math team, still not going to win a teenager any popularity awards? (Gonchar 2014)

However, the questions seem somewhat leading given the title of the Sunday Review essay they were asked to read: "We're All Nerds Now"

(Cohen 2014). This was not the first time the paper of record had made such an assertion. Just a few days before, its online Opinion Pages section brought together seven writers to ponder the implications of an age "when geeks rule." An op-ed *cum* obituary for *Dungeons & Dragons* co-creator E. Gary Gygax declared, "We live in Gary Gygax's world" (Rogers 2008). Similarly, regular columnist David Brooks suggested that the ascendancy of a high-tech economy (represented by Bill Gates and Google's Page and Brin) and a "cool geek style" (represented by musicians like David Byrne, Weezer, and Vampire Weekend) offered a winning alternative to both jocks and "alienated and self-pitying outsiders" that, "in a relatively short period of time," "has flipped" existing hierarchies: "For as it is written, the last shall be first and the geek shall inherit the earth" (Brooks 2008). With its obvious Biblical allusions, Brooks's millennial rhetoric is perhaps unsubtle but it is by no means unusual.

In recent years, popular discourse about geeks and nerds has been overwhelmingly focused on questions of status and mainstreaming. For most of its existence, the social type of the geek and nerd by definition occupied the lowest rungs of the status system. This is evident in many studies of school cultures, from Paul Willis's (1977) "ear'oles" (a term Raewyn Connell lists, along with "nerd," in the "rich vocabulary of abuse" directed at "insufficiently" masculine men and boys; 2005, 79) to Bucholtz's (1999a) "nerd girls." But as these examples from the *Times* suggest, the conventional wisdom assumes a trajectory for geek culture from the periphery of contemporary culture to its centre. These changes are typically explained through economic success in the knowledge economy and a devaluation of traditional expressions of "hard" masculinity. Commentators typically cite the popularity of media forms and genres associated with geeks, ranging from billion-dollar debuts for new video game titles to blockbuster adaptations of fantasy epics like *The Lord of the Rings* and *Harry Potter*. The successful, sensitive, and media-savvy nerd is thus depicted as a new man for the twenty-first century. Indeed, journalist Alexandra Robbins (2011) looks to a carefully curated list of celebrities and entrepreneurs in order to argue that the very same traits that make outcasts of kids in high school predispose them to be innovators and leaders afterwards.[2]

These shifts in the representation of geeks were already inscribed in the film that first introduced broad swathes of the public to the nerd. *Revenge of the Nerds* (Jeff Kanew 1984) not only launched a thousand punning headlines over the coming decades but also provided an influential example of the "hip/square dialectic" (Quail 2011). As Christine Quail

(2011, 463) glosses the plot, "the nerds try to gain social power, or become 'cool,' by starting a fraternity; their nemeses are the popular jocks, who humiliate and hurt the nerds, with the nerds seeking revenge." The nerdy Tri-Lambs win over the campus with a combination of technical prowess and artistic wizardry, establishing themselves as the dominant fraternity by the franchise's third instalment (Kendall 1999a). Similarly, conservative commentator Charles J. Sykes (2007, 110) – in a comment frequently and tellingly misattributed to Bill Gates (xi–xii; Mikkelson 2013) – warns that we should all "be nice to nerds," since we will in all likelihood end up working for one someday. These representations and commentary about them recapitulate the model of subcultural diffusion popularized by the Birmingham School of cultural studies (Clarke 2006; Hebdige 1979). Sometimes, they retain a level of ambivalence or a fear that nerdiness is losing its specificity, as the novelist and lifestyle writer Russell Smith (2007) suggests in a newspaper column: "A geek no longer means someone with no social skills, but someone with specialized knowledge. People say, for example, 'I'm a wine geek' to mean 'I'm middle class,' or 'I'm a finance geek' to mean 'I'm quite rich.' People proudly say, 'I have these dweeby interests' to mean 'I'm educated.' The phrase 'geek chic' has become so overused in magazines it almost means simply fashionable." However, the move from margins to mainstream is more often constructed as a "triumph." Indeed, I would argue that this triumphal narrative has become the dominant way of framing geek culture today, resulting in something like a "normative nerdiness" (cf. Hills 2005). It is basically taken for granted that – as Cohen (2014) would have it – "we're all nerds now," at least within certain, delimited definitions of "nerd."

However, this narrative is deeply flawed. First, it's ahistorical. In searching through the press's discussions of geeks and geek culture to prepare figure 1, I discovered that their triumph has been announced several times already, couched in much the same terms and attributed to the very same causes. While the frequency and prominence of these announcements have undoubtedly intensified, the revenge of the nerds has been imminent for the last thirty-five years, at least. Second, in repeatedly depicting geeks as straight, white cisgender men – thereby erasing actually existing forms of diversity within various geek media cultures (Eglash 2002; Stanfill 2011) – and celebrating a trajectory from allegedly subordinate to allegedly dominant positions, it is highly ideological. For example, Lori Kendall (1999a) observes that stories about nerds and geeks often generate sympathy and humour by parodying the rhetoric of civil rights and gay liberation movements without acknowledging real forms of systemic oppression, a tactic that has recently been adopted by politically reactionary elements in the geek culture wars (see ch. 8). Third and, for my purposes, most importantly, it commits a *category error*. Its conflation of geek culture with media texts (in particular, unusually popular or profitable ones) and overwhelming focus on their integration with mainstream lifestyle trends mean that this narrative tends to overlook actual people and their lived experiences. For instance, in an editorial in the *Journal of Popular Culture* entitled – what else? – "The Revenge of the Nerds," Gary Hoppenstand (2005) contrasts his childhood experiences with his sense that it is now "downright cool to be a nerd." In his view, "the most convincing argument" is the popularity of the CBS sitcom *The Big Bang Theory*: "Even as a child, I have always suspected that one day nerds would make it (finding acceptability, even admiration) and, with *The Big Bang Theory*, that day has finally arrived" (809–10). Despite its perennially robust ratings, however, the show's reception is fraught. Many view it as a celebratory or, at worst, self-deprecating portrait of nerds and, like Hoppenstand, take its ratings success as straightforward evidence that geeks are now part of the mainstream. Others have criticized it as a kind of "nerd minstrelsy" (Dmytrewycz 2012) that ventriloquizes geek culture in order to expose it to ridicule by rehearsing old stereotypes about maladjusted weirdoes. The temptation would be to adjudicate between these viewpoints – is geek culture mainstream or not? – but what difference does it actually make in the lives of the real people who get called nerds or geeks if *The Big Bang Theory*, *The Lord of the Rings*, *Dungeons & Dragons*, or computer programming is popular? The lifestyle trend pieces are largely silent about this question.

Geeks and nerds are very useful for the creators of popular narratives. Like the standard character types of the *commedia dell'arte*, they permit a whole shorthand. They can serve as a foil or sidekick to the protagonist, help differentiate the members of an ensemble cast, or stand in as a misfit or underdog onto whom audiences can project vague feelings of alienation and marginalization. However, we must be very careful about drawing inferences about social reality from media representations. Media certainly express and act upon popular understandings of all sorts of phenomena, but they rarely do so in the straightforward manner implied by the "window on the world" and "mirror reflecting our culture" metaphors (Meehan 2005, 1). All this commentary constitutes a lay theory of geek culture, but one that says more about the rest of "us" than it says about "them." It represents our hopes and fears about the impacts of new technologies, the changing nature of work and gender, and increased (and increasingly individualized) engagement with mediated leisure. To paraphrase Raymond Williams (1989, 11), there are no geeks, only ways of seeing people as geeks.

GEEK CULTURE, MEDIA FANDOM, AND EVERYDAY LIFE

Where do these ways of seeing come from? Reviewing the literature on social types – an analytical concept often associated with the work of Georg Simmel, among others – Oz Almog (1998) distinguishes between social types generated by different sources or mechanisms, including "mythological," "occupational," and "personality" types. Arguably, the nerd or geek contains aspects derived from all of them.

Almog's mythological types synthesize fictional characters and celebrities. The nerd was one of a handful of archetypes that, Martin and Koda (1989) argue, defined men's dress in the twentieth century; the full list – including such entries as the Jock, the Worker, the Rebel, the Cowboy, and the Dandy – reads like a pantheon of mythological types (or the character classes in a terrible role-playing game). As I have already suggested, characters like Gilbert and Lewis from *Revenge of the Nerds* and real people like Bill Gates or Toby Radloff have influenced how we talk and think about the socially awkward, computer-savvy, or media-obsessed people we encounter in everyday life – not least, by teaching us to assume some relationship between these characteristics. But the nerd is also shaped by more concrete factors. For instance, the image of the "computer nerd" or "technogeek" is a variant of the "social construction of the engineer" (Turkle 1984, 197). As Turkle explains, even at MIT, computer science students were outcasts among engineers, and many of them accepted their peers' views of them "as archetypical nerds, loners, and losers" (200). This must be seen as part of a longer trajectory of anti-intellectualism in Anglo-American culture that has tended to view the "life of the mind," which is an occupational category as much as anything else, with contempt (Hofstadter 1966). On the other hand, perhaps features of the individuals who tend to choose these jobs are the real object of disdain. Turkle's (1984, 205) hackers seemed uncanny because they were too much like the machines they worked with. Certainly, specific personality traits – such as introversion, obsessiveness, and a disregard for social cues and conventions – have long been associated with nerds. They are, for example, what Nugent (2008) looked for in literary proto-nerds like Mary Bennett and Gussie Fink-Nottle. Some have even suggested that people we think of as geeks are exhibiting behaviours somewhere on the autism spectrum, though Anderegg (2007) cautions against pathologizing nerdiness in this way. All these "mechanisms," mediated by personal experience and widely circulating representations, undoubtedly contribute to the popular perception of the geek – but they also mystify what they seem to make visible.

However, Almog (1998, under "The Cultural/Subcultural Type") suggests that a fourth kind of social type is identified by characteristics "typical of the individual's culture or subculture," rather than from an occupational category or personality construct. While subcultural types may also be prone to stereotyping (including by other participants), they at least imply a relationship with some concrete referent. This final kind of type opens the door to an understanding of social types as more than a tool for arm's-length cultural analysis, uniting particular cases under a category abstracted from our interactions with or prejudices about engineers and scientists. On this view, people can be recognized as geeks because they participate in geek *culture*. This shift in perspective is crucial because the triumphal narrative of geek culture centres non-geeks and non-fans – what some participants would call "mundanes"[3] – who are hailed as outside observers, given permission to (temporarily) adopt "geek chic" styles when they are in fashion and enjoy things that journalists assure them are "not just for nerds." Yet geek culture is about more than "us" mundanes. Because it is ahistorical, ideological, and ultimately mistakes representations for what they supposedly represent, the triumphal narrative described above attenuates the link between geek culture and the people who may be categorized as geeks and nerds.

My aim in this book is to restore this link and examine the contemporary phenomenon of geek culture from the point of view of ordinary participants in one city's geek culture scene. I want to explore the lived experience of geek culture as "communities of practice" (Lave and Wenger 1991; Wenger 1998) oriented to certain media forms and genres. Pressed to categorize these leisure practices, I would call them examples of fandom, a word that circulates in these milieus as much as "nerd" and "geek" do. Indeed, one of my interviewees preferred it to the latter options, saying, "I guess 'fan' is more accurate, and it's something that's used within science-fiction fandom. It's how people refer to themselves." Kristina Busse (2013) suggests that geeks and fans are often conflated in mainstream media texts: on the one hand, "characters' geek-iness is often shown through their fannish characteristics" (77); on the other hand, nerdy fans are frequently used to stand in for media fandom as such. Yet fans and fandom have been defined in a very specific way within the academic literature, one perhaps narrower than the ordinary language sense of those terms.

Fan studies emerged from a particular constellation of feminist audience studies (e.g., Radway 1984; Ang 1985) and populist approaches to culture (e.g., Fiske 1989a, 1989b; Willis 1990). Pushing back against stereotyped images of science fiction fans as nerdy men, Henry Jenkins (2013), Camille Bacon-Smith (1992), and Constance Penley (1997) drew attention to the genre's female fans. Against a long tradition of both devaluing female audiences and feminizing the audiences of mass culture in general (see Huyssen 1986), they emphasized that these women were not *mere* consumers but active interpreters and appropriators of culture – they were, in Jenkins's (2013) evocative phrase, "textual poachers," using popular culture as a resource to make what media producers wouldn't give them. At conventions, in fanzines and amateur press associations, and through networks that distributed video tapes, predominantly female fans created a participatory culture that transformed the raw materials of mass media into new, expressive forms: fan fiction, fan art, and vidding. These communities became known as *media* fandom, in order to distinguish their emphasis on film and especially television from the older fandom oriented to science fiction literature. They have now largely migrated into online spaces, ranging from early text-based chat rooms and forums to commercial social media platforms like Tumblr and purpose-built ones like FanFiction.net and An Archive of Our Own (see, e.g., Baym 2000; Bury 2005; Hellekson and Busse 2006; Jenkins 2006). While fan studies brought a great deal of richness and depth to our understandings of what people can do with media goods, these accounts of fandom were by no means neutral; Jenkins (2006, 12; Jenkins and Scott 2013, xxix) has noted in interviews that his generation of fan scholars was purposefully attempting to shift perceptions about who fans were and what their communities were all about.

But I would argue that an unintended result of this effort was defining fandom too narrowly. Many read these accounts of *a fandom* or *a set of fan practices* as being about fandom *as such*, thus neglecting or bracketing some communities of media fans and constructing the normative fan as a middle-class white woman writing about TV online. As

Sam Ford (2014) and Rebecca Wanzo (2015) have both suggested, our accounts of fans and fandom would look quite different if we included fans of sports or music within "media fandom."[4] There are different fan communities and different ways of doing fandom, but while heuristically useful, typologies of audience activity – such as Fiske's (1992b) triumvirate of semiotic, enunciative, and textual productivity, Abercrombie and Longhurst's (1998) "audience continuum," or the currently modish binary of "affirmational" and "transformational" fandoms (Obsession_inc 2009) – often fall short. They necessarily end up leaving out some people's experiences and, as Matt Hills (2014a, ¶2.1) notes, "always present the danger of implicitly or explicitly valorizing specific versions of fan practice while denigrating others" by erecting a hierarchy of value wherein some expressions are not merely different from but more fannish than others. If mainstream media have now begun celebrating the male, geeky fan as the ideal consuming subject of contemporary transmedia franchises, then academic efforts to "twist the stick the other direction" perhaps inadvertently reified distinctions among fan practices into an almost ontological divide: good, transformational, and therefore resistive fans who are mostly women, on the one hand; bad, affirmational, and therefore complicit fans who are mostly men, on the other. Within this framework, "nerds" and "geeks" would almost certainly fall in the latter category. Yet the popular construct of geek culture provides a fresh entrée into some of these conceptual difficulties, so long as we commit to moving *beyond* that construct to explore participants' lived experiences. Because fan studies are often focused on specific fan communities – that is, fans of a specific text, series, or character – they tend to create a picture of fandoms as separated, not only from one another but also from a larger spectrum of media-oriented practices. Geek culture is itself a relatively fluid, underdetermined cultural formation and already suggests a broad, variegated topography of fan practices through which people and texts circulate. Thus, geek culture and traditional conceptions of media fandom are not so far apart as may sometimes be imagined. They share some fan objects, practices, and spaces, but do not overlap perfectly.[5] At the risk of oversimplification, all geeks are fans but not all fans are geeks.

What, then, is the underlying substance we are identifying as "fandom"? I want to argue that it involves approaching media consumption as "serious leisure" (Stebbins 1982, 1992, 2007). Robert Stebbins defines serious leisure in contrast to both regular, paid employment (i.e., "work") and "casual" or "unserious" leisure: "Briefly, serious leisure can be defined as the systematic pursuit of an amateur, hobbyist, or volunteer activity that is sufficiently substantial and interesting for the participant to find a career there in the acquisition and expression of its special skills and knowledges [… It contrasts] with a bewildering array of casual forms, such as sitting at a football game, riding a roller coaster, taking an afternoon nap, watching television, observing a fireworks display, going on a picnic, and so on" (1992, 3). The distinction between serious and casual leisure is, however, one of kind rather than degree. For example, Stebbins calls watching television "casual" even though Canadians spend more than twenty-one hours watching television and videos each week according to the 2015 General Social Survey (Statistics Canada 2017). This is a great deal of time to devote to any activity, but one presumes most people, most of the time watch television to entertain, divert, or inform themselves, not to acquire and express "special skills and knowledges." Fans are that portion of the audience that *does* use media consumption as an occasion for creative expression and self-cultivation – this is what distinguishes fanboys, gamers, and Trekkers from comic-book readers, game players, and the occasional viewer of *Star Trek* – without prescribing what that fandom looks like. Fans take their media seriously, which may or may not involve the more specific practices of vernacular creativity. Thus, when I say this book is about geeks and nerds, I mean it is concerned with fans of the media forms and genres conventionally associated with the geek or nerd as a subcultural type.

However, there is still ambiguity in how we talk about fandom. Henry Jenkins distinguishes between scholars who conceptualize fandom as a culture or practice and those who view it as an individual property (Jenkins and Scott 2013, xiv). The former approach is (broadly) sociological, the latter (broadly) psychological. While valuable work has been done theorizing why fans develop their attachments to TV shows, bands, and so on (Hills 2002; Sandvoss 2005), I am principally interested in social action (i.e., "where the actor's behaviour is meaningfully oriented to that of others"; Weber 1997, 113), not individual "activity." This implies a perspectival shift from individual acts or enunciations to the social context that renders them meaningful. My account of geek culture is meant to complement, not compete with, existing accounts of media fandom. Perhaps some of those media fans are only fans of one thing and their fandom stops at the edges of their computer monitors, but I doubt it. They may well be entangled in entirely different social worlds than the ones I describe in this book, but the constitution of geek culture from distinct practices and communities suggests that no fan is an island. My research strategy, drawing on traditions of cultural studies and media ethnography, involved following people who participated in some way in geek media cultures and trying to understand things from their perspective.

"Fandom," like "kingdom," refers to a place: "the *world* of enthusiasts for some amusement or for some artist" ("fandom, *n.*" 1933; my emphasis). This is principally a social world, but one that is also experienced in real places. The research for this book was conducted in a multicultural city of approximately two million people. It is the largest city in its region, with universities, colleges, and an active creative industries sector. Most importantly, it also played host to a vibrant geek culture scene. The study of cultural scenes first gained traction in popular music studies (Straw 1991; Bennett 2004; Bennett and Peterson 2004), though it has since been extended to analyze a broader range of cultural activities situated in urban life (Straw 2004; Woo, Poyntz, and Rennie 2016). In ordinary language, a scene can refer to very different levels of activity – indeed, this flexibility has been seen as one of the concept's strengths – but it necessarily points towards a concern with space and the people who occupy it, with the local and mundane structures that shape how cultural activity unfolds within a particular place or context. While social researchers often discuss fandoms as if they were discrete phenomena – as though media fans are never *also* comic book collectors or gamers or *otaku* or medieval re-creationists, let alone sports fans – the geek culture scene acted as a nexus of niches. It connected these worlds not only conceptually but also in concrete spaces of intersection like stores and conventions.

So, when looking for people to speak with about geek culture, I started by seeking out specialty retail stores and community organizations associated with conventionally geeky goods and activities. Even within this geographically bounded context, however, I could not be exhaustive; there was simply too much activity going on. Organizations were approached based on their prominence within the local scene: one group was primarily concerned with forms of media fandom (Screens & Sorcery), one with comics (King Con), one with gaming (City Gaming Network), and one (the Alternate Universe Club) embraced both media fandom and gaming. Stores were initially approached according to the same criterion of local prominence; however, as I went along I attempted to build points of comparison and contrast into the study. Of five stores, two primarily sold games (Westside Board Games and Plaza Games), two primarily sold comics (King St Comics and Downtown Comics & Collectibles), and one was substantially involved in both markets (Eastside Games & Comics). The stores were in different kinds of neighbourhood (relatively urban versus relatively suburban) and were of different ages (the oldest was established in 1974, the newest in 2008). Table 1 outlines these research sites in a schematic form. More detailed profiles may be found in Appendix A. In each case, I interviewed the store's owner/manager or group organizers and conducted limited passive and participant observation to get a feel for "business as usual" in that place. I also attended two local conventions during the same time frame but did not conduct interviews with their organizers. This work took place between, roughly, September 2009 and June 2010.

After taking some time to analyze the data I had generated in the first phase of the research project, I contacted my informants and asked them to recommend customers or members that they would describe as either typical or atypical of their communities, allowing them to define those terms in whatever way seemed salient to them. Some directly recruited people that they knew, others provided me contact information for likely candidates, and in a few cases retailers asked for a poster they could display instead. I also received some assistance recruiting among fandoms that had not been included in the first phase. From the volunteers, I selected a group of six participants in the local scene, who are presented briefly in Table 2 and in more detail in the appendix. Given the debates about gendered versions of fandom described above and an emerging literature on aging in "youth" subcultures (Hodkinson 2011, 2012, 2013), the interviewees were evenly split between men and women and across three age cohorts or life stages. Most considered themselves to be middle class, although definitions were varied and generally vague; all were Caucasian; and two self-identified as bisexual. Most importantly, they were all involved in a range of geeky media-oriented practices. In order to understand how these practices were articulated together and integrated into the texture of everyday life, it was necessary to talk at length with my informants. I conducted a series of in-depth

Table 1 Phase 1 Research Sites

Primary informant*	Organization*	Type	Est.	Location(s)	Activities
Logan	Screens & Sorcery	Nerdy film society	2008	Movie theatre, artist-run centre	Screening-based events (e.g., retro cartoons, *Ghostbusters*, *Star Trek*, etc.).
Bobby	Alternate Universe Club	University *anime* and gaming club	197?	Suburban university campus	Weekly screenings, game nights, and cosplay workshops. Screenings usually followed by social activity.
Peter	King Con	Bi-monthly comic convention	1989	Rented hall (commercial street)	Small, dealer-oriented con. Free tables for local artists, free admission for children. Annual small-press convention.
Kurt	City Gaming Network	Gamers' networking organization	1996	Various	Annual convention and semi-regular in-store game days. On-line forum for co-ordinating private and public gaming.
John	Westside Board Games	Game store	2002	Commercial street	Demo copies and gaming tables. Weekly board game night.
Hank	Plaza Games	Game store	2003	Shopping mall ("downtown" of suburban community)	Demo/rental copies and gaming tables, schedule of collectible card game (CCG), collectible miniatures game, and board game events. Periodic release events.
Warren	King St Comics	Comic store	2002	Commercial street	No regular, formal activities. Informal social uses constrained by space.
Scott	Eastside Games & Comics	Game and comic store	2008	Commercial/residential area	Regular tournaments and game day/night for miniatures, CCG, and board games. Periodic release events. Informal social uses among comics customers.
Sean	Downtown Comics & Collectibles	Comic store	1974	Major downtown shopping street	No regular, formal activities. Long hours to accommodate downtown foot traffic.

* All names are pseudonyms.

interviews (at least four sessions of an hour or more in length) with each of them. The schedule of questions addressed biographical preliminaries, their views of "geek culture" in the abstract, and a case history of their involvement in each of the practices or communities with which they identified. As much as possible, they were designed to elicit stories and examples of ordinary talk. While interviews are not naturally occurring settings, the length and frequency of our interactions and my own position as a fellow geek, if not always one engaged in precisely the same set of practices, enabled them to approximate a conversation between fellow members. I also conducted a home visit with most participants to view and discuss collections of subculturally relevant goods and engaged in participant observation, shadowing them in their activities as they were willing and able to accommodate. This part of the research took place between April and October 2011 and represents the bulk of my analysis.

Field notes and interviews were fully transcribed and then analyzed using an open-ended, inductive coding strategy. I paid particular attention to symbolic boundaries and identity work, to evaluative talk, and to stories about individual media-oriented practices, but tried as much as possible to keep an open mind as I sifted through my notes and transcripts. I then used my observations and interview data to build up the account that follows.

OUTLINE OF THE ARGUMENT

It should be clear by now that this is not the story of the triumph of the nerds. That discourse was certainly part of the backdrop at the time I was conducting my research. My informants were aware of it and the apparent popularity of their lifestyle and consumption choices. But any culture that merits the term is much more than cultural texts. It is a "whole way of life," and a way of life is *lived*. Consequently, I have tried to understand geek culture, not as a new fad or trend, but rather through the everyday experiences of its participants.

While I have already reviewed how popular culture and the press have talked about who geeks are and what they're like, chapter 1 situates these definitional matters in the identity work that is part of everyday talk-in-interaction. The labels "geek" and "nerd" now have relatively stable denotative meanings but, unsurprisingly, vary in their use from person to person or situation to situation. Drawing on the

Table 2 Phase 2 Research Participants

Code name[a]	Sex	Age[b]	Contact	Practices	Biographical Notes
Barry	M	53	Other	• SF&F fan • medieval recreationist • gamer (RPGs and digital games)	Self-employed research chemist. Roman Catholic, active in Knights of Columbus. Aspiring novelist and screenwriter.
Diana	F	38	Logan	• SF&F fan • gamer (*Dungeons & Dragons*, *World of Warcraft*)	Self-employed but on maternity leave. Master's degree in women's studies about fan-fiction writers. "Nerd family."
Mr Fox	M	25	Sean	• comic-book reader • gamer (*Warhammer*, RPGs, and digital games) • SF&F fan	Video game writer with freelance writing projects. Social circle mainly friends from post-secondary diploma program in game design.
Shiera	F	41	Other	• SF&F fan • gamer (*Star Wars: Galaxies*) • medieval re-creationist[c]	Single mother of three on disability benefits. Interest in Celtic music. Aspiring writer.
Solo	F	23	Peter	• comic-book reader[c] • TV fan • SF&F fan	University student. Interest in working in media/cultural industries.
Wedge	M	37	Logan, Kurt	• gamer (*Blood Bowl*, RPGs, board games) • SF&F fan • medieval re-creationist[c] • comic-book collector[c]	Project manager at software developer. Computer science background. Married with young daughter.

[a] All names are pseudonyms.

[b] Age at time of initial interview.

[c] Indicates a dormant practice at time of research

work of the conversation analyst Harvey Sacks, I argue that these words and others like them are useful precisely because they are vague. For many, they still carry pejorative connotations but they are also sometimes used positively, ironically, or as a neutral badge of subcultural membership. Because of this interpretive uncertainty, the words serve as resources to manage the inferences hearers make about the speakers. They also tended to index normative conceptions of good and bad membership. The various distinctions onto which they were mapped expressed social distinctions between their reference group and the "mundanes," and between different communities or individuals within geek culture. This "boundary work" (Lamont 1992, 2000), and not any specific content or beliefs about technology or pop culture, is the true meaning of "geek" as revealed in ordinary talk-in-interaction, and many of the surprising or contradictory definitions can be accounted for by considering the social context of the interview situation and the tactical goals accomplished by claiming, denying, or qualifying membership.

If geeks are, as I have suggested, a kind of fan, then geek culture comprises particular kinds of audiences. However, the received notion of a media audience is remarkably undertheorized. Chapter 2 situates my research in the context of what Nick Couldry (2012, 8) has recently called "socially oriented media theory," that is, inquiry that explores how social action is constituted by, through, and around media. One version of that project would study media in terms of the practices they enable. While practice theory offers a diverse set of conceptual tools drawn from different intellectual traditions, I have found the theory of practice advanced by moral philosopher Alasdair MacIntyre (2007) particularly helpful in my analysis of geek culture. MacIntyre is a neo-Aristotelian virtue ethicist, and his moral theory revolves around the idea that social practices – defined as a "coherent and complex form of socially established cooperative activity" (187) with distinctive goods, representing a tradition that is embodied in a contemporary community of practice supported by a set of institutions – furnish conceptions of the good life and cultivate the dispositions required to achieve them. These are "focal practices" (Borgmann 1984). Fellow practitioners recognize and can reason about the means and ends of their shared practice, and this provides an intersubjectively valid basis for normative judgments. Most importantly, in acknowledging that ethical norms are bound to practically constituted communities, MacIntyre ties ethics to social organization in a unique and powerful way.

When viewed through this lens, geek culture is a space in which practices oriented to particular media and cultural goods enable and extend possibilities for human flourishing.

With this theoretical and conceptual background established, the remainder of the book analyzes geek culture as an interrelated set of social practices. MacIntyre argues that practices are defined by their distinctive goods or ends. Hence, my analysis of contemporary geek culture begins with questions of value (chapter 3): What is perceived as valuable within geek culture? I discuss two broad categories of subcultural capital: knowledge and collections. These are field-specific forms of *cultural* capital because they embody or objectify competences, such as the ability to feel and express tastes and to make subculturally defined distinctions between good and bad objects. MacIntyre stresses that practices are thoroughly historical objects, a premise with two implications. First, people as individuals have a history or career with the practice. Chapter 4 addresses participants' trajectories within geek culture from their introduction, through a process of deepening engagement, towards some form of conclusion. These autobiographical narratives are fundamental to the production of personal and collective identities. Second, individual trajectories coalesce into scenes or communities, which instantiate the practice over time. Chapter 5 looks at community-making as a dimension of social practices. The mutual orientation to shared objects provides normative ideals that guide and regulate conduct. Because these practices involve communication, it is also worth noting that community-making is being transformed by new capacities for computer-mediated communication. However, communities of practice are not self-sustaining – they depend upon what MacIntyre terms institutions for their continued flourishing. In chapter 6, I examine the intermediary role that local institutions like retail stores and clubs or societies played within the scene. One of their crucial functions is to make resources – a mix of MacIntyre's "external goods" and what Russell Keat (2000, 144) terms "equipment goods" – available to practitioners. They are gatekeepers, or better yet, "gamekeepers" (Hills 2002) who work to maintain the terrain on which producers and consumers of culture meet. However, they were once ordinary participants themselves, and the attitudes and tastes they share with other geeks are prerequisite to the success of their mediating practices. Having raised the issues of institutionalization and of necessary infrastructure, chapter 7 further explores limitations on participation that interviewees experienced, as well as strategies they developed for avoiding or ameliorating them. Because of their dependence on these material resources and conditions, we see that imagined communities have very real costs. In response to critics, MacIntyre has speculated as to whether there's such a thing as a bad or evil practice. These musings have, however, been rather uncompelling. Rather than seeking an inherently vicious social practice as a limit case of the theory, it might be better – and it is certainly much more urgent – to examine how robust social practices of this kind sometimes produce negative or even pathological outcomes. Unfortunately, geek culture has provided several notable examples of this phenomenon in recent years, mostly circling around "identity politics" and legitimate membership, some of which are discussed in chapter 8. Finally, a conclusion draws these threads back together through a reading of Evan Dorkin's "Eltingville Club" comic strips.

As someone who might well be described as a geek or nerd, I have an interest in providing a rich description of this contemporary subculture in its specificity. I want to do justice to the experiences and perspectives of my interviewees, in whom I recognized a lot of myself and people I have known over the years. Geek culture is interesting enough that this exercise would be worth it for its own sake, and, given the increased prominence of comics, games, sci-fi, and fantasy in our contemporary media, I think it would be a timely one. However, popular writers have already done a lot of that work, cataloguing and describing the social type of the geek in print and, especially, in the burgeoning "geekosphere" of online commentary. But geek culture can also be a means for understanding the broader, human possibilities for connection around media and cultural goods. I think that attending to this example can teach us something about how people use media to build meaningful communities in societies where traditional "sources of the self" (Taylor 1989) have been joined by identities and affinities rooted in new kinds of experiences, not least among them the experience of an omnipresent, immersive media – what Mark Deuze (2011) calls "media life." This is, to say the least, an expansive topic and, as discussed above, my research strategy necessarily sacrificed breadth for depth. Thus, I cannot guarantee generalizability by an appeal to large sample sizes but only warrant my account through the quality of the analysis itself. I do not offer a grand theory of media audiences but only a case study that I hope provides a productive vantage point on specific features of social life that strike me as important.

In *Envisioning Real Utopias*, Erik Olin Wright (2010, 10) puts forward a program of "emancipatory social science," where "the word emancipatory identifies a central moral purpose in the production of knowledge – the elimination of oppression and the creation of the conditions for human flourishing." Central to Wright's program is the examination of what he calls "real utopias," that is, "utopian ideals that are grounded in the real potentials of humanity, utopian destinations that have accessible way stations, utopian designs of institutions that can inform our practical tasks of navigating a world of imperfect conditions for social change" (6). However, Wright's real utopias are still somewhat unusual and remote from our immediate experience. I want to point instead to the ordinary "utopias" that exist all around us. They may not be able to furnish the *conditions* of human flourishing, but they offer a glimpse of what one might strive for, if perhaps in an unexpected guise. Stephen Duncombe (2007) has written of the need for those interested in emancipation to take the utopian desires embedded in consumer culture seriously, for "consumer culture – its crafted fantasies and stimulated desires – speaks to something deep and real within us" (16). Geek culture speaks to me, and I think the passion and enthusiasm of its members echo even more widely and more profoundly.

These commitments have been written off as trivial in the past. Ironically, their very depth and richness often become grounds for suspicion, as in the dismissive imperative to "get a life" (Jenkins 2013). Even now, in a more receptive climate, they are still largely assumed to be frivolous. They are "just" hobbies, after all. But in their daily reproduction through a particular set of sociocultural practices – that is, distinctive ways of doing things, including characteristic goals, norms, and standards – geek media cultures provide the context for people to do something important, perhaps the most important thing: define their own conception of the good. Paying close attention to their experiences will shed new light on how we might think about popular culture and consumption as central – though no doubt contradictory – elements of life in modern society. Geek culture is not special or virtuous as such. With respect to Wright's (2010) reformist project, it provides few lessons in institutional design or recipes for social change, and, notwithstanding the media's rhetoric of triumphalism, the revolution won't start or end with the geeks. But we can certainly learn something from them about how people pursue the goods they value in discrete (and not always hospitable) local contexts: about how the relative autonomy or heteronomy of markets, the availability of space, the personal and organizational dynamics of the communities formed in them, and the temporalities of circulation through them enhance or reduce possibilities for human beings to achieve their purposes and projects. This is something geek culture shares with any organized social activity in which human beings invest time and care. Indeed, my argument is that participating in such practices and the communities that inevitably form around them is precisely how we get a life.

1

Talk Nerdy to Me

The Meaning of Geek Culture

Picture a Venn diagram made up of three circles representing intelligence, social ineptitude, and obsession. In the overlapping segments, you find the popular labels "nerd," "geek," "dork," and "dweeb" (Fig. 3). Thus, a geek is characterized by the mixture of obsession and intelligence and a dork is obsessive and awkward but not particularly smart, while nerds are a triple threat. One site posted this image under the headline, "FINALLY: The Difference between Geek, Nerd, and Dork Explained by a Venn Diagram" (Great White Snark 2010).[1] That headline has two significant implications.

First, its all-caps shout of relief assumes we were *waiting* for someone to tell us the differences between these terms, but there is no shortage of such guides. For instance, a number of infographics have been produced and circulated to further show relationships between these concepts. They range from simple comparisons between nerds and geeks to complex field guides. One well-known example is the "Geek Hierarchy" by Löre Sjoberg ([2002?]), a flowchart indicating which geeks perceive themselves to be "less geeky" than others. In this context, where the least geeky were professional science-fiction writers and the most were "people who write erotic versions of *Star Trek* where all the characters are furries, like Kirk is an ocelot or something, and they put a furry version of themselves as the story of the story" – to be geekier is clearly not a good thing. Another take on the concept, the "Nerd Classification Index," locates various nerdy sub-types on a plane defined by the axes of extrovert–introvert and popular culture–academic without imposing any judgments on them (Rhodes 2014). If visuals aren't your thing, you could turn to the "Geek Code," a proposed standard for representing geeky skills and knowledge – everything from programming languages to fashion sense and from political views to opinions on

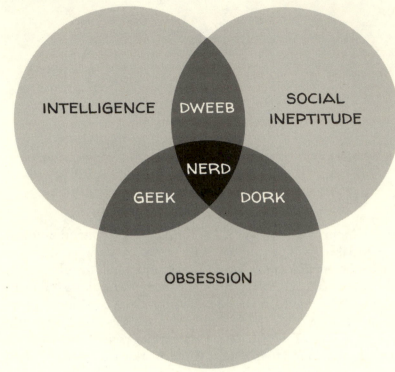

Figure 3   The difference between geeks, nerds, and dorks, "explained." An example of geek culture's quasi-scientific explanations of itself. (Illustration by the author based on a viral meme, ca. 2010.)

Babylon 5 – in a block of text that could be appended as an email signature or posted in an online profile (Hayden 1996) – and if you are at all concerned you don't rate one, you have your choice of the Geek Test and the Nerdity Test to prove it (see Kendall 1999a, 2011; McArthur 2009). If anything, geek culture offers too many taxonomies of the phyla, families, and genera composing geekdom.

Second, the headline assumes that this diagram *explains* something. In appropriating the form of a logic diagram, it creates an impression that the substance of geek culture is well known and well defined, that it is stable and perhaps even quantifiable. But like the flowcharts, graphs, and composite indices cited above, it merely restates preconceived notions. What are we to make of these artifacts that offer themselves as explanations? As Randall Munroe's own entry in this genre reminds us (see Introduction), they ought to be seen as expressions of geek culture rather than knowledge about it. They are, in essence, stories participants tell themselves with every like, upvote, and reblog. As such, they're as prescriptive as they are descriptive or explanatory. While they can't be taken at face value, that doesn't mean they have no value. Like all people, geeks act in the world on the basis of more or less coherent (though not always correct) assumptions about themselves, society, and other people. Their implicit and explicit assumptions constitute "lay theories" (Morris, Ames, and Knowles 2001), which are both "rival explanations" and themselves "objects of explanation" for the social researcher (Sayer 2005, 70). Thus, the goal of analysis is not only to provide superior descriptions of social life but also to explain the explanations given by everyday, practical reason.

To that end, this chapter explores some lay theories of geek culture that are embedded in participants' ordinary language. I begin by demonstrating the fundamental conceptual instability of "geek" and "nerd" as identity constructs. It quickly becomes apparent that they mean – or can be made to mean – different things for different people. In response, I attempt to account for these variations by examining the context in which they were made. Through the lens of membership categorization analysis, the varied uses of these labels appear as strategic responses to problems of impression management. Rather than straightforwardly indexing subcultural identities, they do discursive work that constructs such identities and negotiates their meanings – not least, as "subcultural" or not.

IT'S ALL GEEK TO ME

I have already traced some of the history of the labels "geek" and "nerd" through dictionaries and compilations of dialect and slang. However, denotative definitions rarely capture the nuance that words acquire in use. Even "definitions" embedded in media representations, while perhaps more subtle and open to interpretation than a dictionary entry, are to some extent determined by their narrative function. Since there is a widespread belief in a significant distinction *between* "nerd" and "geek," I found asking people whether they used them differently a particularly fruitful way of getting them to talk about the gradations of meaning that these words could hold in different circumstances.

A common response reserved one of the words for the object of someone's interests and the other for the ways they pursue or express them. As Barry put it, "'Geek' kind of refers to the interest, and maybe 'nerd' kind of the approach." Thus, a geek might be interested in sci-fi, while a nerd was defined by a particularly studious approach to any given interest. Solo said she considered them more or less interchangeable, though they were once more distinct with nerds again defined by personal characteristics, such as awkwardness or intelligence, and geeks by their tastes: "I'd find myself saying, 'Oh, I'm sort of a nerd,' and then I'd say, 'Well, no, actually I'm more of a geek because I'm not that smart. I'm not smart enough to be a nerd. Nerds are more socially awkward, and geeks just like nerdy things.'" These comments suggest that certain things are geeky/nerdy a priori, while others are not but can be made the object of a nerdy/geeky interest:

> DIANA: I think that if you're a fan of video games, I think that that makes you [a geek], but just playing? My parents play first-person shooters, weirdly enough, but does that make them nerds? I don't think so. But they're not fans of it. They're not obsessively hunting it down [...]
> BEN: Um, would that apply to something like tabletop role-playing? Is there a way to play *Dungeons & Dragons* –
> DIANA: And not be a nerd? ((laughs)) I don't think so. Maybe it's just the fringe, the peripheral thing. Like, computer games. Computers can be used in ways that aren't nerdy, right? Because they're just useful. There's no way to play D&D that isn't ... its only purpose is to be nerdy. ((laughs))

When discussing video games, Diana considered the quality of engagement with gaming more important ("they're not fans of it"), but the object itself became paramount when discussing role-playing games like D&D ("its only purpose is to be nerdy"). Objects and activities conventionally associated with nerds can, at least theoretically, be separated from a nerdy interest in them if they are perceived to have some other use or are diffused enough among "normal" people. Other media goods and practices, however, are perceived as exclusively subcultural or "fringe." However, the use of such closely related words for describing both the content and form of leisure interests confuses rather than clarifies things, as in Solo's seemingly paradoxical statement that "geeks just like nerdy things."

In other comments, interviewees restricted themselves to discussing approach, with "nerd" and "geek" distinguishing between different styles of engagement. In these cases, the contrast was usually between relatively individualized and social, specialized and broad, or obsessive and casual engagements. Some considered geeks to be more social, while nerds were seen as loners: "But for me 'geek', 'geek' tends to be … someone who is very interested in a subject, can be quite vocal about it, and is social about it, I guess? Whereas, to me, a nerd is more … the social aspect isn't quite as strong, and it's more a personal intellectual pursuit, like you might have a book nerd or a literary nerd or a philosophy nerd or something like that. Someone who gets really engrossed in a subject, but it tends to be a more personal pursuit, rather than a group or a social or sharing with others sort of thing" (Wedge). Others offered a similar opposition but flipped the terms of reference – for Diana, a "geek" was "very passionate about one thing" while "nerds are more generalists." Of course, this is not merely a question of definitions. Distinctions between relatively individualized and relatively sociable forms of engagement, like all of these distinctions, have an evaluative character, and several participants mapped evaluative judgments onto the meanings of "geek" and "nerd," with positive connotations more often attached to the former than the latter:

> I would also tend to see sort of … "nerd" as a bit more negative connotation for me, just just because of the sort of all-encompassing nature that I have assigned to that, I guess, where they tend to not have a lot more, a lot of other interests. So, they tend to be kind of one-dimensional. (Wedge)

> And "geek" just has a more positive connotation for me, so I'm not offended by the use of them, but I will probably use the word "geek" more than "nerd." (Diana)

There were some exceptions, however. Shiera initially claimed that "when someone calls themselves a nerd, they're not usually meaning it in a positive way and they're also not pointing to their friends and going, 'We're all nerds.'" She later corrected herself, saying she had encountered some people at conventions who used nerd in the way that she uses geek. This led her to conclude that, although "they're not quite interchangeable," the terms' meanings are "getting closer." For his part, Barry feared that both "nerd" and "geek" carried "implications of somebody being overly preoccupied with something at the expense of so-called real life."

Perception by outsiders was not interviewees' only concern; the terms could also function as a kind of membership badge. As Diana, who elsewhere described herself as a "closet nerd," said when I asked if she used either label, "It depends on what group of friends I'm with [...] Like, when I'm talking with my geek friends? Yeah! Like, when we're playing D&D and stuff, those are terms that we use, you know." This was certainly borne out in the interviews themselves. Even participants who explicitly denied using "nerd" and "geek" in everyday speech used them repeatedly while talking to me about their leisure activities and the people they meet through them. In settings where members don't have to worry about the evaluations of outsiders, the terms can be used unproblematically, and even as fodder for good-natured ribbing or self-deprecatory humour:

> I certainly tend to put a more positive spin on the term myself. I've probably used it in sort of a negative connotation myself, but it's not, it would probably be more of a joking sense or something like that, for me. (Wedge)

> I think there's this weird kind of self – again, self-deprecating trend to reinforce geek culture by clinging to those stereotypes of social awkwardness. And often as a joking thing [...] or informing your behaviour based upon it. Like, for example, the stereotype is that when people get together to play games, there's Mountain Dew and pizza and Cheetos and stuff like that [...] I see people kind of reinforcing that, like, "Oh, I'm a geek, I'm going to a role-playing game, I should reinforce that tradition by getting some junk. And when I talk about games and promoting events, I should be like, 'Grab your Cheetos!' and stuff like that."(Kurt)

> So I just kind of generally say that we [Screens & Sorcery] organize events that are ... well, nerdy. I usually use the n-word. (Logan)

Their status as both insults when uttered by outsiders and accepted self-identifications among insiders led some to draw explicit and more serious parallels to the "reclamation" of language as a tactic of identity politics:

> DIANA: Or ... what else would we say? If you're making fun of someone, just gentle mocking, you could say, 'Oh, such a nerd.' But not in a derogatory way. Like, that would be a positive ...
> BEN: So, it's a little ironic, I guess?

DIANA: Yeah, or like an insider. You know, like, I [as a bisexual woman] can call somebody a fag whereas a homophobic person can't call them a fag. Just reclaiming the term kind … kind of thing.

Yeah, language evolution and the reclamation of pejorative terms. I noted that most of the studies of course have been around racial terms or gender terms […] For the most part, they state that reclamation of a term is done by the community itself […] They've reclaimed the term, I think, fairly successfully. One of the things that I noted in that study was that they talk about … when you reclaim or […] when a group reclaims a term of self-reference … usually it's only members of the group can use it without it being insulting. And the classic is the n-word. You can't use that … unless you are and fit, and it, then it becomes a term of brotherhood, of shared "we've both been through the same wringer," and that's what it does for them, it allows that. (Shiera)

Although examples of racist, sexist, and homophobic slurs are well known and were perhaps simply ready to hand, the fact that Diana and Shiera drew parallels to these politicized interventions in language use (i.e., cases of self-conscious re-appropriation rather than simple semantic change) also suggests that at some level they conceive of nerd culture on the pattern of marginalized minority groups subject to stigma and discrimination (see Kendall 1999b). Whether or not they are right and the comparison is justified, it indicates the complicated status that this "other n-word" and related labels have among participants in contemporary nerd culture.

Is it better to be a geek or a nerd? Does one mean good and the other bad? Is one about what you're interested in and the other about how you express your interests? Are they basically the same in the end? These questions don't have single, consistent answers. Despite the presence of these terms in media and everyday discourses, interviewees' explicit attempts at definition were quite varied and their usage was at times contradictory. From this, we might infer that the speakers were confused or that these words are ultimately meaningless. However, all participants used the terms fluently – as a fellow speaker, I could follow along and understand what they were saying – and there were some recurring patterns in how they were used. So these definitional troubles point to the limits of focusing solely on *what* was said rather than examining the social work these statements accomplished in the immediate contexts in which they were produced.

IDENTITY AS PROBLEM

When Sue Widdicombe and Robin Wooffitt (1995) set out to test whether social psychological theories of identity could explain why young people joined subcultures, they assumed – as anyone with a passing familiarity with subculture theory might – that members would have a strong sense of who they were and who they were not. However, when they approached young people who looked like they might belong to specific youth subcultures, they were surprised to find that respondents refused invitations to identify with those groups. In making sense of these denials, Widdicombe and Wooffitt "started to treat these data not as accounts produced by 'punks,' or 'gothics' or whatever" but re-framed their analysis to examine how "specific subcultural identities became salient in specific moments in the accounts" (2). That is to say, identity is not a stable object we hold in our heads or inscribe on our bodies but something we do when interacting with others. This move offered an entirely different approach to group identity, foregrounding how such identities are produced (or not) as a result of interaction. Membership categorization analysis (MCA) was the major theoretical resource for this change of perspective.

As initially formulated by Harvey Sacks (1972, 1979, 1992), membership categorization analysis takes categorization as a basic method for the ordered production of social life (see Hester and Eglin 1997; Antaki and Widdicombe 1998). Rather than reasoning everything out from first principles, we use categories to organize our knowledge and guide our actions. Three principles of classification are relevant here. First, we describe people in terms of more or less exhaustive collections of categories: "By that I mean that whatever number of categories a set contains, and without regard to the addition or subtraction of categories for that set, each set's categories classify a population [...] The names of the sets would be things like sex, age, race, religion, perhaps occupation. And in each set are categories which can classify any member of the population" (Sacks 1992, 40). For example, the categories "baby," "mommy," and "daddy" are conventionally heard as part of the collection "family," whereas "shortstop" would (usually) be heard as referring to a different collection (1972, 219). Second, Sacks explains that "a great deal of the knowledge that members of a society have about the society is stored in terms of these categories" (1992, 40). The MCA literature refers to features or behaviours that are seen as characteristic of some category as "category predicates." These predicates are reversible in that people both apply membership categories on the basis of observed characteristics and ascribe or predict characteristics based on assigned categories. Third, Sacks asserts that "any member of any category is presumptively a representative of that category for the purpose of use of whatever knowledge is stored by reference to that category" (41). Once a person or situation can be classified by a category, they are assumed to be a typical member of that category. Taken together, these principles constitute a powerful, if fallible, method of practical reasoning.[2]

Sacks (1992, 172) once wrote of a group of teenaged hotrodders, "What we want to see, in formulating the problem that they have, is what it is that they seem to see as the things they have to come to terms with." With these three principles of MCA in mind, what problems did my interviewees have with words like "geek" and "nerd"? What did they have to come to terms with? As Lori Kendall (2011, 510–11) writes, the "crucial question" is whether you are a good nerd or a bad one: "The bad nerd – asocial, bitter, too smart for his own good – might cause harm. The good nerd – lacking in social skills but still friendly, willing to use his intelligence to help others – just needs a little 'dating advice.'" But, under the condition Matt Hills (2005) calls "normative fandom," where there is an expectation that "everyone has to be a fan of something" (40), it becomes difficult to tell the difference. That is, "geek" and "nerd" have become ambiguous categories that potentially belong to more than one collection. On the one hand, we have their traditional uses within status systems, such as those constituted by school cultures (Milner 2004; Bishop et al. 2004; Robbins 2011), to designate one group of people among others. If heard this way, they name a "crowd," "subculture," or "identity," and a relatively low status one at that. On the other hand, the triumphal narrative has introduced another sense. If heard this way, the very same words can describe a quality of interaction with some text, genre, or practice. Particularly when qualified (e.g., "music nerd" or "reality-TV geek"), they seem to belong to a collection like "kinds of consumer" or "audience segments" and often carry connotations of expertise or authentic passion. However, as Hills (2005) argues, this second collection has not replaced the first – some fandoms are still perceived to be "sad" – so both are available and more or less reasonable hearings of the same words, depending upon the context in which they are employed.

Because my interviewees were fully aware of my research questions from the start, they came into the interview pre-categorized as "nerds" and "geeks," and these identities were already salient. As a matter of course, people "display their orientation to the kinds of inferences which may warrantably be drawn about them by virtue of their membership of categories" (Widdicombe and Wooffitt 1995, 70). While the stated purpose of the interviews was to learn about their experiences in geek culture – that is, to infer predicates *from* them – it also inevitably created opportunities for those categories' predicates to be applied *to* them, but they could not know for sure (at least at the beginning) how I was using and hearing these categories. When *I* addressed them as nerds, were they good or bad? Therefore, the "problem" they faced was one of damage control: how to limit the scope for negative characteristics to be inferred from their categorization as "geeks" and "nerds"? Two strategies suggest themselves – one that expands the boundaries of the category and one that restricts them.

"Regular People Talk"

An obvious way to limit negative inferences is simply to refuse the "presumptive representativeness" of category membership. But outright refusal was not a realistic option in a situation where they had already volunteered themselves as exemplars of geek culture. Instead, some interviewees attempted through our interactions to take up the "job" of "doing 'being an ordinary person'" (Sacks 1984, 414–15) despite their participation in geeky activities and events. In essence, they attempted to dramatically expand the category's membership until there was no meaningful distinction between insiders and outsiders. This is a kind of anti-essentialist argument that attempts to disrupt the normal work of predicating characteristics on a category.

My interview subjects often affirmed their normalcy, particularly when asked to generalize about geek culture. For example, Mr Fox strenuously insisted on the basic ordinariness of so-called nerds and geeks:

BEN: So, if that sort of popular image – the glasses with the tape on them, the pocket protector, the slide-rule – if that's this sort of ridiculous stereotype, are there any … images or characters that you feel better reflect your experiences of […] what the people you really encounter in comic-bookstores and video game related events are like?

MR FOX: You got a mirror? That's what people who are nerds are like. Having a … different hobby than most people doesn't change how you look. You're still a regular person. There's a whole spectrum … You don't like the same thing in nerd culture that you wouldn't like in any other culture. You know. There's jerks, idiots … just generalized humanity.

MR FOX: We talk about everything […] We have the ((laughs)) normal topics of conversation of any group of friends. "What's so-and-so up to? Can you believe this happened in the world?" Regular people talk. A lot of *Warhammer*, though, because … my friends are big into that.
BEN: So, regular people talk, plus *Warhammer*.
MR FOX: Plus *Warhammer*. And video games. And comic books.

In these extracts, Mr Fox deftly redirects my questions about him and his friends by denying that there is anything to comment on. When activities that might be viewed as distinctive to geeks are mentioned – such as his references to *Warhammer*, comics, and video games in the third extract – he treats them as if they were just more instances of "regular people talk." Similarly, Solo repeatedly described herself as "the everyman," and Barry responded to a question about people becoming "too involved" in fan activities by saying, "It's the same for everything." Widdicombe and Wooffitt (1995) identified similar tactics in their interviewees' attempts to dodge categorization as members of subcultures. Not only did these putative punks and guessed-at goths not offer the expected tribal labels when asked to describe their style, but the ways they chose to talk about, frame, and categorize their activities tended to emphasize their continuity with those undertaken by ordinary people. Widdicombe and Wooffitt (1995), Hodkinson (2002), and Locke (2012) all point to this dilemma, distinctive perhaps to modernity, of reconciling the norms of expressive individualism with group membership – and particularly membership in groups from which people are liable to infer unthinking conformity. Re-conceptualizing one's group as so broad that it potentially encompasses everyone is one way to resolve this problem – after all, what inferences can one make about the "everyman"?

"I'm Not Like That"

Notwithstanding frequent claims of utter normalcy, interviewees still made distinctions among their contemporaries. A second strategic possibility is to assign negative traits to some other category while reserving positive ones for a newly purified category – that is, to preserve a positive self-concept by othering. This can complement the first strategy. Introducing a division between "basically normal" participants, on the one hand, and "abnormal" ones who can be associated with all the negative predicates, on the other hand, was one way to address this dilemma: "You will see big groups of normal-ass looking people who are like, 'Yeah, we are not stereotypes. See, look at us all. There's diversity, cultural … ethnic and everything. We're all different people from all walks of life who share a common interest. It doesn't make us weirdoes.' […] Unless you're a cosplay guy. Those guys are weirdoes. Oh, Crystal is not gonna like that. She's a … friend who cosplays" (Mr Fox). According to this account, nerd culture is a microcosm of society at large and so diverse that nothing concrete can be said about them, except for one sub-group that can be easily dismissed as "weirdoes"; however, this group includes a friend of his, which immediately calls this judgment into question. Similarly, Solo believed that members of "mainstream culture" perceive her as a "hardcore" participant, but her own judgment is quite different: "I look at me and I'm like, 'The people I've seen!' Like, I'm not like that."

Distinctions between insiders and outsiders, authentic members and poseurs, or hardcore and casual participants are fundamental to both lay and professional theories of subcultural groups. However, David Muggleton argues that these binaries are illusory: "there are no 'hardcores' and 'preppies' in any 'realist' sense, only members who construct themselves as the former and their contemporaries as the latter, a process which […] is reciprocal in its effects" (2000, 101–2). This situational logic points to the problem of policing the border between "normal-ass looking people" and "weirdoes."

GOOD NERDS OR BAD? SYMBOLIC BOUNDARIES

The membership categorization analysis perspective contends that categories and categorization are important means for managing information about the social world, but such information isn't neutral. It is implicated in the reproduction of social divisions. As Michèle Lamont's (1992, 2000) studies of upper–middle class and working-class men in France and the United States suggest, any exercise in drawing boundaries between people – whether moral, socio-economic, or cultural in nature – is freighted with significance. These "symbolic boundaries" often divide us from our contemporaries on the basis of personality traits. The process of ascribing traits may be bound to membership categories, but how we respond to them is certainly tied into socially and culturally specific hierarchies of value. In order to elicit examples of "boundary work" in action, I borrowed from Lamont's studies and asked interviewees to talk about their fellow geeks, focusing on those they like or dislike and consider similar to or different from themselves. People draw on a variety of principles and criteria to decide whether someone is a "good" nerd or a "bad" one (Kendall 2011).

If the frequency with which a characteristic was mentioned is any indication of its importance, then my interviewees thought being interesting was the most desirable characteristic for someone to have. However, a specific construction of "interestingness" was evident in their responses: They said they like and admire intelligent people ("When I think about my friends, there's a certain level of intellectual capability and flexibility," Shiera) who are good conversationalists and can speak with authority on a range of topics ("I don't enjoy spending time with people that [...] can't hold a conversation or don't know about a lot of different interests," Wedge), expressing distinctive, reasoned, and unconventional opinions ("My gaming group, for instance, is – if you ask all four of those guys the same questions, you would get crazy different answers. So, that's what I like about my friends … is their diversity of opinions," Mr Fox). These qualities not only distinguish individuals but were also used to describe geek culture and fandom in general, which were described as more rational and discriminating in their tastes than the "average" person. Such beliefs are inscribed in the (often tongue-in-cheek) use of terms like "mundane" to describe non-fans. However, this obviously contradicts claims that nerds are just like everyone else.

Shared tastes are also important to interviewees' boundary work. For example, although he emphasized the diversity of opinion amongst his peer group, when Mr Fox was asked to describe someone he considered similar to himself (according to any measure he should like to use), he cited someone who "shared a lot of the same opinions about comics, movies, that kinda thing." It is in terms of both ideational contents ("opinions") and the objects to which they are applied ("comics, movies, that kind of thing") that Mr Fox marks out common ground. These points of reference provide many of the opportunities to perform "being interesting" in the way discussed above: "If you don't have anything to talk to someone about, then what kind of a relationship can you have with them? You don't have to share every single hobby or every single interest, but you have to have some kind of common ground, or else you're stuck saying, 'Nice weather.' ((laughs)) You know? Like, you're stuck at the very superficial, so you have to be able to relate to each other with common thoughts, common interests, that kind of idea" (Diana). That is to say, everyone agrees on the importance of being interesting or a good conversationalist, but this is defined tautologically in such a way as to privilege those who already participate in nerdy activities: You are an interesting person if you care about the things that I find interesting. The tastes and experiences they have in common allow them to get beyond the "very superficial." This suggests the importance of the events, venues, and personal connections through which they are able to encounter others who share their interests (ch. 6). However, mere professions of shared interests are often insufficient; how they are invoked is paramount.

Participants expected their peers to make genuine and unselfconscious expressions of "enthusiasm" or "passion" for their interests. Like interestingness, this value was described as if it were constitutive of nerd/geek identity:

> Enthusiasm is a big, big, big factor in maintaining a friendship that starts out based on an enthusiasm, a fandom. [...] When I'm low and down, I don't want someone to go, "Oh, I know how you feel, I'm low and down, too"; I want someone to go, "I'm sorry to hear that – look at this cool thing!" Not to distract me but to be excited about – genuinely excited about something they just did or saw or read. I want to be – and that fires me up, that gets me – that's my kickstart. So, enthusiasm's a big part of why my friendships with the people that I have the deeper friendships with, why they work. (Shiera)

> BEN: Can you unpack the idea of, you know, "being a cool guy" a little bit more?
> MR FOX: Oh, god. ... All right, being a cool guy? is ... I would say it's earnestness.
> BEN: Earnestness?
> MR FOX: Yes. A frankness about yourself, you know, you're like ... you make no excuses and you don't try to cover the genuineness about your opinions about things. You don't try to cover up, you don't try to enjoy things ironically. You just say, "Yes, I enjoy these

things. I enjoy comic books. I'm a fully functioning adult who en-joys graphic novels or films or games." It's just being who you are and not trying to cover it up.

This "genuine enthusiasm," in turn, indexes a larger set of oppositions. It was, for instance, closely associated with positively valued character-istics such as reasonableness and breadth. Without these, nerdy enthu-siasm can become fanatical, on the one hand, or narrow-minded, on the other:

> Fanboyism is the biggest thing 'cause … you can't rationalize with those people! You can't present an intellectual argument to them. It's fanaticism is essentially what it is. You can't argue with that. You can't beat crazy with smart. You either have to out-crazy it … or walk away. (Mr Fox)

> I think we all have this trait, and it is – it doesn't build friendships, it-it is to insulate, it's to [become] insular. "I love this and it's won-derful and it's fantastic, and I don't care what you think about it because I love it and it's wonderful and it's fantastic" … to not be open-minded, to be close-minded … I think it was endemic in the early days of the establishment of geekdom, in the *Star Trek* versus *Star Wars* … the versus. (Shiera)

These negative traits are also closely associated with stereotypes of so-cially inept geeks. For example, responses to prompts about people and character traits that interviewees disliked often turned on problems of etiquette – that is, people who became so wrapped up in their own in-terests and concerns that they failed to treat others properly:

> DIANA: So, I guess it's willing to learn – knowledge of the game, willing to learn, and at least some social, sociability ((laughs)) you know. At least somewhat social and not a total … I don't know what to say that isn't going to be offensive! ((laughs))
> BEN: Well, what comes to mind first?
> DIANA: Like, just a total – not a total geek! You know, like just able to interact socially with people.
> BEN: "Dork"? Is this [when you would use "dork"]?
> DIANA: No, it would be "geek," actually. "Geek" would be the, like, ((nasal voice)) "Eeee! That's not how you do it!" You know, that

kind of geek. But it's more like some sociability, like ability to interact with people and not … and not be so stuck in their ways
that they can't – just ability to be part of a communal, a communal
storytelling. Like, as with the one person that's in the game that I'd
love to get out, I'll never game with him because he's not part of
the communal storytelling.

There is a distinctively moral evaluation going on when Diana describes
this "geek." Although she talks about the "ability" to interact with people and to participate in the communal storytelling experience that is
a role-playing game, the tone she adopts – both her palpable frustration with this member of her gaming group and the nasal voice she
used to depict the "total geek" – suggests not just a failure that anyone
might make, but a personal failing. Positively valued traits are portrayed
as taken-for-granted features of these "good nerds," while negatively valued traits constitute a moral boundary that dismisses both "bad nerds"
and uninteresting "mundanes."[3] To put it another way, boundary work
obeys a logic that is situated in particular relationships – those given by
geek culture's place in the social world as well as the interview context
in which these data were generated.

Such value judgments are more than simply expressions of personal, or even collective, likes and dislikes. They are a mechanism by
which people articulate collective identities. In a well-known passage
from his *Rhetoric of Motives*, Kenneth Burke (1969, 20–1) reminds us
that no two people are identical, but they can nonetheless identify
with one another:

> A is not identical with his colleague, B. But insofar as their inter-
> ests are joined, A is *identified* with B. Or he may *identify* himself
> with B even when their interests are not joined, if he assumes that
> they are, or is persuaded to believe so.
>
> Here are ambiguities of substance. In being identified with B, A
> is 'substantially one' with a person other than himself. Yet at the
> same time he remains unique, an individual locus of motives. Thus
> he is both joined and separate, at once a distinct substance and
> consubstantial with another [...]
>
> A doctrine of *consubstantiality*, either explicit or implicit, may be
> necessary to any way of life. For substance, in the old philosophies,
> was an *act*; and a way of life is an *acting-together*; and in acting to-
> gether, men have common sensations, concepts, images, ideas, atti-
> tudes that make them *consubstantial*.

When interviewees used terms like "geek" and "nerd," when they portrayed their activities as basically ordinary and unremarkable, and when they distanced themselves from others who violated their own sense of propriety, they were negotiating not only the discursive framing of geek culture but also who they acknowledge as their peers. Indeed, this perception of shared interests and substance can overcome other important boundaries. For example, as a conservative Roman Catholic, Barry occasionally encounters significant disagreement with other fans over political and religious opinions, as well as differences in lifestyle; however, shared interests provide a means for temporarily setting aside those disagreements. In these cases, his identification with one membership category ("fan" versus "mundane") trumps others ("Christian" versus "atheist," or "conservative" versus "liberal," etc.). As the MCA perspective would have it, identity is a matter of categorization and ascription, of being placed into a group that shares certain characteristics. But to the extent that we identify ourselves with the ascribed categories, it is also performative – created through, as Burke would have it, an "acting-together" in everyday life.

So, what does it mean to call yourself a geek or nerd? It evidently depends on who's asking. For some, this subculture is now perceived as part of the mainstream – indeed, as the beating heart or roaring engine of contemporary pop culture. For others, "nerd" is still a pejorative, a way of putting people down for how they look, how they talk, or the things they're into. It's baggage that some would prefer to lose. The people I spoke with were understandably wary of media stereotypes of geeks and nerds. They knew them well and could easily improvise their own versions on demand:

> I think for me "nerd" is … and will always be *Revenge of the Nerds* because, again, that's what I grew up with. (Diana)

> The stereotypical one is … ah basically someone that is intelligent, someone that has a large social problem, that doesn't know … that's not a jock. (Hank)

> Um just kind of like … the thirty-year-old undershaven guy living in his mom's basement playing video games in his underwear while eating Cheetos kind of things. (Kurt)

You do run into the occasional troglodyte, which is that slovenly unkempt guy who spends nine hours a day playing *Warcraft* or whatever – trolling message boards. That is an unfortunate stereotype that does actually exist. (Mr Fox)

Called upon to classify their communities and peers – and, as Pierre Bourdieu might note, to thereby classify themselves – they enacted a set of tactics that, I argue, preserved their ability to negotiate the application of category predicates. They could be claim positive traits associated with geek culture and fandom – curiosity, imagination, openness, and genuine enthusiasm – while distancing themselves from negative ones – awkwardness, close-mindedness, tribalism, and obsessiveness. Philosopher Ludwig Wittgenstein said that the meaning of a word is its use, and so the "meaning" of these labels depends on what the speaker is trying to accomplish in the moment of the utterance: Is he trying to keep others from assuming he's never kissed a girl? Is she trying to keep them from dismissing her knowledge of video games? Much of what we do in everyday life is a matter of managing others' impressions – that is, how they categorize us and what they assume about us based on those categories. All of our position-takings do discursive work. They construct us for others as particular kinds of people. To the extent that this is how people *use* "nerd" and "geek," their meaning *is* this process of managing and negotiating the inferences others are liable to make about us.

This is not to say that "geek" is a sign without a referent. Following Sacks, I have already argued that people organize information about the social world with reference to membership categories, including "geek" and "nerd." When used to classify and make inferences about the world, categories are also components of "lay theories" (Morris, Ames and Knowles 2001) or "cultural models" (Holland and Quinn 1987). According to Morris, Ames, and Knowles, laypeople's practical reasoning can be compared with the reasoning of scientists insofar as their "theories" posit the existence of things and of relationships between them, are used to explain, describe, and interpret, and may be altered (if not straightforwardly falsified) by evidence. Geeks, nerds, gamers, and fans are all social types, or models that are abstracted from particulars. Some are deliberately constructed by scholars, while others occur more or less "naturally" as part of the folksonomies of everyday life (Almog 1998, under "Ambiguity in the Meaning of Social Type"). As models, types exist beyond any concrete individual they might be used to describe, but they do not constitute "groups" in the traditional sense for, as we have seen, their membership is a contingent matter of categorization. They are certainly identities, but as Burke's (1969) "doctrine of consubstantiality" suggests, identity is not quite what we thought it was, either. Talk of "identities" is "usually concerned with 'cultural identities,' identities that form in relation to major structural features of society: ethnicity, gender, race, nationality, and sexual orientation" (Holland et al. 1998, 7). However, these features are emergent, continually reproduced social phenomena. This is the underlying ontological argument being made in the turn from talking about "race" to "racialization," from "gender" to "gendering," and from "class" to "classification." If we want to understand how are people organized into groups as a matter of institutional practice or individual sense-making, then we need to understand the conceptual domains constituted by categories and types.

Thus, while sensitizing concepts like identity or subculture are still valuable (McArthur 2009; Woo 2015), I want to move forward on the assumption that geek culture is a cultural model or, more specifically, what Holland, Lachicotte, Skinner, and Cain (1998) have called a "figured world." This concept is grounded in cultural anthropology but draws on the social psychology of George Herbert Mead and the Russian theorists Mikhail Bakhtin and Lev Vygotsky. Figured worlds offer a conception of identity that is "specific to practices and activities situated in historically contingent, socially enacted, culturally constructed 'worlds'" (7). These social worlds are "figured" in that they include "figures, characters, and types who carry out its tasks and who also have styles of interacting within, distinguishable perspectives on, and orientations toward it" (51). When multiple actors share a figured world, it provides frames of reference that make actions intelligible and reasonable; when they don't, the result is "confusion and prevarication" (52). That is to say, a figured world is both a *lay* theoretical model – "a socially and culturally constructed realm of interpretation" where certain kinds of things happen for certain kinds of reasons (52) – and a *play* theoretical model, a "collectively realized 'as if' realm" (49) with its own *dramatis personae* and conventions for acting.

The various field guides and infographics with which I began this chapter are pictures of a figured world. These artifacts help us to see it as its members do – or, perhaps, as they want us to. As this chapter has argued, ordinary talk can also furnish an image of this world and the roles people are expected to play in its characteristic forms of social activity. However, in arguing that these are pieces of a model of geek culture, I have for the moment only displaced the problem of explanation to another level, and this is perhaps where the goals of lay and academic theorizing diverge. Every model is a model of something, and if anything is to be *explained*, then theory must eventually be related to practice.

2

Taking Geek Culture Seriously

A Practice-Theoretic Account

Nothing symbolizes geek culture quite like a comic-con. The first comic book conventions were organized in the 1960s as comic book fandom grew out of the older community of science fiction fans; today, these events often function as "entertainment" or "pop culture" expos, bringing together passionate fans of a wide range of more or less geeky media. Charles-Clemens Rüling and Jesper Strandgaard Pedersen (2010, 319) suggest that film festivals "are rich in symbols that take value beyond the concrete event," and the same could easily be said of comic-cons: the exhibit hall and artists' alley, star-studded panels debuting teaser trailers for blockbuster movies, photo ops and autograph signings with cult stars of yesteryear, elaborate costumes, and interminable lines all say something about how people relate to media.

Science fiction and other fan conventions long signified the supposed pathology of media fandom – the infamous *Saturday Night Live* sketch in which *Star Trek*'s William Shatner commanded his own fans to get a life, for instance, was predictably set at a con. However, the rise of "geek chic" discourses has been intertwined with a re-evaluation of comic-cons. San Diego's Comic-Con International and several other major conventions now routinely admit over 100,000 attendees, while smaller and more targeted cons have sprung up in cities and towns across North America; the "fan event" sector as a whole is responsible for US$500 million in ticket sales and an estimated $3–6 billion in total economic impact, according to research conducted for the online ticketing platform Eventbrite in 2013 (Buell, n.d.). But it is not just their size that exerts this gravitational pull. No longer imagined as dreary hotel ballrooms with sad losers grubbing through collections of memorabilia, cons have become a premiere, almost glamorous, site for promoting big-budget, high-concept entertainment franchises – a Cannes for the rest of us. Entertainment media cover them with a level of detail and excitement that would have been unimaginable thirty years ago, as a major comic-con today necessarily involves big announcements and reveals about coming attractions, opportunities to interview and photograph Hollywood stars, and a compelling visual spectacle.

As difficult as it proves to formally define, we know geek culture when we see it, and it is uniquely visible and palpable at a comic-con. Events like the San Diego Comic-Con are "not just the pop culture industry in microcosm" but "the pop culture industry incarnate": "Everyone and everything relating to comics and their connection to wider entertainment industries is here, under one roof, in person. For five days in July, Stan Lee, Steven Spielberg, the cast of *Twilight*, the makers of bestselling video games, graphic novelists reviewed in the *New York Times*, the publishers of the first comics fanzines of the 1960s, the proprietors of the most-read comics blogs and news sites, hundreds of dealers and exhibitors, and throngs of hard-core fans all occupy the same space and breathe the same air" (Salkowitz 2012, 19). Comic-cons not only provide a space for industry and audiences to interact with one another but also actively articulate different industries and different audiences together into what business analyst Rob Salkowitz calls "the pop culture industry" but we could equally call geek culture. It is an almost carnivalesque space in which play and fantasy seem like the most important things in the world. From these dedicated collectors, cosplayers, and people willing to camp out for hours or days to catch the first glimpse of a new movie, we can gather hints of what it means to take media consumption seriously. The active, creative audiences that gather at a comic-con or other fan convention represent much of what makes geek culture meaningful and attractive to its members. An account of media fans like the people we conventionally call geeks and nerds is necessarily an account of media audiences, but outside of special, bounded spaces like comic-cons the audience is something of a mirage.

AUDIENCES, EMPIRICAL AND ABSTRACT

This is perhaps a surprising claim. In everyday life, we routinely and unremarkably make assumptions about audiences when talking about media, culture, politics, technology, and so on: "In our everyday language we are used to saying that one can draw or attract an audience; one can move, grip, or stir an audience; an audience can be responsive, enthusiastic, unsympathetic and so on. In all these cases, the audience is implicitly granted an autonomous, supra-individual existence. In common sense language, then, the objective status of audience is treated as self-evident; audience is assumed to be a given category" (Ang 1991, 27). Furthermore, every theory of media, communication, and culture has something to say – if only implicitly (Livingstone 1998) – about the people who use media, receive messages, and experience culture, and whole industries exist to measure and report what audiences are doing and thinking. Yet despite the manifest importance of the audience to any theory of media and communication, there are fundamental difficulties in conceptions of the mass media audience. As Douglas B. Park (1982, 247) writes, audiences are "obvious, crucial, and yet remarkably elusive."

John Fiske (1992a, 358) observed that "'audience' suggests a priority that is misleading, for an audience can exist only when hearing something." The aural metaphor underlying the audience concept foregrounds a particular sense and implies a limited range (i.e., earshot). The term is thus an odd fit for many of the media forms and experiences onto which it is transposed, though there are no obvious candidates to replace it that aren't at least as problematic (Livingstone 1998, 204–5). However, the problem runs deeper than an awkward metaphor. Most importantly, talk of "audiences" typically elides an important distinction, namely, that the audience of a performance – say, a speech, play, or concert – has a concreteness that the audience of a newspaper article, television show, or musical recording does not. The former comprises real people interacting with one another in a definite space and time, while the latter may be geographically and temporally dispersed, being added up from innumerable discrete moments of consumption. Like "geek culture" and "fandom," this audience in general is a conceptual abstraction, a "taxonomic collective" that, by "lumping people together [...] turns them into 'audience members'" (Ang 1991, 29).

Cinema audiences provide a particularly useful illustration of this distinction because they are often both at once. Films have empirical audiences, some number of real people who gather together in a particular movie theatre at the same time. These people can profoundly affect your perception of the film – you laugh and cry and gasp in surprise together, or maybe someone spoils it by whispering, eating loudly, or forgetting to turn off their phone. However, films also have an abstract audience. This is the sum of all those empirical audiences in all those movie theatres (and eventually in airplanes, at home, etc.), whether conjured by filmmakers imagining their potential viewers, marketers doing their best to attract them, or reviewers attempting to anticipate their responses. Notably, there is no necessary connection between any of these concrete audiences and their abstract representation. Indeed, the latter "implies a denial of the messy social world of actual audiences" (Ang 1991, 30), as "the idiosyncrasies of the individual people making up an audience, as well as the specific interrelations between these people," are flattened out by a view from nowhere (29). However, an abstract audience may be regarded as an actor (at least within particular institutional circuits, such as systems of ratings measurement; Meehan 2005) in ways concrete ones never can. The transformation of concrete audiences into abstract ones is a key way that viewers, readers, listeners, and players are "positioned by particular forms of mass communication, with particular possibilities for interactivity and engagement, with particular kinds of meanings prioritized and legitimated over others" (Livingstone 1998, 197).

Rejecting the naïve view of media audiences as a social group, Sonia Livingstone (1998, 206) proposes that "audience researchers could usefully conceive of audiences in terms of the relationship between media and people." We need accounts of audiences that restore those messy social worlds inhabited by real people, for the audience is "identified by what its members *do* rather than by what they are" (Fiske 1992a, 351; emphasis added). In *Family Television*, David Morley (1986) argued that television viewing had to be understood as a practice unfolding in a particular social context, namely the home and the social relationships constituted by the family; however, as Ito et al. (2010) demonstrate in their ethnographic studies of young people's relationships with digital media, the family is only one social frame for practices of media consumption. Some are structured by institutions like the worlds of school and work, others by peers or particular interests. Building on this approach, which sees media consumption as a differentiated set of practices, this chapter establishes a theoretical and empirical framework for studying media audiences based in theories of practice, notably the work of Alasdair MacIntyre (2007).

THE PRACTICE TURN

A "theory of practice" sounds like an oxymoron, but philosophers have been thinking about action since at least Aristotle (Knight 2008b). Eclipsed for some time by rationalist and idealist conceptions of the self and society, practice has re-emerged in recent years. Some have even marked a "practice turn" in social theory (Schatzki, Knorr Cetina, and von Savigny 2001). In the last chapter, I suggested that the "geek cul-ture" construct represents a figured world, "a socially and culturally con-structed realm of interpretation in which particular characters and actors are recognized, significance is assigned to certain acts, and par-ticular outcomes are valued over others" (Holland et al. 1998, 52). Dorothy Holland (2010) has explicitly connected this concept to theo-ries of social practice.[1] If figured worlds are mental representations, they are representations of concrete "domains of activity" (280n6), for "only in these spaces of local practice do social formations come into contact with persons and stand to shape or be shaped by them" (278). That is to say, this represented world not only guides action but is also grounded in practical experience.

According to its strongest advocates, practice theory holds out the promise of the transcending antinomies that have bedevilled modern social and political thought. However, a grand, unified theory of prac-tice is not yet on offer, for the concept can be found in (or re-con-structed from) a wide range of theoretical and philosophical resources, many of which are conventionally viewed as incompatible with one another. Scholars as different as the American pragmatists, Georg Sim-mel, Ludwig Wittgenstein, sociology's Chicago School, Norbert Elias, Harold Garfinkel, Michel Foucault, Pierre Bourdieu, and Anthony Gid-dens (to name only a few leading lights) can all be read as prefiguring some aspect of the practice turn. Despite these diverse sources, certain family resemblances may be found among practice approaches. Un-surprisingly, they assume that coherent, distinctive, and more or less or-ganized practices are the basic units of social analysis. According to Theodore Shatzki (2001, 2), theories of practice share a "belief that such phenomena as knowledge, meaning, human activity, science, power, language, social institutions, and historical transformation occur with-in and are aspects or components of the field of practices. The field of practices is the total nexus of interconnected human practices. The 'practice approach' can thus be demarcated as all analyses that (1) de-velop an account of practices, either the field of practices or some sub-domain thereof (e.g., science), or (2) treat the field of practices as the place to study the nature and transformation of their subject matter." This "field of practices" is an attempt to reconfigure some of social the-ory's basic components. On this view, practices are not new objects of inquiry but a better account of how the social world is continually re-produced and transformed. Macro-level theoretical constructs – like "structure" or "the state" – are simply ways of describing chronically reproduced practices, while micro-level phenomena typically attributed to individual agency are only intelligible in terms of the ordered social practices of which they are a part.

Schatzki's definition clears away a great deal of conceptual accretion but leaves us with a wide-open field – can we be more specific about what it means to take practice as the fundamental building block of social life? To begin with, we are talking about particular social *practices* rather than *praxis*, or human activity in general (Reckwitz 2002). Schatzki (1996) further distinguishes between "dispersed" and "integrative" practices. The former are "dispersed among different sectors of social life" and include such practices as "describing, ordering, following rules, explaining, questioning, reporting, examining, and imagining" (91). Based on these examples, we can understand a dispersed practice as a set of social competences that people use to accomplish something in everyday life; however, it is important to note that these practices have a level of coherence – provided by "teleoaffective structures" that comprise "ends, projects, tasks, purposes, beliefs, emotions, and moods" (89). It is because of this coherence that we can recognize dispersed practices such as reason-giving or joke-telling in action. Integrative practices, by contrast, are "the more complex practices found in and constitutive of particular domains of social life," examples of which include "farming practices, business practices, voting practices, teaching practices, celebration practices, cooking practices, recreational practices, industrial practices, religious practices, and banking practices" (98). Practices of this type articulate behaviours, competences, intentions, activities, and other dispersed practices together in such a way that someone involved in one could not explain their conduct without reference to the whole practice.

I want to suggest that some practitioners further elevate integrative practices, making them not only descriptive of a domain of social life but also foundational to a distinctive kind of personhood. Following the philosopher Albert Borgmann (1984), let's call them "focal practices." "To focus on something," Borgmann writes, "or to bring it into focus is to make it central, clear, and articulate" (197), and focal practices are "practices of engagement" that concentrate our attention: "The human ability to establish and commit oneself to a practice reflects our capacity to comprehend the world, to harbor it in its expanse as a context that is oriented by its focal points. To found a practice is to guard a focal concern, to shelter it against the vicissitudes of fate and our frailty" (207). Where dispersed practices comprise distinctive forms of social behaviour, integrative ones typify complexes of activity like farm-

ing, teaching, or cooking. Focal practices, in turn, are not only definitive of a kind of activity but "guard in its undiminished depth and identity the thing that is central to the practice" (209). These practices touch
on the ends of a life organized around some set of focal concerns.

It is important to note, however, that formally identical behaviour
can, at different times and for different people, be articulated into any
of these categories of practice. Let us take Fiske's (1992a) practice of "audiencing the show," for instance. Alan Warde (2005, 150n6) suggests that
we might think of consumption as "a dispersed practice, one that occurs
often and in many different sites," but not as an integrative practice because most of the time people "consume without registering or reflecting that that is what they are doing." Much of the activity around media
is presumably consumption of this sort: as a kind of casual leisure, audiencing is typically a dispersed practice that entails behaviours (e.g.,
looking or listening more or less attentively) and competences (e.g., understanding the conventions and codes employed), as well as uses and
gratifications. There are also media-related integrative practices – reading a daily newspaper, following a TV series, cinema-going, or supporting a sports team, for instance – which have distinctive "understandings,
know-how and teleoaffective structures" (150n6) that incorporate and
build upon simpler forms of media consumption. But the kind of "serious" consumption that we associate with fandom represents another
order of practice, one which entails relationships with other participants,
a longer and more committed career, and a reflexive awareness of being
engaged in a practice that precedes and will outlast the individual practitioners. To be a fan, the kind of fan who actively "belongs to a fandom,"
is to be a particular kind of person – or, even better, to make media the
focus of a particular kind of life. Alasdair MacIntyre offers a theory of
practice that describes these kinds of commitments. Applied to media-
oriented practices, MacIntyre helps us answer what is, in my view, one of
the most fundamental questions for media and communication scholars: what does a good life lived in, through, and around media look like?

MACINTYRE'S THEORY OF PRACTICE

Alasdair MacIntyre is a preeminent advocate of the neo-Aristotelian
"virtue ethics" approach in moral philosophy. He began his career as a
member of the British New Left, raising questions about the moral and
ethical grounding of political critique (MacIntyre 1998), though he has
spent most of his working life in the United States. In his most famous

text, *After Virtue*, MacIntyre (2007) proposes that the modern world has somehow lost the ability to talk coherently about what we ought to do. Moral discourse has become unmoored from reason, and disagreement is interminable. MacIntyre's return to Aristotle and, later, to Thomas Aquinas is meant to give a new foundation for morality. Central to this project is his conception of social practices as the ground of human flourishing. As Kelvin Knight (2008a) suggests, MacIntyre thus introduces an important twist to Aristotelian teleology: "What is novel about *After Virtue* is not its famous rejection of Aristotle's 'metaphysical biology' but its proposition that some new teleological justification of morality must be elaborated in its place. What the book substitutes for 'metaphysical biology' is social theory" (40). His key insight is that every "moral philosophy [...] characteristically presupposes a sociology" (MacIntyre 2007, 23).

For MacIntyre as much as for Aristotle, a human life is understood in terms of the ends it seeks to attain. However, these ends are not – as Aristotle supposed – biologically given but socially produced. Social practices create contexts in which people discover, elaborate, and reason together about ends: "MacIntyre proposes his sociology of practices as the presupposition of a 'narrative' and teleological conception of the self, in which the person's desires are educated and her actions unified through her quest for the good life. This good is not stipulated at the start of her life but something that, insofar as her life is coherently recountable and intelligible, she progressively understands as she advances toward her goals, so that she can explain how she advanced from who she was to who she is, and to what future condition she intends to progress" (Knight 2008b, 42–3). This account of morality is constructionist (i.e., moral ideas are not eternal absolutes; they come from somewhere and can change) but not relativist (i.e., moral ideas are legitimate; they are more than the advantage of the stronger) because practices have their own, historically bounded rationality. They provide the basis for making normative claims that are intersubjectively valid but not merely conventional. MacIntyre thus stakes out a middle ground between moral minimalism and universalism, with the implication that moral notions are precisely as "universal" as the social practices that provide their ground by defining a community of moral reasoners.[2] That is to say, focal practices are not merely routinized activities but are related to conceptions of human flourishing in particular ways: "By a 'practice' I am going to mean any coherent and complex form of socially established cooperative activity through which goods internal to that form of activity are realised in the course of trying to achieve those standards of excellence which are appropriate to, and partially definitive of, that form of activity, with the result that human powers to achieve excellence, and human conceptions of the ends and goods involved, are systematically extended" (MacIntyre 2007, 187). How broadly can this definition be applied? MacIntyre does not address contemporary media specifically in *After Virtue*, but his definition embraces (among others): "arts, sciences, games, politics in the Aristotelian sense, [and] the making and sustaining of family life" (188). And there are good reasons for adding media to this list. Referencing MacIntyre's definition, Nick Couldry writes that media "are surely a practice in this specific philosophical sense. What we do with media *matters* for how humans flourish overall" (2012, 190; original emphasis). Indeed, it is difficult to imagine any contemporary practice that does not, in some respect, involve the media or communications technologies – if not substantively "media-oriented," they are at least "media-related" (Couldry and Hobart 2010). Because, as MacIntyre insists, his definition of practice is not only a philosophical but also a sociological concept, it provides a rubric for both normative evaluation and empirical analysis. It refers to objects we can observe in the social world. In particular, a focal practice involves (a) goods and virtues, (b) communities and traditions, and (c) institutions.

Goods and Virtues

As mentioned above, MacIntyre's moral philosophy revolves around goods – not material objects, but the fundamental ends or purposes of human life. The good life is one where you do what is best for you, not simply as a generic human being but as someone engaged in some set of practices. These practices define particular goods for their practitioners. Indeed, every practice involves two different kinds of goods, those internal to the practice and those external to it. In *After Virtue*, this distinction is established with the memorable thought experiment of teaching a precocious seven-year-old to play chess (MacIntyre 2007, 188–9). At first, the child must be encouraged and cajoled to participate, and so a treat – a piece of candy, say – is offered every time she plays. In time, however, she may come to appreciate the artfulness of the game, the particular kinds of strategic thinking it calls forth from her, and the satisfaction of having played well. As she does, the sugary inducements become less and less important to her. In this illustration, then, the collection of skills and pleasures "which cannot be had in any way but by playing chess or some other game of that specific kind" are goods internal to the practice of chess (and games of that specific kind), while the candy, which represents such "real world" incentives as money, status, and power, is a good external to it.

The distinction between internal and external goods accords with powerful and widely held moral intuitions about the importance of activities or projects undertaken "for their own sake," rather than for the material or status rewards they might furnish. Thus, healthy practices, ones where their characteristic internal goods are actively cultivated and widely available, are autotelic (literally, "ends in themselves"), and are understood as such by its practitioners. While external goods may be achieved through other means, internal goods are only realizable in particular practices and are only recognizable to practitioners who have experienced them (MacIntyre 2007, 188–9). Importantly, internal goods are also, in a way, public goods: "External goods are [...] characteristically objects of competition in which there must be losers as well as winners. Internal goods are indeed the outcome of competition to excel, but it is characteristic of them that their achievement is a good for the whole community who participate in the practice. So, when Turner transformed the seascape in painting or W.G. Grace advanced the art of batting in cricket in a quite new way their achievement enriched the whole relevant community" (190–1). Because practitioners in a given practice share in one another's achievements and share the experience of pursuing and (sometimes) achieving these goods, there is an intersubjectively justified framework for evaluating – or, at least, for reasoning and arguing about – success or failure with respect to the practice's distinctive ends. They thus provide a basis for squaring the circle of making moral judgments when there is an objective diversity of conceptions of the good.

The internal goods of a practice are intimately connected to virtues. Although MacIntyre's work is deeply informed by his Christian faith, he does not mean the religious virtues of hope, faith, and charity. *Arete*, the Greek term we translate as "virtue," also means "excellence," and in the vocabulary of virtue ethics, they are not simply about being a good person in some Pollyannaish way. They are dispositions that lead us to act in particular ways, dispositions that aid our ability to realize or achieve specific goods, given the constraints of concrete situations. If goods are articulated and realized through practices, then so too are virtues. According to Couldry (2012, 199), "An ethics of media in a neo-Aristotelian approach is oriented to identifying the multiple dispositions that we would expect of those who act in and through media," to which we must also add those who act and build their lives around media.

Communities and Traditions

Because internal goods cannot be realized outside the practices in which they are embedded, the novice must undergo an "apprenticeship" before they can effectively pursue those goods for themselves. Thus, practices are never individual projects, even when practitioners are working alone. They are by definition social because practices are necessarily rooted in communities and traditions. As MacIntyre (2007, 194) writes: "To enter into a practice is to enter into a relationship not only with its contemporary practitioners, but also with those who have preceded us in the practice, particularly those whose achievements extended the reach of the practice to its present point." This is, in part, a pragmatic issue of reproduction – identifying a practice is a merely academic exercise if no practitioners actually do it – but MacIntyre's point is subtler.

Communities are custodians of the standards of excellence applicable to a given practice, both maintaining and developing them over time. The history of the practice, as narrated by its contemporary practitioners, inevitably enacts normative conceptions of good practice. These are communicated by how the story is told: the changes and developments (both positive and negative) that are picked out as points of inflection say something about how the community is defining the nature of their practice; the people and achievements that are consecrated serve as role models for others. This ongoing, historical conversation is essential to practices and to their ability to function as a nursery for relevant virtues. Without it, a practice is mere activity.

Russell Keat (2000) argues that the "community requirement" – MacIntyre's "apparent 'insistence' that [productive practices] should form an integral part of the way of life of a local *community*, with their participants consequently regarding their own good as inherently related to that of its other members, and vice versa" (123; emphasis in original) – is excessively influenced by a nostalgic attachment to traditional communities. He seeks to rescue the theory of practice from a reliance on a vanishing social form by rejecting this community requirement. Although MacIntyre does indeed suggest that practices were more central to life before the rise of the liberal state, this historical claim is independent of the general theory. Moreover, when discussing specific practices, he does not limit himself to some bygone historical period.

For instance, key examples (cited above) include painting and cricket. In each case, the "relevant community" is the one constituted by the practice: the community of painters or the cricketing community (MacIntyre 2007, 191). That is to say, we are talking about "communities of practice" (Lave and Wenger 1991; Wenger 1998), not generic "local communities." These communities are defined by mutual engagement, a joint enterprise, and shared repertoires (Wenger 1998, 73), rather than the affective unity of will that Ferdinand Tönnies attributed to *Gemeinschaften*, and community in this sense is hardly extinct.

MacIntyre certainly believes that specific social structures can be inimical to focal practices, but the corollary is that other social structures can encourage their formation, and this strengthens the claim that his conception of community is not fundamentally anti-modern. Rather, community is an ongoing achievement. It is a stance that is taken towards one's relationships with others, and one that can be detected in many corners of geek culture. Communities are not confined to a lost golden age; they may look different today, but we are arguably witnessing a renaissance of community-making as digital communications technologies further the deterritorialization of interest-driven practices beyond local peer groups (Ito et al. 2010). There is, therefore, no reason to set aside the community requirement, which is nothing more than the observation that focal practices invoke real and imagined others as a prerequisite to their day-to-day performance.

Institutions

Communities are necessary for the achievement of internal goods, but they do not stand alone. Practices and their communities must also be supported by what MacIntyre terms institutions: "Chess, physics and medicine are practices; chess clubs, laboratories, universities and hospitals are institutions. Institutions are characteristically and necessarily concerned with what I have called external goods. They are involved in acquiring money and other material goods; they are structured in terms of power and status, and they distribute money, power and status as rewards. Nor could they do otherwise if they are to sustain not only themselves, but also the practices of which they are bearers" (2007, 194). As I suggested above, the distinction between internal and external goods parallels a pre-existing discourse of the intrinsic and extrinsic motivation, and that same discourse tends to devalue external goods. Doing something for money, power, or status is not typically a praiseworthy motivation, but external goods are not all bad. Indeed, they are useful and often necessary.[3] People need them in order to reproduce their practices, and institutions play the crucial role of distributing them among the community of practice. Moreover, institutions stand between practitioners and what we might call "meta-institutions," such as the market and the state, which dominate the larger economy of external goods.

The problem of institutions is decisive, and the history of geek culture and its constituent communities has often been described through the creation of clubs, conventions, and amateur publications. Local fan communities exist in a symbiotic (though not entirely untroubled) relationship with whole industries that are run to a greater and lesser extent by people who also have a history as practitioners – though they now occupy positions that may well change their relationship to the practice in question. Thus, clubs and societies, comic-book stores, game shops, distributors, and companies that actually produce media texts and objects are all involved, in their own ways, in sustaining geek culture. Like the institutions that MacIntyre describes, they acquire money and other resources, develop a hierarchy of insiders and outsiders, if not necessarily leaders and followers, and eventually redistribute the capital they have collected as "rewards." They may not do these things perfectly or even very well, but because they do them the geek culture scene remains available: societies and conventions are able to meet for their activities, stores remain open and are stocked with goods, and so on. The social worlds that they compose also support the broader and more dispersed community of nerds and geeks, enabling them to pursue and enjoy the goods internal to their practices.

So the problem turns out to be, not external goods as such, but rather the confusion of means and ends. As Knight (2008a, 44) puts it, "A teleological ordering of social relations would subordinate institutions to practices." Institutions cannot simply hoard external goods for themselves; if they are functioning as institutions, they must redistribute those goods in ways that provide appropriate support and incentives for practitioners, accord with applicable standards of excellence, and are consistent with the shared pursuit of the internal goods that give rise to them in the first place. The problem of institutionalization turns out to be about distributive justice, and problems of justice are rarely settled easily. They are certainly never settled once and for all. This is all part of the "struggle for organization" that characterized the growth of, first, science-fiction fandom and then later communities of geeky practice (Wollheim quoted in Gardner 2012, 69).

To summarize, internal goods contribute to human flourishing and to the development of virtuous character but can only be acquired through practices. Practices and communities are mutually constitutive, and the adaptation of one to the other requires the continued support of institutions. Institutions help sustain practices over time so that they and their distinctive goods remain available to new entrants to the community, but they can also become sources of vulnerability if they pursue external goods at the expense of internal ones or if they distribute them badly. A well-ordered practice provides a space and context for us to articulate and develop life projects that are good for us, not as generic subjects, but as ourselves, people with particular goals, ideals, commitments, interests, and passions.

It may seem presumptuous to speak of morality or human flourishing with respect to reading comic books, watching anime, or playing RPGs, just as a Catholic moral philosopher will strike many as an odd figure to bring into a conversation about geek media culture. This is because, as Jonathan Gray (2005, 849) argues, media studies has largely abandoned the moral register: "Indeed, to talk of morality in media studies itself is to approach a rarely discussed topic [...] and to utter the word morality in conjunction with television is often to invoke a discourse most dear to right-wing media panic groups. Numerous studies of fans barely mention morality, as the moral text appears deeply submerged, and perhaps morals and ethics are rarely mentioned when everything is perceived to be fine. However, the strong presence of a moral lens through which many [Television Without Pity] viewers claim to watch some television suggests the significance (even if often unstated or hidden) of this lens in media consumption." Media studies is certainly involved in moral projects – indeed, some of the field's most significant bodies of work demonstrate a sense of moral purpose: ameliorating harmful media effects; challenging sexist, racist, and classist representations; improving democratic deliberation; and so on. However, they are rarely understood in such terms. Media scholars are expected to have a "politics" but they don't typically have a "morality," for as Gray suggests, moral talk has been rendered a highly suspect discourse.

Recently, there has been a new conversation about media and morality. The media ethics proposed by Luc Boltanski (1999), Roger Silverstone (2007), Nick Couldry (2006, 2012), and others is not about the goodness or badness of texts and their effects. This view of media ethics is also distinct from the applied ethics of journalists, advertisers, and other professional communicators, focusing instead on "the general issues that media as a human practice raises for anyone involved in it" (Couldry 2012, 187). These are questions about the consequences of media and mediated life for ethics in general, as Silverstone (2007, 109) says: "Everyday life is a moral space [...] And now the everyday includes the media." However, it is not only that media are inescapable features of daily life and, therefore, need to be accounted for when we talk about life in contemporary society but also that media must be numbered among "the *ethically significant 'practices'* in which humans are involved" (Couldry 2012, 186; emphasis in original). When we orient ourselves to media, what we do with and around them is morally consequential.

Geek culture, as I am defining it, is a social space generated by a set of focal practices, their associated communities of practitioners, and the local institutions that sustain them. The geek culture scene is a kind of public sphere – for some it is imagined as a counterpublic, while for others it only constitutes a subpublic (Warner 2002), but it is in any case a "space of appearing" (Silverstone 2007) where people work out what is important and valuable to them. Through the activities taking place within it, participants are brought into contact with others who are made significant by their shared orientations to a practice and its objects. The "ethical connection" (Maffesoli 1996, 18) forged in these communities does not mean that every member is beyond reproach, or even that participating makes them better people than they would otherwise be, but it does suggest an immanent tendency towards "seriousness" in Stebbins's sense (1992, 8) – that is, towards "such qualities as earnestness, sincerity, importance, and carefulness." The broad sweep of MacIntyre's theory of practice helps us think about the contributions that media and the activity that takes place around them can make to our lives and our capacity to act as moral agents. Geek culture may have a selective appeal, but insofar as participating in these social worlds means participating in a practice or practices, it opens out onto a much broader vista of human significance. Members' mutual, practical orientation to particular objects constructs a horizon within which they encounter one another. It is on this basis that "geek culture" coheres as an object of knowledge, both to practitioners themselves and outside observers.

If cultural studies has a signature concept, it is undoubtedly the active audience. Research on media reception, and especially on that of the most dedicated and affectively engaged audiences (for which the media fan has been the paradigm; Jenkins 2013), has gradually built up a picture of media consumers as active interpreters negotiating the meaning of mass media texts for their own purposes or pleasures. That there are no cultural dopes is, by now, axiomatic. The encounter between audience and text is always complex and contingent, even if much audience activity is far less oppositional than some scholars hoped and most is inconsequential or uninteresting to anyone else. Indeed, it may be that the "active audience," abstracted away from specific practices and contexts that made that activity meaningful, is an untenable generalization. It is only when activity is channelled into a specific social form that it becomes an object available for analysis, that it becomes *action*. This is the difference between fandom as a subjective or emotional state experienced by individuals (an audience "in itself") and a fandom as a community (an audience "for itself"), between people who play games and gamers, between casual and serious leisure.

As MacIntyre defines them, practices are characterized by a particular relationship to internal goods, communities, institutions, and so on. The meaningful action that unfolds within geek cultures – and not the symbolic expressions captured in science fiction and fantasy novels, superhero comics books, or video games – are their contents. Traditional "content" is certainly important to participants: it is a subjectively meaningful ordering principle that people use to define the boundaries of their practices. If we are to distinguish between social action and mere activity, we need to understand what people themselves think they are doing and why. This is impossible without reference to the objects around which people are acting, of which the media are significant as both "resources for defining collectivities" and "means for constructing [them]" (Couldry and Hepp 2017, 175).[4] For example, the practices of soap opera fans, sports fans, and sci-fi fans are formally quite similar – similar enough that we can call them all "fandoms" – but they are experienced differently. Some of this difference is indeed attributable to the content of the media goods in question, of the particular demands they make on their audiences, but much is the result of contextual and contingent factors that have shaped the history of fan practices in individual fields. Nonetheless, it is because they are engaged in one of these practices rather than another, and rather than "mundane" media-related practices, that someone will call upon a particular body of attitudes, competences, and teleoaffective structures.

We know that participation in geek culture can be a deeply meaningful experience. For at least some people, geek culture and its many tributaries and distributaries constitute an important way of thinking about who they are. In *Why Things Matter to People*, Andrew Sayer (2011) argues that social scientists have tended to neglect the values and concerns that shape people's actions. But, Sayer writes, "the relational quality of human social being is [...] evident in the capacity of individuals to form attachments and commitments, whether to ideas, causes [...] traditions, practices or other people" (124). It is in this sense that we are "beings for whom things matter" (5), beings who express our deepest concerns through focal practices.

Paul J. Booth has argued that describing fandom as a practice "ignores the major focus of fandom as an identity as well" (2015, ¶3.7). Certainly, our picture of fandom is incomplete if it does not consider the sentiments that frame and motivate action. However, personal identity can be highly idiosyncratic. One could speculate endlessly about the "why" of fandom (J. Coulson 1994), but such speculations all too easily get caught up in the internal debates and struggles, position-takings and post-hoc rationalizations, and the infinite regression of representations that shape everyday social experience. Thankfully, identities and meanings do not reside in the mind alone. Although they are obviously in some sense "subjective," they also have an objective existence. They circulate and can be observed in interactions between people, have real effects on how social life unfolds, and leave traces in material spaces, organizations, and biographies. Thus we might replace Sayer's philosophical question (i.e., "why do things matter to people?") with an empirical one: *how* do things matter to people? Or, as Couldry (2012, 35) phrases it, "what are people doing that is related to media?" This shift in emphasis is crucial because practice is necessarily prior – in the sense of temporal or logical priority, not necessarily of importance – to identity. From a practice-theoretic perspective, doing always precedes being.

During the twentieth century, the media favoured by geeks were routinely written off as unserious, trivial, and even isolating. It was pop culture that didn't even manage to be all that popular. However, a set of social practices grew up around them as people talked and hung out, exchanged letters and fanzines, and attended club meetings and conventions. People drawn to the spaces and communities associated with these practices have enabled them to continue to develop and change along with the media. Despite the stereotypes of lonely nerds in their parents' basements, taking geek culture seriously *as a culture* orients us to collective rather than individual meaning-making and to activities that could not exist without people acting in concert to reproduce and innovate those activities. The figured world of geek culture, as a cultural model, has its complement in a set of social worlds constituting a cultural scene. As a sensitizing concept, thinking in terms of scenes offers a "view of the sociocultural domain as made up of agents in relationship around shared practices of meaning-, place- and community-making" (Woo, Rennie, and Poyntz 2015, 5). First, scene thinking points towards a "microsociology" of cultural production (Straw 1991, 375). Will Straw argues, for instance, that cultural scenes are produced by "systems of articulation" that manage the twin pressures towards conservation and innovation, and include such prosaic factors as liquor licensing, noise by-laws, and the real estate market. The resulting scene is a nexus of niches, a space where multiple communities of practice are articulated together by the shared (physical or virtual; Grimes 2015) institutions through which practitioners circulate. Second, scenes remain "overproductive signifying communities" (Shank 1994, 122), places where cultural activity is greater than the sum of its parts. Cultural scenes are typically seen as the locus of a kind of effervescent sociality, such as that associated with music scenes and "club cultures" (Thornton 1996), and this is the side of scene thinking that attends to the ephemerality and fluidity of social life, though they may also live on in collective memory. Third, as the theatrical metaphor suggests, scene thinking also acknowledges that media fans are not only audiences but also actors in their own right. For its participants, the geek culture scene sets the stage for a production of everyday life.[5]

Approaching geek culture as a generative context for social action, a figured world that makes identities available and salient, and a scene of practice, rather than as a form of personal identity, reorients our attention to the "observable aspects" of fan practices (Sandvoss 2005, 6). The remainder of this book examines some of the things that some people we call nerds or geeks are actually, literally doing with and around the media. Taking MacIntyre's account of what, following Borgmann, I'm calling focal practices as a point of departure, it attends to how people develop and express conceptions of value, narrate the progress of their life, and conceptualize themselves as members of communities. Further, it examines how these communities are supported by various local institutions and constrained by external limitations such as time, space, money, and other demands.

3

Values and Virtues

What Is Best in Life?

"What is best in life?" In a memorable scene from *Conan the Barbarian* (John Milius 1982), the eponymous Cimmerian is asked this question and replies, "To crush your enemies, see them driven before you, and to hear the lamentation of their women." I certainly don't want to endorse Conan's answer, but explicitly asking what people value is a worthwhile exercise.

Value is a sometimes subtle but always important part of lay theories. Every claim or description of the social world incorporates assumptions about the good. Furthermore, processes of valuation go hand in hand with projects of identity formation: Conan is a barbarian precisely because he values crushing his enemies, et cetera. "Value," in the sense of what we esteem, is intimately connected with "values," in the looser sense of "cultural values" or "moral values." Hence, to speak of value is to speak of ends and goods – what is the goal of some action, not only in the shorter-term horizon of instrumentality but also in the longer-term horizon of value-rationality?

As discussed last chapter, Alasdair MacIntyre (2007) asserts that social practices are defined by the distinctive "internal goods," linked by habits or virtues to conceptions of human flourishing, around which they are organized. Goods internal to a practice are the specific pleasures, achievements, and accomplishments that can only be realized within that practice. They make the effort involved in any practice worthwhile. They're what its practitioners *value* about it. There is room for individual agency and disagreement – remember that MacIntyre is concerned with the grounds of moral reasoning and debate – but all this is to say that value and values are not produced in a vacuum. Rather, people determine what they value in their lives in the context of particular projects and in terms of the social practices in which they participate.

Pierre Bourdieu is one of our most important and insightful thinkers about value and valuation. In Bourdieu's thought, social fields are defined by the distribution of certain socially valuable traits, skills, and resources, which he refers to collectively as "capital." On the one hand, the position of agents *within* the field is determined by how much and what kinds of capital they possess (Bourdieu 1985, 724). On the other hand, and perhaps less frequently commented upon, it is the circulation of particular types of capital that creates fields as distinct social arenas in the first place (725). Fields coalesce around the social agents who are competing with and for the capital that they all treat as valuable. It is like learning the rules of a game, rules that stipulate not only what one may or may not do but also the game's victory conditions. Bourdieu calls this investment of value the *illusio*: it means "to be invested, taken in and by the game. To be interested is to accord a given social game that what happens in it matters, that its stakes are important […] and worth pursuing" (Bourdieu and Wacquant 1992, 116). Some agreement about and investment in these stakes is necessary to the social competition that unfolds within a field.

In *Club Cultures*, Sarah Thornton (1996) extended Bourdieu's ideas to more local processes of valuation, such as those taking place within subcultures. Her key example was "hipness," which, she argued, functioned as a form of *sub*cultural capital amongst the British ravers she studied. For these clubbers, being on the cutting edge of youth culture defined an alternative status hierarchy: "Just as cultural capital is personified in 'good' manners and urbane conversation, so subcultural capital is embodied in the form of being 'in the know,' using (but not over-using) current slang and looking as if you were born to perform the latest dance styles" (11–12). This competitive "alternativeness" – the constant search for fashionable but not too fashionable tastes that strike the just-right balance between individualism and conformity – can be seen across a range of youth cultures (e.g., Hodkinson 2002, 38–41; Widdicombe and Wooffitt 1995). It is certainly present in geek culture, but it often appears in more subtle guises. Nerd culture presents its own logics of valuation, its own specific subcultural capitals. While two of the three fundamental kinds of capital (namely, economic and social capital; Bourdieu 1986) doubtless play important roles within the subcultural scene, they function in more or less the same way that they do in the general economy of practices – all other things being equal, it is good to have more economic and social capital than less. Cultural capital, however, takes field-specific forms that demand particular attention.

Some scholars have drawn critical attention to Bourdieu's seeming assumption of a single hierarchy of "legitimate" cultural forms and tastes (see Fiske 1992b; Peterson 1992). However, such criticisms often fail to separate the general theory of cultural capital from particular empirical cases. It would be a mistake to reduce cultural capital to the forms it took amongst the *grande bourgeoisie* and intellectuals of 1960s France. But even in a fractured, contested space of lifestyles, the theory of cultural capital can help us understand how value, prestige, and status function by sensitizing us to the work accomplished by displays of skill and avowals of taste. Brown's (1997) discussion of comic-book fandom, for example, identifies two main forms of specific cultural capital – knowledge and collections – that were valued in that subculture. Evidence from my interviews and observations suggests that they hold their value across a range of geek cultures.

"IT IS KNOWN, KHALEESI": KNOWLEDGE

Fan studies scholars have repeatedly drawn attention to the importance of knowledge in determining authenticity within fandoms – and especially in those fan groups, such as comic-book collectors (Brown 1997) or cult movie fans (Jancovich 2002; Hunt 2003), conventionally imagined as "masculine." Demonstrating knowledge about the practices in which they engage is one important way that participants assert their right to be included within subcultural spaces.

"Knowledge" here represents a broad catchall encompassing several particular forms of value. Whether expressed as trivia, good taste, or intertextual referencing, we are talking about an embodied form of subcultural capital.

Trivia

The most obvious forms of valued knowledge are facts and trivia. Indeed, for some interviewees, these defined nerdiness as such – Hank described a nerd as someone who "knows the most useless trivia out there." As Nathan Hunt (2003, 185) notes, discussions of fans frequently revolve around questions of fannish knowledge: "either fans are denigrated for their obsession with apparently useless trivia or else their concern with this information is valorized as a form of radical cultural criticism." But neither view captures how trivia actually works socially within fan cultures as a source of legitimacy and cultural authority:

"Trivia are important exactly because its value can be recognized only by insiders. Their possession is therefore a form of cultural capital through which fandom is able to claim special access to, and knowledge of, specific texts and groups of texts and, in so doing, to make claims of ownership of them. In the process, they also enable fans to distinguish themselves from the 'phantom menace' of the mainstream consumer, and so present themselves as discerning, rational and cultured. Finally, trivia are also used in competitive struggles within fandom in which different sections of fandom not only vie with one another for status but also provide a sense of affirmation and solidarity through masculine contests of homosocial competition" (198). Trivia are not trivial in the context of fan practices and the communities oriented to them. But neither does their value come solely from an instrumental relationship to knowledge or an imagined political subjectivity of resistance. Rather, they are used socially as tokens of competence in a language-game of connoisseurist consumption that constitutes much of the interaction within geek media cultures.

A good command of relevant facts distinguished people within the interactional settings I observed. Knowing actors or plot points from TV series, for instance, can serve this function in media fandom, as understanding the minutiae of game rules and mechanics does in gaming cultures (Hank and Scott both pointed to the detailed knowledge of individual cards among CCG players) and knowing about creators and "continuity" (i.e., the diegetic histories of fictional characters and worlds) does in comic-book fandom. Solo, for instance, claimed to frequently use her knowledge of comic-book characters and their origins as her "in" to geeky spaces and conversations, and she took higher levels of knowledge (e.g., of spin-offs and tie-ins, like the *Star Wars* expanded universe) as indicators of greater involvement with a fan object. As a counterpoint, game store owner Hank sometimes found his encyclopaedic knowledge of board games to be a disadvantage, as it meant that many of his customers would bypass his employees to speak directly to him – but this is a very particular sort of problem to have.

Like all forms of capital, the value inhering in subcultural capital can only be realized if it circulates. Extensive knowledge of *Magic* cards or superhero origins really is "the most useless trivia out there" if you never find opportunities to display it. Conversational markers like the sentence adverb "actually" have become conventionalized – even parodied – indicators that someone is about to interject a piece of trivia, as Solo notes when describing how she responds to challenges about superhero trivia: "Somebody has always instigated me, and then I'm like, 'Well, actually … fun fact!'" Although one would presume that facts related to particular nerdy interests would be the most valuable because they are most salient within these communities, it also seemed important to the people I spoke with to demonstrate their general knowledge of science, history, literature, and so on. Informants like Barry and Shiera offered little bits of trivia as an aside to nearly every conversation. When inserted into conversation, the etymology of umbrella, the source of synthetic vanilla, or the popularity of puce in seventeenth-century Normandy became valuable commodities in the market of subcultural capital. Thus, the ability to perform the role of a knowledgeable person was more important than any particular piece of trivia.

Taste

The category of knowledge also embraces one of the main uses of cultural capital described by Bourdieu, namely, enabling agents to make "correct" and "appropriate" aesthetic judgments. Although taste is often regarded as an idiosyncrasy for which no rational account can be given, tastes are not equally distributed in the social space – this is, after all, the lesson of *Distinction* (Bourdieu 2010). Full participation in a practice presupposes the internalization of shared orientations or frameworks that constrain aesthetic reason in particular ways. The operation of these situated aesthetics may be seen in the discussions and debates that are everyday aspects of nerds' social interaction.

The exchange of aesthetic judgments about comics, their creators, and movies was a common feature of talk at King St Comics. Although Warren said that he and his staff try not to judge their customers' tastes, these conversations were sometimes quite blunt, as when one of the staff commented loudly and sarcastically while sorting the week's shipment: "That Batman vampire thing doesn't look retarded at all!" Taste is not fundamentally a private matter but circulates publicly within practical communities. Moreover, these discussions of taste also assume some familiarity with the object under discussion.

Thus, the most significant dimension of taste as a form of cultural capital is knowledge of the canons – albeit, loosely defined ones – of subculturally relevant media texts. Individual judgments rely on a shared framework of important works and creators, against which particular cases can be evaluated. Being familiar with lists of "great" sci-fi and fantasy novels, comic book sagas, classic D&D modules, and video games, or of great writers, artists, designers, developers, and so on, and being able to argue about their composition, are important skills for getting by in geek culture.

Intertextuality

Finally, it is not enough to demonstrate *familiarity* with the canon of relevant texts; one must also display *mastery* by playing with them. Mark Allen Peterson (2005, 130) argues that intertextuality is not a property of texts but a performance by their audiences: "People are never only audiences constructing readings of texts, they also seize upon, remember, replicate, and transform elements from the media they consume. They quote dialogue, emulate styles, and whistle tunes they learned from television, radio, or the movies. Some of this intertextual borrowing may be random, idiosyncratic, and personal, but the bulk of such intertextual play is socially patterned. Knowledge of particular kinds of media texts and an ability to display this knowledge competently is a form of cultural capital valued highly in many social fields." Geek culture is clearly one such field. Distinctive "patterns" of intertextual play are dispersed practices (Schatzki 1996). It would be difficult to assess whether nerds engage in them more than others do – they are certainly not unique to these communities – but making and recognizing media references is a ubiquitous feature of social interaction within nerd cultures, and they are thoroughly integrated into the focal practices that constitute them.

The ability to participate in the performance of intertextuality distinguishes insiders and outsiders, consociates from mere contemporaries (Schutz 1967). Indeed, it is a key way of identifying with others (Burke 1969) and turning contemporaries into consociates (Zhao 2004). For example, during participant-observation at Plaza Games, I played a game called *Neuroshima Hex* with a group of store regulars. I was on a team with Norton, who I had briefly met in the store the week before. As Norton laid down a tile that could push away adjacent enemy tiles, he looked up at the group and said, "You know what this reminds me of? 'I am the pusher robot.'" I immediately gave the counter-sign: "Shoving is the answer." We both laughed, confirming that we both knew the same reference, taking us out of the board game into a language-game of intertextual play that forged a momentary bond. It felt as though we were now familiar with one another because we were both familiar with the same text.

Such referencing need not be verbal. Many participants like to wear nerdy t-shirts, buttons, or other merchandise. By encoding media references on them, nerds are able to use these items as tokens of belonging. This can be quite literal, as in the case of SF&F Con attendees that wore shirts – what one member called his "club colours" – showing their affiliation with the international *Star Wars* costuming club, the 501st Legion. However, they not only provide an opportunity to show affiliation (i.e., objectified social capital) but also to display distinction from one's peers through the selection of especially "clever" shirts. During participant-observation at Downtown Comics & Collectibles, one of the clerks was helping a customer to find a book he wanted. When the customer checked out, the clerk (who was wearing a Cookie Monster shirt) asked him where he got his Mario shirt, and they spent a few minutes talking about their favourite t-shirt websites. The moment of recognition allowed by wearing one's heart on one's sleeve (or chest) enabled these two people to transform a purely economic transaction into a more communalized one by disguising the stranger-relationality that formal market relations demand (Warner 2002, 57). While relationships among attendees in "ethereal" cultural spaces like gaming shops (Kinkade and Katovich 2009) may or may not become intimate friendships, exchanging references supplies scripts for interactions that contribute to an atmosphere of sociability and camaraderie within them – so long as one is able to catch the reference – without the need for particularly well-developed interpersonal social skills.

However, because not just anyone is taken for a consociate, we can also understand such interactions as a moment of evaluation, of the person as much as the t-shirt and the intertextual knowledge that it represents. Referencing not only divides fans from mundanes, but positions individuals within a community of practice. One common version of this was shouting humorous comments (often involving intertextual references) during presentations or film screenings. I'll call this "MSTing," after the television series *Mystery Science Theater 3000* (MST3K), which layered acerbic, mocking commentary over old B-movies. I observed MSTing most frequently at events hosted by organizations that held screenings, such as Screens & Sorcery and the Alternate Universe Club. At the first AUC weekly anime screening I attended, the audience was mocking the quality of the animation and voice acting within moments of the show beginning and they continued to pepper media references, including other anime and Internet memes, throughout the evening. The membership extended this practice to the club's business meetings as well, which consequently felt rather anarchic. They frequently interrupted with comments that in turn often occasioned a chain of responses, leaving club officers (or, at least, those few who were not themselves caught up in the diversion) at times helpless to keep to the agenda. That being said, participants engaged in MSTing seem to be contributing – or, at least, to see themselves as contributing – to the experience of reception rather than undermining it; a successful example would evoke laughter and follow-up comments, showing that the contribution had been recognized and received as intended. However, I also had a strong sense of a competitive undercurrent, suggesting that this was not merely a mode of consumption but also a valued form of capital.

The category of knowledge embraces several discrete manifestations of subcultural capital, only some of which might routinely be described as "intellectual." Under this concept, I have discussed forms of discursive consciousness – "know that" related to particular, valued domains – and practical consciousness – the "know how" used to make intelligible judgments and interact with others in expected ways. Categorizing them together in this way highlights the fact that even relatively abstract cultural competencies are embodied: the feel for making intertextual references at the right moment; the physically manifested sense of enjoyment, boredom, or revulsion evoked by a particular text; and the ready-to-handedness of the spouted factoid. The ability to use knowledge as cultural capital is more like a muscle that must be trained and exercised than like a piece of data stored on a computer drive.

"WHERE DOES HE GET ALL THOSE WONDERFUL TOYS?": COLLECTIONS

Like intertextual referencing and trivia, collecting is by no means unique to geeks, but it is nonetheless an important dispersed practice within geek culture. As Lincoln Geraghty puts it: "In many ways fandom is about the display of one's passion for a media text [...] Collecting objects, keeping them, organizing them and displaying them is then by its very nature about the process of distinction and accruing cultural capital" (2014, 181). More specifically, collections – not only in their simple existence as owned things but also in the care that goes into their organization, maintenance, and display – serve as an objectification of their owners' cultural capital. For instance, two customers I interviewed at Plaza Games told me they had spent thousands of dollars on collectible miniatures for a single game. All the comic-book retailers started out as collectors, and comic-book fans were observed seeking to complete runs of series or acquire rare variant covers. Indeed, personal collections often formed the core of new comic book stores. Similarly, Screen & Sorcery's Saturday Morning Cartoon events developed out of private screenings Logan held with material from his collection of VHS tapes, and Hank boasted a collection of 500 board games and 15,000 comics.

In my own observations, I distinguished three ideal-typical collectors, distinguished by their disposition towards the act of collecting itself: I call them completists, hobbyists, and speculators.[1] These ideal types may be understood as particular "rationales" deployed by collectors, and in each collecting becomes more autonomous from the practices in which it is embedded than the last. Completists seek to acquire complete sets of goods that others might purchase more haphazardly but it is having them that's important. Hobbyists interpret their focal practice as mainly about collecting and the thrill of the hunt for elusive objects. Finally, speculators collect principally with an eye to return on investment. Although completists and hobbyists may be interested in the economic value of their collections, this concern remains informed by the aesthetic and other values internal to their practice, while speculators primarily pursue external goods (i.e., economic profit), potentially disregarding the practice's internal norms of good taste and quality. In my research, evidence of speculation was only apparent within the comic-book community,[2] while completist and hobbyist collecting were more widely dispersed throughout the cultures studied.

All three types of collector are opposed by an orientation towards the use-value of objects. As Walter Benjamin (1999, 9) puts it, the collector "makes his concern the transfiguration of things. To him falls the Sisyphean task of divesting things of their commodity character by taking possession of them." Once the insistent need to be useful has been removed, the commodity may be re-enchanted as part of the collection. In this new context, it may serve as a symbol of personal or collective identity (McCracken 1988; Geraghty 2014), an index of the collector's expertise and discernment, or both. However, the immaterial labour that produces collector's value also opens the door to the item's re-fetishization. Hence, collectors of all types are always speculators *in potentia*, rescuing objects from the curse of usefulness but delivering them to another master.

The opposition of use-value and exchange-value was relatively repressed within gaming practices, as participants I observed did play

with goods they had collected. I observed little to no fear of deprecia-
tion among players of miniatures games, including collectible miniatures games, and although there is a secondary market in CCG cards
enabled to varying degrees by different game stores (some do not sell
individual cards, others help facilitate trades and deals among customers, and still others actively sell cards priced at what the collectors'
market will bear), the most evidence I saw of concern to preserve cards'
condition was a conversation at Eastside's *Legend of the Five Rings* night
about different techniques for shuffling cards that might minimize
warping them.

In the comic-book sub-field, however, this opposition is quite evident due to a split between "readers" and "collectors" within the participant base. While collecting – especially that of completists – is not
necessarily incompatible with identifying as a reader, comic-book retailers noted that "people who collect them tend to be a little bit pickier about condition," even if "their comics aren't gonna be particularly
worth anything," while "the readers are more casual about it" (Sean). In
response to collectors' "pickiness," Warren keeps his store's stock of
graphic novels and trade paperbacks in plastic sleeves in order to maintain their condition. Although these books are not scarce and are thus
very unlikely to appreciate in value, "there are people who are collectors
and who are very particular, and if there is even the slightest ding, you
know, bent corner, crease, then it's going to hurt the potential for the
book to sell." Nonetheless, he recognizes that this makes it more difficult for customers to browse, an activity fundamental to shopping for
comics, especially among those more interested in entertainment than
building a collection. Interviewees reported that the distinction between readers and collectors has become more polarized within the
comics field. Warren and Sean both perceived most of their customers
as primarily readers, and this is reflected in contemporary comics' emphasis on story and continuity.[3] At the same time, collecting and reading have become increasingly differentiated due to the widespread
availability of re-prints of old comics – meaning that readers need not
become collectors in order to access these "classics" – and to the rise of
the Certified Guaranty Company (CGC), a service that evaluates the condition of comic books, assigning them a numerical grade, and then
"slabs" them, sealing them in a protective case from which they cannot
be removed without invalidating the grade. CGC comics represent the
triumph of exchange-value over use-value among collectors, making
them very "liquid" commodities (in Sean's words) but also preventing

you from reading them. However, as Sean explained, should one still desire to read the stories it is possible to acquire a "beater," or reading copy, of even quite valuable comics.[4]

The acquisition of this specific cultural capital typically presupposes economic capital (though we can imagine exceptions, such as someone inheriting a collection), and Kurt, the president of the City Gaming Network, was critical of the consumerism he saw in geek culture: "Where does geek culture congregate and what does it congregate over? It congregates in stores and places of business, and it congregates over collections and collectibles and status that's driven by possessions and material goods." However, a collection's "quality" is principally determined by knowledge and taste. For example, while part of the pleasure and the skill of wargaming is assembling and painting an army of figurines, it appears from a conversation observed at Eastside Games & Comics' weekly *Warmachine* game day that few players (at least in this particular scene) ever completed the task for all of their miniatures. When one player set up his army for a match, someone at a neighbouring table commented that this was the first fully painted *Warmachine* army he had ever seen. In contrast to the many players who field unfinished miniatures, a completely painted collection was remarkable and therefore distinguishing for its owner. This is not a *collectible* miniatures game – the manufacturer does not impose scarcity on the market as part of the structure of the game – so what was valued in these collections was the know-how represented by the process of skilfully selecting, assembling, and painting the models, not their capacity to stand in for economic capital. It is for this reason that I understand collections as at least partially and perhaps even principally an objectified form of cultural capital, rather than a display of "pecuniary strength," as Veblen (1948) might have it. While a certain amount of disposable income is needed to participate in many activities (see ch. 7), I did not find evidence that economic capital as such operated as an axis of distinction, and I suspect that most participants who still talk about their collections' economic value are deploying a discursive frame for their activity that they believe will be more acceptable and legitimate to others.

Collecting is a kind of fan activity. With Lincoln Geraghty (2014), I want to push back at the tendency within fan studies to marginalize collectors and collecting practices within accounts of fandom: "As is so often argued, fandom is active, it is participatory and it is creative. Therefore, the act of consumption (personified by the purchase of mer-

chandise) is the antithesis of being a real fan because fans are not passive consumers – they are supposed to be producers, makers and doers"
(180). Collectors of comic books, toys, or other licensed merchandise
seem like the epitome of the bad "affirmational" fan (Obsession_inc
2009), whose enthusiasm is expressed by purchasing and is, therefore,
more or less perfectly absorbed by media companies. But, as Geraghty
rightly points out, collectors are indeed producers, makers, and doers.
If nothing else, they produce collections as a kind of "transformative
work," placing these objects in new contexts in a way that can be analo-
gized to the fan-fic writer's appropriation of someone else's characters
for new purposes. Once lodged in my collection, a Funko Pop vinyl
figurine is no longer an anonymous, generic product, however routinized its licensing, design, and production may be: I selected it for a
reason, it now sits in relationship with the other objects in my collection (e.g., am I collecting Funko Pops related to various media that I
enjoy, or does this stand as one kind of object among several related to
the same media property?), and it can be taken as a sign of my (sub)cul-
tural capital. That is to say, collecting is not only a personally meaningful activity that appropriates aspects of popular and material culture
for individual identity work but also a means by which people articulate and objectify important (but always contestable) distinctions between more and less valued objects.

THE ECONOMY OF RECOGNITION

There is a basic truth underlying these examples. When others recognize the value of your knowledge, skill, or collections, they are also recognizing your value. This mutual recognition is one way we identify
ourselves with others (Burke 1969, 20–1). But consubstantiality is not
the same as equality. As Bourdieu's metaphor helps us to see, knowledge and collections, when recognized as capital by members of a particular community for whom they are valuable, may be "cashed in" to
better one's position within that field. In my observations, this most
often took the form of conversational precedence, namely, the ability to
have others listen to you. They allow participants to claim status among
their fellow geeks.

However, attempts to draw on reserves of cultural capital can also go
awry; indeed, the rule may be more easily observed in the breach than
the observance. Asking interviewees about people "doing it wrong" supplemented my own observations of failed attempts to gain recognition.

At the same AUC screening mentioned above, for example, a woman sat by herself in the row in front of me. She would periodically lift her head and make a comment, loud enough that it was clearly not intended to be *sotto voce* yet not quite loudly or assertively enough to enter into the stream of comments among the dominant wiseacres. In this case and others I observed, failed contributions were simply not acknowledged or commented upon. However, a poorly timed comment may result in a loss of face. For instance, during a well-attended panel at Anime Con, an audience member interrupted the presenter to offer a correction: PAX, a gaming convention that he had just mentioned, had moved to the east coast of the US from Seattle. The presenter immediately retorted that there were now two PAX conventions, one in Seattle and one in Boston.[5] This attempt to demonstrate superior knowledge in front of a large audience ended up exposing a significant gap.

Interviewees often downplayed status competition. When raised explicitly, they denied the very existence of "poseurs" and attempted portray geek culture as a tolerant, pluralistic sphere where differences of taste didn't signify.[6] However, it could also be seen that participants subject their peers to continual scrutiny, as in the snide comic-shop commentary cited above or this extract from my conversations with Mr Fox:

> MR FOX: If you're a fan of ... cinema in general, you have to hit, you know, there are certain highlights you *should* see that make you seem more authentic. Like *Citizen Kane* or the original *King Kong*, *The Maltese Falcon*, *Plan 9 from Outer Space*. Things like that. *This Island Earth ... The Day the Earth Stood Still* [...] If you go out of your way to see films that old, which are actually not that easy to track down? Then it shows a genuine interest as opposed to just like ... bandwagon jumping.
> BEN: Could you talk a little bit more about what bandwagon jumping would look like in the context of movie fandom? [...]
> MR FOX: These are not conversations I have with my friends ... because they're all Philistines [...] Oh, well ... if someone claims to be a big movie buff who's only seen stuff that's come out recently, like the big pop culture stuff? Like, claiming ... yeah. About that. Claims to know more than they actually do about the history of cinema.

For Mr Fox, who elsewhere claimed there was no such thing as a "poseur" in his communities of practice, the failure to demonstrate "properly" subcultural knowledge (versus the "big pop culture stuff" that a merely mainstream audience member would know about) invalidated one's "claim" – not only to a domain of knowledge but also to standing within the social world corresponding with that domain. The standards against which others are judged are both intersubjective, in that they are the object of collective discussion within the community, and unavoidably idiosyncratic, in that each participant is likely to have slightly different ideas about what one needs to know to be a "real" fan, a "real" gamer, and so on.

REGIMES OF VIRTUE

In his introduction to *The Social Life of Things*, Arjun Appadurai uses the suggestive phrase "regime of value" to describe how objects are "enlivened" through transactions. Acts of exchange presuppose an agreement that, for some "specific cultural and historical milieu" (4), this is how much something is worth. While people may vary in their estimations of a given act, object, or person – we grumble when we feel cheated and exult in a bargain – people who share a regime of value have an overlapping consensus about the *criteria* that should be used to judge them. It captures something like the idea of an evaluative schema, but one embedded in ritualized interactions, institutions, customs, and material culture. What can we infer about the regimes of value active in geek culture based on how they talk about their media-oriented practices?

As I have suggested, interviewees repeatedly emphasized the importance of expertise, whether embodied in performances of knowledgeability or objectified in collections of material objects. Matt Hills (2002) has called academic researchers to task for portraying fans as feral cultural studies scholars generating sophisticated, critical readings and vernacular cultural theory (or, "meta") as a kind of folk art. Because academics inhabit a regime of value that privileges the rational subject above all else, fandom could only be recuperated for the scholarly public by portraying it as "a perfected university seminar" (John Michael quoted in Hills 2002, 10) – "perfected" because participants are self-motivated, genuinely interested in the topics they've chosen, and never come grubbing for grades. Hills argues that this may be only a form of protective coloration adopted when fans deal with sociologists, a "discursive mantra" designed to chase away accusations of irrational passion, which they know non-fans view with disdain (67). He is right to sound a note of caution. These intellectualized values are not the only way of being a fan, as the idiomatic phrase "to geek out" should remind us.

Yet there was an undeniable affinity between the forms of valuation I observed and what Bourdieu calls the "scholastic disposition" or "scholastic point-of-view" (Bourdieu 1990b, 2000). Indeed, many of the attitudes and habits we call "nerdy" or "geeky" are traditionally academic or scholarly but lack the imprimatur of academic and other cultural institutions: "Their ambivalent relationship with the educational system, inducing a sense of complicity with every form of symbolic defiance, inclines them to welcome all the forms of culture which are, provisionally at least, on the (lower) boundaries of legitimate culture – jazz, cinema, strip cartoons, science fiction [...] – as a challenge to legitimate culture; but they often bring into these regions disdained by the educational establishment an erudite, even 'academic' disposition" (2010, 361). There is something very familiar in this description of the new petite bourgeoisie training their "schooled" gaze on lowly artifacts like sci-fi and comics. My observations seemed to confirm Henry Jenkins's (2013, 277–8) assertions that "fandom involves a particular mode of reception" and "a particular set of critical and interpretive practices," comprising close attention to a text, "a mixture of emotional proximity and critical distance," and "preferred reading practices" that are "playful, speculative, subjective." As Michael Saler (2004) writes in his study of Victorian and Edwardian proto–science fiction, "those who use the ironic imagination do not so much willingly suspend their disbelief in fictional characters or worlds, as willingly believe in them with the double-minded awareness that they are engaging in pretense" (139). Replete with paratextual elements such as footnotes, maps, photographs and realistic illustrations, and translations from imaginary languages that invited their readers to fantasize but to do so rationally, these texts "were the precursors of the internally consistent virtual worlds of our contemporary media, like *Star Trek*, *Star Wars*, and online computer gaming worlds, all of which have become imaginative habitations for millions" (145). They reward readers who engage with them on their own terms – who are willing to simultaneously immerse themselves in the narrative worlds they present while holding them at enough distance to not only play *in* them but also *with* them. Intriguingly, Bourdieu describes the scholastic disposition as "very close to the 'let's pretend' mode of play which enables children to open imaginary worlds"; it "makes possible all intellectual speculations, scientific hypotheses, 'thought experiments,' 'possible worlds' or 'imaginary variations'" (2000, 12–13).

The scholastic disposition follows from Bourdieu's general theory of socialization. He argues that we all develop habits and dispositions – a habitus – that accommodate us to our social and material conditions (including our trajectory through the "social space," i.e., whether we're upwardly or downwardly mobile). The condition of the middle and upper classes by definition entails a relative "freedom from necessity" that is prerequisite to the distanced, intellectualized, and playful "scholastic" attitude towards the world. The life of the mind, in other words, is predicated on the taken-for-granted satisfaction of the body's needs. Although most of my informants described themselves as middle-class at the time of the interview, they did not in fact come from any single class background. Some were raised in solidly middle-class, professional families but others grew up poor and rural. However, most had completed at least some post-secondary education, and two had graduate degrees. Moreover, their attitudes towards schooling and education were strikingly similar. While modern educational systems have been criticized as an Ideological State Apparatus (Althusser 1971), a locus of disciplinary power that enforces a "hidden curriculum" of compliance (Foucault 1995; Apple 1990), compulsory schooling and improved accessibility to higher education also temporarily suspends the imperative to productive labour: "This time liberated from practical occupations and preoccupations, of which the school [...] organizes a privileged form, studious leisure, is the precondition for scholastic exercises and activities removed from immediate necessity, such as sport, play, the production and contemplation of works of art and all forms of gratuitous speculation with no other end than themselves" (Bourdieu 2000, 13).

When asked about their academic performance, most interviewees portrayed themselves as bright, hard-working students. In general, they said they liked school and had good experiences there (at least with respect to academics). They described supportive and encouraging home situations. Some of their parents specifically valued academic achievement, while others were less wedded to formal measures of success but nonetheless encouraged their children to pursue their interests and to excel on their own terms: "Yeah, I don't think that they put on any pressure at all. I think a lot of that came from probably my dad's experience. He's quite smart and went to university, but was never ... never ashamed that he left university to go to a trade. And, because he worked as a plumber, that was always highly valued, as well. There was never a … never a negative connotation to not going to school or at least, learning was always a positive thing but it didn't have to be a school-based learning or anything like that. And as long as you did things that you enjoyed, there was no real pressure to, like, make money or you had to do well in order to advance yourself or anything like that" (Wedge). Solo was a notable exception, describing herself as a "lazy" student. When interviewed as an undergraduate student, she felt habituated to the education system, saying, "I think I'm used to school, and there's … pieces that I like, but [...] I've never been overly engaged in it." Nevertheless, when asked what these pieces were, she sketched a romantic view of education consistent with the others': "I like learning. I like knowing things. I like knowing that, in three months from now, I will know more than I know now [...] Especially the last couple of years, just knowing more about the world and sort of getting a bigger perspective on what other people, you know like re-occurring things about our society and stuff like that? I like that sort of thing. That's part of why I'm a history major."

Interviewees embraced the intrinsic rewards of learning and generally accepted the education system's legitimating ideologies. Even without the inducements of assignments and report cards, these students would have been interested in the world around them and eager to learn more. However, they distinctly rejected the system's attempts to discipline learners. This became particularly clear in descriptions of favourite teachers. They were not necessarily the ones who explained things particularly clearly and certainly not the ones who gave easy assignments and exams; rather, they recognized when intellectually precocious students were being frustrated and made accommodations for them. The "best" teachers were the ones who got out of the way:

[That] drove me crazy in elementary school. We studied the Egyptians, and we spent three weeks on the Egyptians. I'm like, "This is a culture with thousands of years of history, and we're looking at mummies. I want to know about how they trained their chariot horses, I want to know how they farmed in the desert, I want to know about how you make papyrus – I don't care about mummies! I care about every other aspect! I want to know what pigments they used on the paints that they put on the carvings that people didn't even know were painted" – it was a recent discovery. So, it drove me mad that we had to move on. And my teacher, I had a great teacher in grade 6, she was like, "Great! We're going to move on to something else, you can stay on this. You're going to keep writing reports on whatever interests you." And that was great, that self-directed, that kind of encouraged that aspect of myself. (Shiera)

Yeah, exactly, like … I can remember in public school I had a great teacher for English, and so he'd give essay assignments […] and I hated them. I hate just writing an essay on something that I don't care about. And he would let me write, like, creative writing, like write sci-fi stories or that sort of thing instead of – because he saw the benefit of writing and you're still doing all of the grammatical studies and that sort of stuff, but it doesn't necessarily need to be focused on something that the teacher assigns. (Wedge)

The actions that endeared particular teachers to them were those that excepted them from forms of observation and discipline to which their classmates were subject. Shiera was given permission to remove herself from the classroom (and the watchful eye of her teacher) in order to study whatever she found interesting at her own pace in the school library, and Wedge's licence to write sci-fi stories instead of essays meant that his work was literally incomparable with that of his peers. But these exceptions were in the service of an ostensibly higher purpose – their own sense of what education ought to be.

These "habits of the head" may not constitute a habitus in the strictest sense, since they cannot be traced to a common set of material conditions experienced by all members. However, similar experiences of the social institution of schooling seem to have inculcated some shared orientations that were subsequently activated by geek culture's focal practices. It's no wonder that the labels "geek" and "nerd" are strongly associated with the peer cultures produced within the education system, that these are also the years when people appear most likely to embark upon "careers" within geek culture (ch. 4), and that most people I spoke with also undertook programs of self-teaching later in life. Nor is it surprising that "reason," "rationality," and all the related mental faculties figured prominently in my interviews as normative discursive frames. For example, interviewees would talk about "doing research on," "studying," or "learning about" something as a way of communicating their passion about a topic or activity. Common-sense distinctions between pleasure or emotion, on the one hand, and reason, on the other, might suggest that thinking this much is precisely evidence that one is not having fun. Yet it would be exceedingly difficult to maintain such a claim in the face of a group of geeks making puns, discussing deck-building strategies for their favourite collectible card game, or debating the finer points of comic-book canon, any of which could be described as both fun and intellectual.

I have already suggested that value (i.e., beliefs about what something is worth) and values (i.e., beliefs about what is worthy) are deeply interconnected, but what of virtue? A new account of the virtues is, after all, Alasdair MacIntyre's (2007) ultimate concern. As he notes, different thinkers have proposed variable and incompatible lists of virtues. Indeed, they harbour quite different conceptions of what a virtue is. If we expect the virtues to be universal, this presents something of a problem, one MacIntyre attempts to solve through his appeal to social practices. What is considered a virtue varies between places and periods because they are related to historically and socially bound practices: "A virtue is an acquired human quality the possession and exercise of which tends to enable us to achieve those goods which are internal to practices and the lack of which effectively prevents us from achieving any such goods" (191).

The "excellences" that have been traditionally called virtues are dispositions that are nurtured by and through practices. Like the habitus in Bourdieu's thought, these are transposable dispositions (Bourdieu 2010, 20), such that "someone who genuinely possesses a virtue can be expected to manifest it in very different types of situation" (MacIntyre 2007, 205). Practices can thus be expected to exhibit characteristic definitions of good people as well as "regimes of value" that define good things. For instance, as discussed in chapter 1, interviewees raised traits like open-mindedness, curiosity, and genuineness when I asked them about peers who they liked and admired. Meanwhile, debates and disagreements among geeks suggest that rationality, reasonableness, notions of merit, the disinterested cultivation of skills and craft, and respect for (if not *obedience* to) the authorial intent of cultural producers might also be counted among geek culture's "catalogue of virtues" (181).

This is not to suggest that every nerd – or even the average nerd – is a moral paragon. As Jenkins (2013, 282) admits, fandom's utopian impulses are often frustrated: "Fans react against [...] unsatisfying situations, trying to establish a 'weekend-only world' more open to creativity and accepting of differences, more concerned with human welfare than with economic advance. Fandom, too, falls short of those ideals; the fan community is sometimes rife with feuds and personality conflicts. Here, too, one finds those who are self-interested and uncharitable, those who are greedy and rude, yet unlike mundane reality, fandom remains a space where a commitment to more democratic values may be renewed and fostered." I would not go so far as to say that "mundane reality" is incapable of nurturing democratic values, but Jenkins is right to suggest that fandoms are spaces of commitment – cultural spaces that are constituted by, and in turn nurture, commitment. They may not start out being about openness to creativity, tolerance, human welfare, or other such virtues. It is much more likely that they start out being about *Star Trek* or *Warhammer* or Robert Jordan's *Wheel of Time* novels, but because these commitments are shared, they locate their bearers in spaces that must be shared with others. If they want to be able to continue to access and enjoy the practice, they must learn to live and to disagree with their fellow practitioners. That is, a mutual orientation to practices creates a social framework that provides standards for action that can be brought to bear within the community – if they can't agree, they may at least be able to agree about *how* they will disagree. Ideally, MacIntyre suggests, goods internal to practices and the virtues that enable them develop in tandem. In this way, practices are schools of the virtues as much as sources of particular pleasures.

As the critical theorist Herbert Marcuse once pointed out, it is easy to make judgments about true and false needs – that is to say, about what is truly worthwhile and valuable – in the abstract, but to dictate them to others is problematic, to say the least. "Any such tribunal" would be "reprehensible" (Marcuse 2002, 8). It would be reprehensible because all sorts of decisions flow from such determinations of value, decisions not only about how to value things and allocate finite resources but also about how to value *people*. It is through the dismissal of cult media, science fiction and fantasy, comics, games, and so on as low culture, ephemera, and kids' stuff (among other labels) that fans were also dismissed as cultural dopes, obsessive collectors, and developmentally arrested adolescents (Jensen 1992). Likewise, it is from a double movement in popular culture – of geeky media texts' changing status among other taste publics, and of the extension of geeks' enthusiastically obsessive mode of expert consumption into new domains – that geek culture has emerged as an object of discourse outside of its own subcultural worlds.

But we need to understand these processes not only as macro-level trends working their way through mass-media markets but also as worked out, reproduced, and challenged through micro-level interactions in everyday life. We are not only talking about the fate of games or comics or speculative fiction as whole categories but how individual objects and, in the case of collections, assemblages of objects are valued by particular people and groups of people. We are also talking about how the ability to make and advocate for such distinctions tends to distinguish individual participants within geek-culture spaces – or, as discussed above, how failures to do so can also "distinguish" us. Geek culture is, among other things, a "taste culture" (Gans 1999) defined by a particular orientation to particular objects. Thus, its publics are interpellated by *both* the selection of relevant media or genres as focal things *and* by the distinctive ways that value is generated around them.

Theories of cultural capital help us to better understand the importance that things and ways of doing things have for participants. They express and reproduce values, and they therefore influence the structure of these communities – for if something is good, it must be worth pursuing. However, in adopting this perspective, there is a risk that culture becomes no more than an arena of struggle and competition for valued symbolic resources. A further theoretical problem is that cultural sub-fields – understood as spaces of social contestation and, therefore, only as an aggregation of moves and counter-moves in a zero-sum game of status seeking – would have no internal order. Yet geek culture does appear to have some coherence. The tastes that shape its canonical works and valued commodities are not perfectly consistent, regular, and predictable, but neither are they entirely arbitrary. How can we theorize perceptible "elective affinities" without falling back into essentialist explanations (which are not really explanations at all)? How do people learn to value certain things in certain ways? From what point of view does this become, for us or for anyone, what is best in life?

While internal goods and the virtues or habits that enable us to achieve them are obviously central to MacIntyre's theory of practice, there is more to a practice. As Beadle and Moore (2006, 335) explain: "the establishment of internal goods is a necessary but insufficient condition for the identification of a practice – the neglected conditions being around the role of the practice in the narrative of an individual's life, the tradition of the community to which individuals belong and the interconnected role of institutions." The next three chapters will take up these "neglected conditions," examining how participants establish talk about their "careers" in geek culture, how they discursively and practically articulate these individual and individuated narratives with a sense of community, and how institutions like retail stores, clubs, and conventions are situated within the local scene.

4

Careers

Boldly Going On

In an article on *Magic: The Gathering* players, Kinkade and Katovich refer to that culture which gathers periodically in game stores for tournaments and other events as "ethereal" – a culture that is "not necessarily bound to strict correlations between time and space" (2009, 4). Insofar as these gatherings, like many events within the geek culture scene, have a loosely defined base of participants with a great deal of turnover and contribute to a network distributed across many such sites, their appraisal isn't wrong. Even relatively dedicated players will be unable to attend every event and will probably see new faces whenever they do. Contrasted with social groups grounded in geography, ethnicity, or "objective" interests, it is easy to think of those sprouting up around leisure activities as ephemeral or somehow less substantial. But as Kinkade and Katovich argue, a pattern can be condensed from these events as "regulars" pick up understandings and habits over time. From a certain point of view, ethereal cultures start to look quite solid indeed.

Perhaps the perspective from which this is easiest to see is that of biography. For although subcultural events like game nights, tournaments, and conventions are not strictly tied to space and time, human beings certainly are. In interviews, I asked people to recount some features of their life history but mostly concentrated on their careers in various fandoms and subcultures. While we mostly associate "career" with occupational roles, a generalized notion of the career as "pattern of movement" was a key exploratory concept for scholars working in the Chicago tradition of sociology (Becker 2014, 185; Barley 1989). A career is a trajectory between social roles, sometimes but not necessarily ordered in a hierarchy. For example, Jean Lave and Etienne Wenger (1991) develop a model of learning based on apprenticeship. They push back against idealist conceptions of learning as the transfer of knowledge between minds.[1] Rather, learning is practical and always situated in concrete social settings. A learner necessarily moves through a series of roles in the community of practice, from outsider to full participant and from novice to expert. But, as Barley (1989) notes, careers not only define one's position in some social world but also offer "scripts" to their occupants. This notion of a career can be applied to those who never occupy paid or other formally defined positions in geek culture's institutions (see ch. 6).

Barley's (1989) conception of the career script accords with the narrative conception of the self advanced by Alasdair MacIntyre. MacIntyre argues that identity (or, as he puts it, the "unity of a life") is not a thing people possess but rather a story they tell about themselves and how they got to where they are today (2007, 205). Our sense of selfhood is, in the final instance, our capacity to order experiences into a relatively coherent narrative. Indeed, it is the specifically narrative form – beginning, middle, and end – that I want to emphasize as I examine how participants construe their experiences in geek culture over time: how they first came to join in a community of practice, the people they met and things they learned as they became more involved, and how they moved on to other related practices or perhaps retired altogether. The stories composing these narratives will certainly be selective accounts, emphasizing some aspects of their teller's biography and neglecting others. They do not constitute an objective history but a collection of anecdotes arranged in order to create a certain impression, for themselves as much as for others. Nonetheless, how individuals narrativize their paths through the field, looking both backwards and forwards, provides insights into the possibilities and potential costs offered by participation in geek media cultures.

ORIGIN STORIES

When talking with people about specific practices they pursued, I usually started by asking how they first became involved or what their earliest memories of the practice in question were, but asking for post hoc accounts can be tricky. Interviewees frequently fell back on conventions like "I was always interested in that" or, to quote Diana, "I can't remember ever not reading science fiction and fantasy."[2] Locating the source of geeky interests is made even more difficult by the fact that themes and imagery derived from science fiction, fantasy, and superheroes saturate children's media culture, and so the precise moment when isolated acts of consumption come into focus as a social practice, when the "naïve" viewer or reader becomes a fan, is hard to pin down. More recently acquired interests and activities depend on tastes and dispositions formed in earlier practices and, in most cases, ultimately recede into the mists of personal history. Nonetheless, two common features of these origin stories can help us understand how people are initiated into geek culture. Both are present in the following extract where Solo explains how she got into comics:

BEN: Okay, so having had this interest in superheroes, grade 12 you get into comics. Can you tell me a bit about what that was like, what that process was?

SOLO: I met a boy who was a fan from when he was a little kid, so … It probably started a little bit earlier. Like, I was interested in it, and then I met him and he was really interested in it [...] Yeah, I don't know, I met a boy and we bonded over this mutual sort of nerd connection (perhaps), and then he got … It was like, because I was new at it and he'd stopped for a while, and then I was really interested and it like brought him back into it [...] So that's probably when I started buying graphic novels. Er, and I started off buying trades because I was like, "I don't need to buy individual issues. I find that kind of ridiculous. I just want to know the story; I don't need to make money later." And then I started going to comic cons because of Peter, who was my teacher, so that connection was there. And there it's mostly trades – er, it's mostly floppies, so I bought some … sets.

BEN: Sort of bundles that the dealers put together?

SOLO: And then, for some reason, I just went on this crazy – I think I read *Identity Crisis* in a hardcover [...] and then I got, I went on this mission to find 52 in back issues, so I got all the 52s, and then that led into needing to have, like, *Final Crisis*, and then that led into needing to have *Blackest Night*.

Notably, this account of her origins as a comic book fan and collector is, like most that I heard, an account of being recruited into the practice.

Significant Others

First, no matter when they started the practice in question – in childhood, as a teenager, in university, or six months ago – other people dominate these recruitment accounts. When interviewees explain how they got involved in a cultural practice, they tell stories that feature significant others as their main characters. Although the real origins of Solo's comics fandom precede the seemingly chance encounter with the "boy" ("It probably started a little bit earlier. Like, I was interested in it, and then I met him and he was really interested in it"), her *story* begins with a person and a "mutual sort of nerd connection." I collected several accounts that followed this pattern. Friends, friends of friends, siblings, and parents feature prominently in them. Often, these people are simply eager to share their tastes with others, such as Hank's brother who introduced him to comics and gaming; sometimes, they have more pragmatic motives, as with the mothers of Solo and Eastside's Alex, who created *Harry Potter* and comic-book fans, respectively, out of their concern to find reading material their children would accept. Diana's version is particularly notable:

> BEN: Can you remember your … what's the earliest memory you have of engaging with the science fiction and fantasy genres?
> DIANA: ((laughs)) My dad loved *Dune* … just loved it and pushed it on me and pushed it on me and pushed it on me and forced me to read it. And I hated every page. *Dune* and *The Hobbit*, every … like, he sat down and read it to me. So, I don't know how old I would be, but the age when you'd still be reading to your kid at night, he sat down, and I hated every single page of *The Hobbit* and the same with *Dune*, every single page of *Dune*. That's my first, earliest interaction. You'd think that would turn me off, but it didn't.

Diana's stories about her father stick out because she returned to them when asked about particularly meaningful or significant experiences having to do with her science-fiction fandom: "Just all through, reading science fiction with my dad, you know, that was important. That's important to me." Thus, despite initial resistance to the SF&F fare proffered by her father (and belying her claim, quoted above, not to remember a time before she read it), reading together enriched their relationship. This way of accounting for the origin of a leisure interest is so common and habitual that Barry twice inserts hypothetical others into this story of joining his first fan club: "I'm trying to remember if I knew somebody in it or … probably it was a poster in a library. I hung around libraries a lot, and I know that they were publicizing there. And that was a society that was specifically devoted to science fiction and fantasy ... Before that, it was ... a really solitary activity. I mean, reading comics – okay, yeah, comics you talk about, trade them with your friends and talk about them ... a little bit [...] But as far as science fiction or fandom *culture*, I guess that was my first exposure to fandom culture, and a science fiction society *is* ... fandom culture, capital 'c.'" Whereas Diana's case shows how the introduction of geek culture practices can be used to strengthen and enrich existing relationships with significant others, Barry used the field of fandom as a means to establish new relationships. He reported using nerdy practices strategically to join communities and social networks again later in life, such as his decision to look into the Society for Creative Anachronism (SCA) after moving to the city, and that the majority of his social interactions within geek culture were facilitated by groups and organizations such as the SCA, a Tolkien fan society, and so on.

The tendency to "socialize" their recruitment is notable for two reasons. One, despite prevailing cultural norms privileging the performance of individualism and authenticity,[3] interviewees did not hesitate to name others as the source of something they treated as an important part of their own identity. Two, there is an obvious affinity between this way of talking about their recruitment to specific practices and their more general understanding that shared tastes lay the foundation for shared experiences and, thus, a kind of community. Theories of consumption, including closely related theories of postmodern identities, often elevate the individual to the position of both prime mover and final cause. However, most of the conversation focuses on hedonistic consumption – optimists pointing to subjective experiences of agency produced by the thrill of shopping, and pessimists lamenting the emptiness of such acts – but, as Miller (1998) notes, the majority of our consumption is not hedonistic in nature. Rather, we mostly shop and consume to meet our basic needs and those of the people who share our lives. In most cases, then, consumption is also a channel through which we express care for and confirm our relationships with the people who matter most to us. The accounts I collected suggest that participation in geek culture is similarly Janus-faced. On the one hand, as forms of leisure these activities fulfill the needs and desires of individual participants. On the other hand, they are also oriented to significant others. This does not seem to in any way reduce their felt authenticity or integrity.

Passive Voices

The second feature of these stories is that interviewees typically portrayed themselves as objects acted upon by external forces, rather than as active agents. We saw this above when Solo said that "for some reason" she fell into reading and buying, first, the DC Comics crossover event *Identity Crisis* and then its successors *52*, *Final Crisis*, and *Blackest Night*. She describes the chain of events with the construction "that led into needing to have *x*." Her local comic shop closed shortly thereafter, curtailing her participation, but it's quite easy to see how this chain could continue indefinitely, drawing her deeper and deeper into comic book culture: after *Blackest Night* she would have "needed" to collect *Brightest Day* and then *Flashpoint*, which would have led into the New 52 line-wide relaunch and a whole series of crossover events after that. As she recounts things, at least, these purchases were entirely out of her control.

To put it another way, these accounts – like passive sentences – seem to lack a subject. Instead, impersonal processes work themselves out through their narrators' lives. A great deal of emphasis is placed on the conditions or situation in which their interest was sparked, but their own active agency is given a limited role, if any. The most generous reading of the accounts might suggest that the situation had qualities or affordances that called out for a response from them. When Mr Fox explained how he started reading comic books, his first purchase was explained as a function of a "need," despite no pre-existing history of comics reading; he "ended up" collecting comics "and then just kept going." Diana used similar wording when she described getting back into *Dungeons & Dragons* after years away from the hobby: "Yeah, started playing there and just kind of went on from there." Her narrative skips from the initial point of contact to full-fledged participation. There is no reflection or point of decision. In several cases, the speakers have relatively little to say about the qualities of these initial experiences – they don't even mention *liking* these things or activities, as if it weren't important at all. Rather, they talk as though they were caught up in an inevitable chain of events. Despite being constructed as accounts of external processes initiated by other people, there is no sense of alienation present in them. That their recruitment was not under their control is not treated as a problematic or even a remarkable feature of the narratives fitting this pattern.

These two features don't quite add up. If the recruitment process is a means of establishing or enriching relationships with significant others, then it cannot truly be an impersonal process. And yet these ways of narrating their careers as practitioners appear cheek-by-jowl in the accounts I collected. Because they distance the true subjects from their actions, both could be understood as another way for speakers to normalize themselves and minimize opportunities for negative inferences to be made about them. But in weaving narratives that involve people who are important to them and processes that extend through time, they are also expressing an intuitive understanding that engaging with geek culture involved them in something bigger and more complex than individual preferences and tastes.

IF YOU LOVE IT SO MUCH, WHY DON'T YOU MARRY IT?

In moving onto the next stage of a leisure career, I want to evoke two different ways we use the word *engaged*. On the one hand, it describes a quality of active participation – as Barry says, some TV shows are "quite passive" while others, like *Star Trek*, are "engaging." On the other hand, it implies commitment, as in an appointment (e.g., "a prior engagement") or an engagement to be married. In leisure careers, these two senses go hand in hand: to be engaged by an activity or interest is to become ever more committed to it. Based on her study of fandom and convention-going, for instance, Kington (2015, 224) reports that respondents' levels of fan activity were positively correlated with the number of fandoms in which they participated, the number of different kinds of fan activity they did, the variety of convention types attended, and the number of different kinds of convention activity they did. That is to say, fandom seems to exert a kind of gravitational pull upon people once they are caught in its orbit. However, in my interviews, this ever-increasing engagement was expressed as an issue of quality – for example, emotional investment – as much as sheer quantity of time or financial resources. Which sense of engagement comes first is like sorting out the chicken and the egg, and the paradox only strengthens the sense that depth of commitment and richness of participation are intimately woven together.

Given their life circumstances and the differing demands and temporalities of the practices themselves, interviewees described a wide range of levels of engagement. Most interviewees had at least one activity that they reported absorbing significant amounts of time on a daily or weekly basis:

- Barry spent several hours a day consuming sci-fi literature and media or working on his own novel, travelled to SCA events most weekends during the summer, and towards the end of the data collection period began running a weekly RPG session that required several hours of preparation time in addition to the block of time in which we played;
- Diana read SF&F novels and watched movies for an estimated eight to ten hours a week, played in a weekly D&D campaign, and logged into *World of Warcraft* nearly every spare minute that her infant daughter was sleeping;
- Wedge played in two weekly RPG campaigns and a monthly miniatures game that requires a fair amount of maintenance between playing sessions;
- and Shiera joked that she "lived" at the computer, playing *Star Wars Galaxies* and helping administer a guild, which involved monitoring problems and liaising with developers to address them, for many hours every day.

At the other extreme, several interviewees described practices that were more or less dormant, reduced to a taste – for comic books (Solo) or miniatures games (Mr Fox), for example – that was only rarely indulged. However, even where active engagement had waned, interviewees frequently professed an enduring sense of affinity with that activity. Despite being unable to participate in the fandom, they still thought of themselves as fans.

Once initiated into practice, one's identity as a practitioner exerts a determining influence on their next steps. This is not an instance of constraint so much as "setting limits" and "exerting pressures" (Williams 2001, 153). As Bourdieu (1996, 168) notes, a field is a "space of possibles," and one's trajectory through it makes some "moves" seem more obvious or even natural than others. Wedge provides good examples of how a series of engagements with different practices and groups can form relatively straightforward, linear narratives. As he thinks back to his initiation into each practice, the causal chain regresses to playing *Dungeons & Dragons*:

Well … probably a lot of it came from … playing D&D, I would guess, just … because I got interested in that sort of thing, it's hard to tell … like ((laughs)) how early on I was watching what shows and that kind of thing. 'Cause I can remember that time period when I grew up ... there was a fair number of like fantasy movies and like ... *Dragonslayer* and *Beast Master*.

Well, I think really, really it was ... I'm sure it was D&D, really. When I started playing D&D, that was pretty early on, so I don't think I would have been reading *Lord of the Rings* or *The Hobbit* or something like that before that. But I think by playing D&D then I started looking for that kind of stuff.

We have a Celtic festival in my hometown, so somebody who was a member of the SCA in Toronto had come out, who was from our hometown, and he had like fights with kids with like foam swords, so that's how we got interested in it. So I was already interested in the fighting, but I was always interested in that historical period through role-playing.[4]

Such narratives are sometimes portrayed as a matter of random chance, but in this account contingency seems to be erased and events are instead presented as organic developments. Because it is experienced – or at least recollected – as a more or less unproblematic process of getting from there to here, it may even be recast as a generic psychological process, another instance of "doing being ordinary" (Sacks 1984):

Well, I think it's natural in any human activity that you start by consuming ... In education, you start by being a student, and then eventually you ... get the desire to start giving back and actually ... teaching the stuff or going into it yourself. If you're a fan of science fiction, you might start by reading everything that's ever been written. And then you proceed to writing your fan-fiction or, you know, your own stuff. So, I think there's nothing special about ... fandom in that. It would be the same with everything else. (Barry)

It ... just kinda ... kept going. You know, gradual increase in interest, same as with ... games and comics. You start out with, you know, watching regular stuff and you're like, "I have an interest in this that I'm going to *pursue*," so you just naturally get more into it. (Mr Fox)

As in Wedge's case, deepening engagement with one practice often leads people into some level of involvement with others, whether they are understood as directly related or are simply part of the milieu they find themselves in. For example, Barry often recalled the science-fiction fandom of his youth. The main fan club in his area embraced not only sci-fi and fantasy literature but also other nerdy pursuits, and their annual convention "included all of that stuff: comics, movies, games." Since then, however, there has been a proliferation of more specialized clubs in that scene: "the *Doctor Who* Society, the *Star Trek* group that I mentioned, and the comic collectors, and so on, a whole galaxy of different aspects with common roots but their own interests and their own vocabulary and everything." Sometimes these combinations can be quite idiosyncratic, as in the case of the small-town comic book and hobby shop Mr Fox describes:

MR FOX: I bought my first rocket there.
BEN: At the comic shop?
MR FOX: You know the little model rockets? Man, those are fun.
BEN: I don't think I've ever seen a comic shop that sold model rockets before.
MR FOX: Well, it was a comic/hobby shop. They did everything. [...] They also had a slot car track [...] It was actually a really terrible comic shop.

Personal trajectories can also be unexpected. In one of my conversations with Mr Fox, we discussed our different experiences with webcomics: I began reading them because they were another outlet for my enjoyment of comic books, while he started out reading *Penny Arcade*, one of the pioneers of the "gamer webcomic" genre, because of his engagement with video games (although he was also a fan of traditional print comic books). Geek culture's institutions and infrastructures often maintain relationships with one another – or with third parties that they mutually support or promote – making these sorts of connections readily available, if not always explicitly promoted. Talking to individual participants about their paths through the scene underscores this point, as they frequently move between or simultaneously engage with groups that have no formal relationships.

Lay theories of geek culture are embedded in these accounts. Although the details vary, participants generally described a continuum of engagement, with the norm (in both descriptive and prescriptive senses) lying somewhere between two extremes. As we saw in chapter 1, so-called hardcore fans often served as rhetorical scapegoats for all of the negative inferences associated with the categories "nerd," "geek," "fan," "gamer," and so on. But even within the category of fanatical fans, distinctions are made. They may all be viewed as a little weird, but while some are marginalized for their objectionable habits and prickly personalities, others are tolerated for their authentic, unselfconscious engagement with the objects of their fandom: "Who am I to tell you that you're too something? If you get enjoyment out of it, then you know, run with it. It doesn't mean I won't laugh at you, but, you know, at the same time [...] part of me ... I look at the people that go to conventions, the (kind) where everybody's [i.e., non-participants viewing from the outside] laughing, 'Oh, look at them dressed up in *Star Trek*,' and part of me is like, it's kind of cool, you know? It's kind of cool that you're so involved with your passion and you can wear it right out like that. It's kind of neat, you know? I kind of admire that" (Diana). At the other extreme lie "casual" participants, a category that in fact hides a wide range of commitment levels. In some cases, casual fandom or participation seemingly embraces everyone who can successfully "pass" as ordinary folks – that is, everyone who is not hardcore: "If you play games? You're a gamer. Just like if you read *any* kind of book, you're a reader. If you drink any kinda coffee, you're a coffee drinker kinda thing" (Mr Fox).

In other cases, however, casual participation – in Shiera's vocabulary, being a "dabbler" – is devalued because it is a less involved and therefore less authentic kind of participation. Still other practices are depicted as entirely lacking a "casual" level due to their prerequisite knowledge, expertise, or time commitments (e.g., games like *Dungeons & Dragons* or *Warhammer* versus following a television series). It is perhaps becoming clear that regular, unremarkable participation is a moving target. A "normal" level of engagement is a situated judgment that depends on a great deal of other factors. Nonetheless, "passion" or "interest" remained keywords when people tried to explain why they participated in their given practices and what they believed they shared with their consociates. It is clear that some form of engaged commitment is considered the bedrock of membership and a prerequisite to participation in the nerd-culture scene.

DURABILITY OR DECLINE?

As people move through the field of geek culture, they are frequently confronted with a choice between diverging paths: do I stick with this or give it up? Talking to participants, rather than *ex*-participants, in the geek culture scene, there was a risk of bias towards accounts of continuing, durable involvement, rather than declining participation. Yet my informants talked much more explicitly – and often quite poignantly – of friends who had retired (as it were) from their leisure careers, of groups that had fallen apart, and of practices they themselves had left behind. Some of the reasons why participation might decline or stop altogether will be discussed in chapter 7. For now, I want to look at how participants interpreted these paths and what's at stake in choosing between them.

No one can fully engage with everything. People will draw the line in different places, but they eventually have to make decisions about how to manage the commitments they have shouldered. This is true of most aspects of life, but the costs of walking away from leisure activities are relatively low. They are, therefore, low-hanging fruit as different priorities compete for attention in our lives, and Kington (2014, 224) notes a "slight negative correlation between age and the number of fan-related activities" in which her survey respondents participated. This experience is common enough that sci-fi fans coined a word just to describe it: "There's an expression called gafiation. It means 'getting away from it all.' And that can be when somebody is just, well, it could be money or time or job or whatever, or it could just be that they're starting to get sick and tired of the whole thing, or starting to get into feuds with some individuals. They don't want to go to these events anymore because there's that person there that they don't want to see ever. It can even be an ex or something" (Barry). This definition already suggests two distinct reasons why someone might gafiate: first, the accidents and contingencies of everyday life and, second, changing attitudes towards the substance of participation. His experiences bear this out. As a self-employed person without family living in the city, Barry was less bound by external commitments and so he was one of the last men standing in a number of different groups over the years. However, he found it difficult to stay interested and committed when others' participation flagged. As a result, he had mostly abandoned these other groups, throwing himself into writing a novel, the SCA, and, towards the end of the fieldwork period, a new gaming campaign. Although he was clearly excited about these activities, the tone of regret in his accounts of dying or declining organizations is palpable: "My last regular game seems to have shut down. Actually, I just got an email from the [gamemaster] saying that she has to withdraw from fannish activities for a while because she's on medication [...] They were great games, but ... there were many days when I was the only player showing up, you know?"

The sphere of leisure is beset from all sides. According to Robert Coulson (1994, 11), there has been a long-standing, though somewhat tongue-in-cheek, debate between two rival camps of SF fans: FIAWOL (Fandom Is a Way of Life) and FIJAGH (Fandom Is Just a Goddamned Hobby). Neither of these positions quite captures the ways that participation in the practices of fandom, whether as a way of life or goddamned hobby, relies on a whole host of external circumstances. The person who can maintain the prescribed level of engagement over the long term is rare indeed. For example, by the end of the data collection period, Diana had gone from playing *World of Warcraft* every spare moment to not having played at all for some time:

BEN: So, yeah, how do you feel about firing up *WoW*?

DIANA: Sure. Like I said, I haven't played in a while.

BEN: Is this bad? I mean, am I going to cause you to relapse or something?

DIANA: No. Unfortunately, I'm in a spot where I'm kind of stuck. I don't really have anything to do.

Steve: It's been, what? Two months since we played?

DIANAa: It's been since my mum – since my parents were here [...] I got out of the habit, you know? Because it's such a new one.

BEN: Do you see yourself coming back to it? Do you miss it? Or are all my notes about *Warcraft* just –

DIANA: ((laughs)) Just throw them away! Yes and no. I mean, I could see myself easily going back into it ... I have much less time now because Donna was a lot younger so she was sleeping more so I had much more time, but now she's not sleeping as much so I can't. ((laughs)) You know, the baby doesn't really like it when you don't pay attention to her.

Like Barry, above, two different factors conspired to reduce her ability and desire to play. First, her infant daughter no longer slept as much, significantly reducing Diana's window of opportunity to play. Second, she got stuck in the game; feeling helpless or directionless, she was temporarily unable to achieve the game's pleasures and goods, and she lost interest. While we might assume that the former is much more important, Diana might have been more willing to make time to play if the game was still experienced as rewarding. But she "got out of the habit."

In other cases, changes in circumstance are less personal and, thus, also less manageable. At different times, Solo and Mr Fox had both had their regular comic shops close on them. At the end of her account of being recruited into comics fandom and becoming a regular reader of more and more series, Solo's career abruptly ends when her comic shop of choice closed. There were, of course, other shops in a city of this size, but their locations were less convenient and she just didn't like them as much as her old store. At the time of our interview, she said she might occasionally stop in a mass-market bookstore to buy a trade paperback collection of comics but was no longer engaged with the culture of comic book store regulars. Gaming groups are also fragile. As mentioned above, Barry had had one break up shortly before I started interviewing him, and both Diana and Mr Fox's regular groups ran into difficulties during the fieldwork period. Diana didn't open up about the issues that precipitated its dissolution, though she had previously mentioned personality conflicts among the players, but Mr Fox explained that his game master had moved away: "He was the guy who told all the stories and had everything sorted out, so … it's kinda gone." The logistical problems of co-ordinating schedules in order to have regular sessions prove difficult to solve permanently: "The big problem these days is getting everybody together. Huge problem these days! I don't know if it's we're all getting older or something like that because I guess when we're all students at the same place, okay, because often it's a student situation, they all kind of hang out together, but then people got their own things going in different parts of the city, and it becomes a rarer pastime so those who are interested find themselves farther away in the first place from each other" (Barry). Subcultural studies remind us that teenagers often have more truly disposable income and free time than adults. That Barry, at age 53, still harkens back to his student days underscores the significance of this period of relative freedom for leisure practices of all sorts. Once adult responsibilities enter the picture, the threat of gafiation is always nearby. In small groups, especially, even one member leaving can severely disrupt a practice.

But declining participation is not only a problem for self-organizing groups of friends. Fan Fellowship and Convivium, two local groups Barry mentioned that met for dinner, drinks, and fannish discussion, had a reasonable amount of institutional momentum, but their low-commitment structure made them vulnerable to the vagaries of members' interest levels. Despite their relatively lengthy histories, Barry reported that attendance had fallen, they were now being held less regularly, and he himself had not attended for several months. These might be contrasted with the Society for Creative Anachronism, which Barry repeatedly held up as an example of a healthy, well-organized group that was in it for the long haul. But despite his sanguine views of the bonds of fealty and affection that held the group together, Shiera was concerned that the rise of a rival society of medieval re-creationists that had fewer bureaucratic requirements – and, therefore, seemingly more "fun" – heralded decline for the local SCA. Even the best-organized institutions may be overtaken by forces outside of their control.

In other cases, people feel forced out of fan communities and active practice not by external factors but by the very relationships that constitute the community. Barry and Shiera, who both had long associations with organized fandom, mentioned personal conflicts or "feuds" that push people out or otherwise precipitate their gafiation. These were never discussed at length, but they were alluded to again and again. Shiera noted wistfully that she wouldn't attend SF&F Con, which she viewed as the main fan event in the area, because of an ex's involvement in its organization. And, although she said SCAers don't hold grudges, she was also very wary of being drawn into the society's internal politics, which like all feudal societies have an inescapably personal dimension: "It's a time that I look back on now, and I still want to go to events for the *people*, but I want to make sure I don't get involved in the politics. And it's very difficult to do when you're as intimately familiar with as many different things as I am. Because I have done a lot. But the moment I volunteer to co-autocrat an event, I've gotten involved in the politics, and I'm going to have to deal with that. I'm not going to do that. I refuse." Although Barry said he had mostly managed to avoid feuds and grudges in his time in fandom, the problem seemed to weigh quite heavily on his mind: "Some clubs and just groups of people involved in fandom, they can detonate, okay? Self-destruct with people not talking to people anymore about who knows what." While he was undeniably correct that such conflict is endemic to human relationships, it also seems that the experience of his religiously based conservatism putting him at odds with the left-liberal, libertarian, atheist/skeptic, and neo-pagan types that are often outspoken members of fan communities colours his account. As he put it, "Any trouble that

I've been in has had more to do with people's own lives apart from their fannish activities. Or my life apart from my fannish activities." So, although he tries to restrict conversations to harmless topics of fannish interest, he did admit having gotten into arguments or offended people on occasion. Whether successfully resolved or not, these sorts of encounters can easily rob the pleasure from participating in communities of practice.

The meaningfulness of durable fandom did not generate the same detailed, explicit discussion as accounts of gafiation and disintegrating groups did. I found this somewhat curious, expecting people to be able to articulate the value that long-term commitments to these practices held for them. Perhaps my informants simply had more difficulty projecting forward than they did looking back, but this also points to an important aspect of subcultural careers. Recently, a body of scholarship has begun investigating the experiences of members of "youth" cultures as they age. If subcultural activity is in part made possible by the licence accorded to young people and their greater degree of free time, what happens when punks have to start paying mortgages and goths have to attend PTA meetings (Hodkinson 2011, 2012, 2013)? The "problem" of aging is the relationship between subcultural participation and the rest of life. No longer in the relatively protected space of adolescence, people have to find ways to take not only leisure but also work, family, and other relationships seriously. At the same time, the practice itself may change in significant ways as subsequent cohorts of participants transform it, and some existing members simply may not be as interested in the newer trends. As a result of both external and internal pressures, then, signs of engagement that could once be taken for granted – for instance, that more time means more enthusiasm or passion – may no longer reliably index levels of commitment in later stages of one's career in a practice. Over the longer term, participation and non-participation can start looking more and more alike.

In *Situated Learning*, Lave and Wenger (1991) suggest that the starting point of a career in a community of practice is "legitimate peripheral participation." This phrase suggests a recognized role, like that of that apprenticeship, that is seen as belonging to the group (hence, *legitimate*) but for whom it is not yet appropriate to fully participate in the action (hence, *peripheral*). A different kind of legitimate peripheral participation may also be the end point of many leisure careers. This represents a kind of "post-fandom" experience, where tastes and expertise outlast active engagement. People spoke of long-term relationships they had made or witnessed within geek culture, but these sometimes seemed the exception rather than the rule and, as Shiera explained, it takes work to hold them together: "I have a friend who [...] does a weekly game. He's in his late twenties now, and they've maintained it all the way through from high school. Those are some hardcore geeks. ((laughs)) [...] But the thing is he writes – I think part of keeping that community together is maintaining the interest across the board, so he writes a write-up, almost an episode of what they gamed through. And it's brilliant stuff, it's great stuff, very fun, fun to read." The rewards of long-term participation were, more often than not, momentary and fleeting: a fun conversation or game session, being recognized for your skill and effort, or being exposed to an interesting or moving story in prose, film, or visual art. But every life is composed of disparate moments. Our job is to collect these moments and articulate them together so that we can tell the story of how we came to be who we are today. Like the pictures on a LEGO set that suggest several alternative configurations for the bricks contained within, social practices and careers within them provide guides for the work of narrating identity. All this is to say that experiencing the rewards of participation, at whatever stage of a leisure career, is not an automatic function of putting your time in.

MacIntyre's theory of practice implies that we must learn to be practitioners. Note, for instance, that his example of internal goods involves teaching someone to play a game (MacIntyre 2007, 188). Along the way, the learner is presumed to internalize the game's norms and standards. That is to say, one not only learns how to play but *how to play well*: what moves are regarded as elegant solutions to a given problem, what is and isn't sporting, and so on (see ch. 3). Matt Hills (2014b) has argued that "first wave" fan studies overemphasized recruitment as a process of socialization and learning, at the expense of "the affectively powerful *moment of 'conversion'*" (11; original emphasis). However, given that few of my interviewees organized their own recruitment accounts around a singular road-to-Damascus moment, I think it is more helpful to consider conversion as an ongoing process rather than an act that can be completed in a moment. One understanding of what it means to be a practitioner gradually supplants another, and that understanding is deepened, extended, and perhaps supplanted in turn. This process of conversion cannot be separated from socialization; learning, engagement, and participation overlap to the point that, in my informants' accounts, it is not entirely clear where one begins and the other ends. If "becoming-a-fan narratives" are about "encountering media texts that [...] transform one's identity" (Harrington and Bielby cited in Hills 2014b, 10), we should remember that identity is a narrative that we are perpetually revising – we are always "fixing it in post."

-❤-

In a *Wired* magazine editorial, comedian Patton Oswalt (2010) describes the intensity of his youthful attachments to nerdy media as developing due to two crucial *lacks*. First, the absence of the texts themselves. Oswalt suggests that audiences make meaning when texts leave us wanting more, but this happens less and less today. Second, and less developed in the essay, is the absence of anything better to do: "I was too young to drive or hold a job. I was never going to play sports, and girls were an uncrackable code. So, yeah – I had time to collect every *Star Wars* action figure, learn the Three Laws of Robotics, memorize Roy Batty's speech from the end of *Blade Runner*, and classify each monster's abilities and weaknesses in TSR Hobbies' *Monster Manual*" (¶4). In the normative life course of someone raised in a wealthy society, adolescence is a special time. Teenagers are granted more autonomy than younger children but typically have fewer constraints upon their time compared with working adults. For someone like Oswalt, who (he suggests) was unable to "crack the codes" of high school social life, the imaginative worlds of science fiction and fantasy provided something else to invest time and care into. However, it is the forty-one-year-old Oswalt, not his teenaged self, speaking here. It is from the perspective of 2010 that he looks back at the 1980s as a time when "nerd meant something" (¶1) and prophesies the "death" of geek culture. This is as much an instance of autobiographical narrative as a commentary on geek culture.

As MacIntyre suggests, the self is a narrative construction, but in adopting a practice approach, I have committed to the idea that social practices precede their theorization. It is through practical engagement with the world that objects present themselves to thought. In the case of autobiographical narratives, people, places, and things are made salient because of their relationship to what the narrator is trying to accomplish in the narrative. Actions, attitudes, and intentions – our own as much as others' – disclose themselves and become intelligible because of their role in advancing (or thwarting) the narrative we are trying to lay out. Oswalt's essay, for instance, is full of references to experiences, states of being, and forms of knowledge that are produced by participation in geek culture; as MacIntyre (2007, 189) might suggest, they are goods that can only be recognized by a competent practitioner. Our experiences within communities of practice also present us with a set of explanations that are conventionalized, simply ready-to-hand, or both. Oswalt adopts the style and rhetoric of causal explanation, saying, in effect, "'nerd' meant something in the 1980s *because* x, but now it doesn't *because* y."

Similarly, my interviewees used conventional formulations to describe and explain their careers in geek culture, such as the reliance on other people and this-led-to-that in the stories discussed in this chapter. The circulation of conventionalized tropes like these is, I think, key to how individual narratives become articulated with narratives about groups and collectives. As Laclau and Mouffe (2001, 105) define it, to articulate is to create "a relation among elements such that their identity is modified as a result of the articulatory practice." An articulation is a connection that changes the things it connects. There is nothing natural or inevitable about such articulations. For Stuart Hall (1985), it is the very contingency of the relationship that makes it an articulation in the first place. But how does the articulation between individual and group play out at the level of lived experience? Practice precedes identity, just as individual precedes group – no one, not even children whose fan parents saddled them with names like Kirby and Khaleesi, is born a geek. Yet the group must also come before any practice understood as a "*socially established* form of activity" (MacIntyre 2007, 187; my emphasis). The next chapter explores how people make the diverse and differentiated clusters of activity in the geek culture scene into communities. As we orient ourselves to communities of practice, the stories we tell about ourselves become inseparable from those of the groups – whether local, specific, and concrete or more nebulous and even notional – in which we participate.

5

Making Communities
from Mass Culture

The fate of community is one of social science's original research problems. Scholars writing from a variety of theoretical and political positions have argued that modernity represented a break from the forms of social life characterizing earlier eras. Typically, social orders based on rationalized, functional differentiation are contrasted with ones based on affective experiences of commonality. These concepts were taken to describe the fundamental difference between modern European societies, on the one hand, and their own historical antecedents or some primitive "others," on the other hand. But community is not just a theoretical problem. It looms much larger as an object of anxiety or a symptom of some fundamental social malaise.

The issue is not community per se since, as Raymond Williams (1989, 112) notes: "Community is unusual among the terms of political vocabulary in being [...] the one term which has never been used in a negative sense." Everyone is in favour of community. The problem is the nagging feeling that real, authentic community is slipping from our grasp. Modern societies are said to lack the resources for human fulfillment that were widely available in pre-modern communities, and this tendency reaches its apotheosis in the mediated marketplaces of consumer society. Instead of "real" communities, we have only "lifestyle enclaves" (Bellah et al. 1986), "proto-communities" (Willis 1990), "club cultures" (Thornton 1996; Redhead 1997), and "brand communities" (Muñiz and O'Guinn 2001; O'Guinn and Muñiz 2005) or "neo-tribes" (Maffesoli 1996; Bennett 1999). If community bears the weight of all our hopes and dreams for a humane social order, then things look rather bleak.

In a short essay that was unpublished during his lifetime, Walter Benjamin described the cultural condition of his generation, which had survived the trenches of the Great War and subsequently lived through rapid social and technological change, as "a new kind of barbarism": "We say this in order to introduce a new, positive concept of barbarism. For what does poverty of experience do for the barbarian? It forces him to start from scratch; to make a new start; to make a little go a long way; to begin with a little and build up further, looking neither left nor right. Among the great creative spirits, there have always been the inexorable ones who begin by clearing a *tabula rasa*" (1996, 732). Our problem is much the same. There is no way back to "authentic community," which is always already gone anyway. Yet people continue to find meaning in everyday life. This cannot be easily written off as false consciousness. Indeed, recognizing alienation presupposes at least some frisson of unalienated experience. The meaningfulness of everyday life – and of the social relations it comprises – is a collective accomplishment. Like individual identities, community is a matter of narrative, one that people tell one another about their mutually sustaining relationships, and of practice – that is, of *community-making*. Geek culture provides one example of how to make a little go a long way, as Benjamin would have it. Oriented towards consumer goods and cultural commodities, geek media cultures offer a distinctly modern vision of what communities might look like today.

THE GEEK CLIQUE

When I asked my interviewees to estimate how many of their friends were also geeks, their responses ranged between 60 or 70 per cent (Diana) and virtually 100 per cent (Mr Fox and Wedge).[1] In thinking back to their school days, several interviewees identified as "loners" or said they built peer groups around specific clubs or shared activities, such as drama or music programs. As adults, many of them continued to develop friendships through the local geek culture scene.

Solo provides an interesting case, as she seemingly identified more strongly with geek culture in the abstract than with any particular practice or group. She and her best friends from high school were drawn together by a shared fandom: "Well, I was putting up a *Buffy* poster in my locker, and two girls walked by and were like, 'Oh, you like *Buffy*, too?' And that started my entire circle of friends that continues to this day. So, that's pretty significant." Although she remains close with these girls, they have grown apart somewhat in the intervening years: "I got into comic books and others got into art and others got into science, and you know that sort of stuff changed, too." The majority of her peer group at the time of our conversations, by contrast, was a group of "gamey nerdy boys," whom she met after one of them struck up a conversation about her *Star Wars* t-shirt. But she explained that "they're not the same kind of geek as me." Despite not considering herself a gamer, Solo nonetheless pointed to a shared sense of geekiness that cemented her relationship with the group: "Hanging out, talking, and a lot of the talking is where a lot of the nerdy stuff comes up. So, a lot of it is like, we're not doing anything, but we're like sitting and actively being nerds together. Like just being nerds together." There is a strong implication in the way Solo framed her interactions with friends – and even strangers – that they share a common repertoire drawn from their mutual orientations to geek culture, even when they don't necessarily participate in the same practices within it. At the least, this repertoire facilitates small talk, and sometimes the shared sense of belonging and familiarity that it generates provides the basis for more significant relationships to develop.

But a social circle or group of friends, however close, is not the same thing as a community. Thanks to its vagueness, ubiquity, and universally positive connotations, the word was widely used by my interviewees:

I would use "fan community" or "fan*dom*." And that's about the most general term that I can think of that applies to that sort of thing. Everything else I can think of is kind of subsets of that. (Barry)

One of the things that makes MMOs work is community, and [*Star Wars Galaxies*] has a very vocal, very intelligent – I have a very intelligent community that I'm a part of. So, I'm very involved with them, both emotionally and intellectually. (Shiera)

I think there are certainly geek communities [...] Like, you have the gaming community, which I probably have the most connection with, and that's separated into a bunch of them, but I think most of those people would probably know each other or have met or seen each other, that sort of thing. There's a fairly large sci-fi community, I think [...] And then ... I just saw the other day there was a ... local nerd meet-up something, and – then there's the Reddit ... Reddit kind of meet-ups going on, which I think would probably classify as a geek or a nerd meet-up. And then you've got like the hackspace crowd, which would probably fit in there a little bit. Yeah, so there's ... I think there's a lot of different communities. I don't necessarily know them that well. Unless it tends to be more of a focus that I'm interested in. (Wedge)

However, they also qualified its application. Some practices were viewed as having a community and others weren't ("I mean, I'd say 'fans.' It's like, you know, '*Pokémon* fans.' I wouldn't say 'the *Pokémon* community' 'cause that sounds weird," Mr Fox). While people would readily discuss whether particular groups counted as communities, there was more uncertainty about whether geek culture in general could be called by that name. There were some ways that the relationships fostered by geek culture simply didn't square with their understandings of what a community is. Many recognized it as a social object, but hesitated to attribute to it the intimate qualities typically attached to community:

> "*Geek*dom" is less a ... less of a word that I'd use. It doesn't seem to me to actually exist in the sense of a community. You know, a lot of people [in "geekdom"] have a personality trait that they don't get together. Community is where people get together. (Barry)

> I wouldn't say "community," though. I would never use the term "nerd community." That makes me think of like an old folks' home. It's like, "Oh, at Shady Oaks Community Centre." That's an old folks' home. That's like this horrible place you put nerds. Ugh. That place would smell like Cheetos. (Mr Fox)

However, I had to push interviewees to explicitly formulate why they held the term to be appropriate (or not) for describing a given set of people.

One of community's key characteristics in these accounts was sharing. Communities might share spaces ("In comic books, I think the community is very central to your shop," Solo), activities ("You know, like, they're groups of people that do the same thing, so they can talk about – people that play D&D, that's a community," Diana), goals ("My community in *Star Wars Galaxies* is ... based on [...] shared needs and goals and desires," Shiera),[2] or experiences ("The point about adversity and surviving adversity as being one of the ingredients in a successful community is that ... they have a shared experience," Shiera), but there was a strong sense that they had to share *something*: "Well, I think ...

community is like shared – it maybe depends on your – I think there's community in nerds" (Solo). The choice of focal thing or activity demarcated boundaries between "communities," even if these boundaries were only symbolic or rhetorically achieved. However, shared interests alone are insufficient. Indeed, it is such one-dimensionality that leads critics to dismiss these formations as mere "lifestyle enclaves" (Bellah et al. 1986, 72–3) or "cloakroom communities" (Bauman 2000, 199). Clearly, we want a community to be something sturdier and more robust. When comparing different organizations with which he had been involved, Barry rated two sci-fi fan clubs as more like communities than the Society for Creative Anachronism (SCA):

> BARRY: Organizations like the Fan Fellowship or ... what's the other weekly dining thing that's been going on for longer? Convivium. Those are kind of formal communities because they get together on a regular basis. The individuals are fairly diverse and have diverse interests, but they do still get together and there's some back and forth on different subjects.
> BEN: What makes an organization like that different from some of the other fannish organizations?
> BARRY: I guess you could compare that to the SCA. The SCA is much more organized, scheduled, more different kinds of things happening ... I suppose, more reliable in some sense. If something is announced it usually happens. And more active. You know, people doing more stuff and putting more of themselves in an activity.
> BEN: So, why is that you think of Fan Fellowship and Convivium when I asked about a local fan community?
> BARRY: Because they're more general.
> BEN: More general?
> BARRY: I think if you're talking about ... the concept 'community,' the general comes first. You know, like a family may be extended but everybody's still related to each other there, rather than people on the other side – well, neighbours or whatever. Anyway, Fan Fellowship and Convivium and the conventions like SF&F Con are set up specifically to bring people from different backgrounds together. They're meeting places. They're the town halls, the marketplaces.

Two dimensions of Barry's notion of the priority of the general are important to understanding what these communities share and how they diverge from traditional communities.

First, privileging more general groups means emphasizing people and relationships over the activities that they do when together. A group becomes a community when sociability amongst members overruns the original reason for its constitution. Although Barry doesn't draw attention to it, there is also an implicit contrast here between local, more informally organized groups and the SCA, which is a (not-for-profit) corporation with a board of directors providing oversight to nineteen "kingdoms" and their smaller branches around the world. When Barry described Fan Fellowship and Convivium, he mentioned that they gather regularly, are made up of diverse members, and serve as meeting places; when describing the SCA, he basically says they keep the trains running on time (or whatever the "period" equivalent would be). Fan Fellowship and Convivium are not only more "general" than the SCA but also appear more intimate or personal. While *some* level of organization made Fan Fellowship and Convivium "formal communities," rather than just a private group of friends, they were organized at a more human scale. But under the right conditions, communities can be carved out of such large, bureaucratic entities. While Shiera agreed that the SCA as a whole shouldn't be considered a community, she believed that "individual branches can form communities."

Second, a community is general because it takes all kinds. While traditional communities are often understood as relatively homogenous (at the extreme, bound by blood), Barry suggested that the less narrowly focused a group's interests and activities, the more it was designed to attract people from "different backgrounds," then the more like a community it becomes. He relates this to the givenness of traditional communities, where you may have little in common with other members besides the fact of your membership. That is, in the same way that you don't choose your family, you don't have a say in who will show up at a meeting or convention and make themselves a part of your community:

SOLO: But I think it's also very like close – like, it's friendship-based? It's very friendship heavy where it's hard to say if that's community or not because you're not … like, it's more private? It's less public? Maybe?

BEN: So, you're saying –

SOLO: Like, it's more of a private community.

BEN: – nerd culture is more based on friendships and so is more likely to be closed off in the private sphere, whereas something you'd more easily describe as community –

SOLO: Is public [...] Like, where you're coming into contact, where you're networking and making friends, but also sort of like business associates and that sort of stuff within community.

Contra Zygmunt Bauman's (2000, 172) claim that "the community of the communitarian gospel is either an ethnic community or a community imagined after the pattern of an ethnic one,"[3] my informants asserted that a group must be inclusive and "joinable" in order to merit the term. Of course, not every gathering of geeks meets this standard, but this is another instance where a breach makes the rule plain. If an individual participant or group of them is seen as creating barriers to entry or turning some participants against others, then community has devolved into mere cliquishness.

Although groups described as communities could be quite durable, geek culture's communities of practice differ from those celebrated by communitarians and civic republicans like Michael Sandel (1984) in that their members have relatively few obligations or responsibilities to the collective. For Sandel, people are never the "unencumbered selves" of liberal political philosophy but always "members of this family or community or nation or people." As such, we are bound to others and owe them "more than justice requires or even permits, not by reason of agreements I have made but instead in virtue of those more or less enduring attachments and commitments that, taken together, partly define the person I am." (90) Notwithstanding the strong sense of belonging and attachment sometimes evident in their talk, when I asked people whether their experiences of geek culture involved obligations or duties, I received unusually short, straightforward answers:

> I guess that's something that I do value because I miss it in some of the communities that I'm a part of right now, some of the fannish communities. (Barry)

> No, not really. (Mr Fox)

> *That* is almost completely lacking. (Shiera)

Participants denied feeling any obligations to their consociates "beyond the obligations I voluntarily incur and the 'natural duties' I owe to human beings as such" (Sandel 1984, 90), such as specific promises made to individuals (Barry) or regularly picking up merchandise set aside for you at the comic shop (Solo). By the same token, what one can expect from these groups is much more limited. However, Mr Fox recognized that in certain instances the consubstantiality binding fans together could motivate people to act in ways that they wouldn't for "just anyone": "Like, I guess, a hypothetical, if someone is a big comic fan and is well known in the community, and their house burned down, chances are the comic-book *fans* would send them stuff. They'd be like, 'Well, I've got a few extra comics kicking around.' They'll help him rebuild his collection, things like that. Same thing in the gaming community." Solo alluded to other obligations immanent to fandom. When we talked about movies, she said she felt as though she "should" see *Green Lantern* (Martin Campbell 2011) in theatres, despite trailers that turned her off, and she described feeling bound to watch TV series she followed: "It used to be – ugh! When [*Buffy the Vampire Slayer*] was on TV, it was brutal. I would put off anything to be in front of the TV Thursday night. Everything else, it just would not … I could not miss it." Admittedly, these are not serious ethical burdens – indeed, they are obligations to things rather than people – but they constitute some awareness that participation in the community involves more than just showing up.

IMAGINING COMMUNITIES

Benedict Anderson (2006) taught us that nations are imagined communities. The *idea* of the nation compensates for a fundamental problem of scale – that is, the boundaries of even the smallest nation-state comprises too many people for us to feel emotionally attached to or even really know – by projecting a sense of community onto the symbols and trappings of nationhood. As Bauman suggests, however, not only nations but all communities "are *postulated*": they are "projects rather than realities, something that comes *after*, not *before* the individual choice" (2000, 169; emphasis in original). Bauman means this to deflate the claims of communitarian political philosophers. It seems plainly contradictory to him to say that we must choose to create and defend things that, according to writers like Sandel (1984) are valuable precisely because they precede individual choice.

I want to split the difference here. Communities typically do precede their members, and they undoubtedly rely on resources that are prior to any individual action. However, that is not to say that a community or the experience of membership is a static, unchanging essence. Rather, community is performative; its reality is its regular, even routinized, enactment by members. Various forms of community-making were embedded in participants' everyday activities. To the extent that a tradition-bearing community is essential to the definition of a focal practice (MacIntyre 2007, 191), then dispersed "communalizing"[4] practices enable us to imagine what we do as more than just individual action. Rather, these habits serve to sustain, extend, and repair, as necessary, relationships with others. In my interviews, the project of communalization appeared in three main contexts.

Given the above definitions associating community with persistent or organized groups, it is unsurprising that community-making often took place through existing organizations and institutions. To hear my participants talk about it, some organizations were simply better at producing a sense of community than others, and this was typically attributed to some feature of their policies or how they approached running events:

> I think they [gaming conventions] really foster ... um a good network of people and draw new ... my main goal at throwing cons and helping out with the City Gaming Network and that sort of thing is really to draw new gamers in, give them a place to sort of meet together or connect with other gamers or play new games. That sort of thing. I think ... fostering that sense of community is really ... useful to draw new people in. (Wedge)

> We talk about how to keep a game that is seven years old going, how to keep people coming in and interested, and community support for new players and returning players. We talk a bit about ... what we've learned from what we do. (Shiera)

Similarly, individual members of these groups could act in ways that supported the ongoing reproduction of the community. Some people made building and maintaining groups a priority, most often by pitching in towards shared activities: "In other parts of science fiction fandom, you have people who go to science fiction conventions. That's part of their hobby. They spend, like, every weekend it seems at a different convention. And helping to organize conventions, too, or some aspects of them. Like, organizing ... what's it called? The con suite. Okay? Think of the couple who I mentioned to you. That's what they used to do, organize con suites at the different conventions. Just a place where people drop in and chat, a bit of refreshment" (Barry).

By directing their efforts towards the reproduction of the practice, they conduct themselves *as if* they were members of communities. Group-oriented community-making might also include distinctive ways of supporting novice practitioners. To take the Society for Creative Anachronism as an example again, Barry asserted that its culture emphasized interpersonal bonds and loyalties: "The SCA is kind of a special case because as an organization it has a commitment to the ideals of chivalry. Now, that's a formal commitment. I'm not saying that the other fannish organizations don't have those ideals, but they're not necessarily stated." Obviously, this is partly an element of "the game" of playing at medieval lords and ladies, but it does appear to influence how the group forms its members. As Shiera describes the Society's day-to-day and behind-the-scenes functioning, this fantasy of chivalry and fealty is expressed, organizationally, in an apprenticeship model that not only transmits expertise across membership cohorts but also guides people into roles where they can contribute to the group.[5] Of course, not every member will go to such lengths. As Wedge noted, "Some people will be *far* more committed to … solving problems within a community or that sort of thing."

Other forms of community-making took place outside of the roles provided by formal groups and organizations – though not necessarily outside of contexts they furnished. Michel Maffesoli's *Time of the Tribes* makes the important point that "*experiencing the other* is the basis of community" (1996, 73; original emphasis). Maffesoli pushes back against the tidy functionalism to which social explanation is sometimes prone, arguing that some groups' *raison d'être* is simply to be: "Thus, I believe that the *being-together* is a basic given. Before any other determination or qualification, there is this vital spontaneity that guarantees a *culture* its own *puissance* and solidarity" (81; original emphasis). On this view, individuals *qua* individual come first, and groups, organizations and institutions are merely channels through which their creative social energy circulates. "It is by force of circumstance; because of proximity; […] because there is a sharing of the same *territory* (real or symbolic) that the communal idea and its ethical corollary are born" (16; original emphasis). Stripping away the mystical excesses of Maffesoli's prose, the "proxemics" that generate a sense of community can look quite pedestrian, as in examples of preferential treatment or special care taken towards other members, but they can also be deeply meaningful. Shiera's accounts of her MMORPG-based relationships illustrate this point beautifully:

But, I mean, what do we talk about? Mostly, it's game stuff, but also there's some personal stuff. Friends have ... One of the things about community-building and maintaining is that when a crisis happens, you need to be there for them, you need to be a friend. You know, we've been through deaths in the family, we've been through cancer diagnoses, as a group. The guild that I'm the leader of right now [...] we formed in 2005, so we've known each other a good long while. And while we've had new people come in, they're people who fit that same help/share/bear kind of dynamic.

I have a very intelligent community that I'm a part of. So, I'm very involved with them, both emotionally and intellectually. There's a lot there for me. They also make me laugh, and first thing in the morning, sometimes, I really need that because I'm in a lot of pain. So, that have my morning coffee and sit there, and there's a post from a guy in Australia who's a hilarious writer, and he's making stuff that – it's funny! So, it's enlightening to read. Just lightens the whole mood.

This could be framed in terms of investing in personal support networks to generate social capital. There certainly is a transactional dimension to Shiera's comments about sharing one another's burdens – to say "there's a lot there for me" is, at one level, to make a statement of cost and benefit – but it could also be said that this "being-together" is exactly what is meant when we invoke that nebulous "sense of community."

Finally, any discussion of contemporary community-making practices would be incomplete without reference to new media and communication technologies. Although these technologies are often the subject of a great deal of hype, I was surprised to find that digital communication appeared as a taken-for-granted rather than disruptive or revolutionary feature of everyday life. Its novelty and convenience wasn't lost on my interviewees, but new media were ultimately subordinated to old problems and goals, such as maintaining relationships over distance or coordinating meetings and events.

From one point of view, digital communication simply provides another set of tools and platforms for groups and individuals to organize themselves, much as they are used in the workplace. Electronic mailing lists, Usenet and Internet Relay Chat, message boards and forums, blogs and social networking sites are successive re-mediations of the fannish correspondence culture that started out in the letter columns of pulp magazines and comic books. Digital resources can also ease the work of running in-real-life events within the local scene. For example, the meetings of Westernesse, a Tolkien fan club Barry occasionally attended, were co-ordinated through the web app Meetup.com, and Shiera remarked that a labour-intensive project she implemented while still heavily involved in the SCA – and which she viewed as an important instrument of community-making within the Kingdom – could, today, be accomplished quite easily with a wiki that decentralized the collection and maintenance of information. In these cases, new technologies are being enrolled into long-standing community-making practices.

However, many interviewees also remarked upon online communities and their role in changing geek culture in recent years. I'm refraining from calling them "virtual communities" because, despite persistent fears that computer-mediated communication is turning its users into digital anchorites, cultivating a seething underbelly of misanthropic sociopaths, or regressing us into texting simpletons, communities organized through or around the Internet (whether supplemented with face-to-face interaction or not) do not seem to be viewed as necessarily any less meaningful or authentic than offline ones. Indeed, Shiera ranks her "guildies" in *Star Wars Galaxies* as having much more communalized relationships than the ones she experienced in the SCA, which is of course primarily oriented to interacting "in real life." Digital resources and communication channels also weave geek culture through everyday life, particularly for those whose working day is spent in front of a computer and so have relatively constant access to a flow of digitized information and discussion. Blogs, podcasts, listservs, and forums accelerated the circulation of information about geek culture: "With the Internet, you get knowledge a lot faster, you know. So, you have this nerd hive brain kind of thing that – before the Internet, where did you get this knowledge from? You know? You had to go to a bookstore, you had to go to a, you know, *geek* social place to find out, you know, where now you can stay at home. I can get much more information than I ever would have had being on the fringes of the community than … I can be almost as informed as somebody in the heart of the community if I want to be" (Diana).

It seems that fandom is no longer a "weekend-only world" (Jenkins 2013, 277); geek culture is now a constant presence wherever and whenever they have access to the web. But Barry, for one, feared that new modes of interaction, which encouraged extensive, diverse, but ultimately only periodic and glancing contact, don't foster the level of commitment that fan communities need in order to thrive in the long run: "There's a lot less face-to-face interaction, I guess, in terms of clubs and conventions [...] Now, it's more casual, loose ... you don't know the people you're talking to, or at least you've never met them. I mean, that can be a good thing. You're talking to people who are farther away, in other cultures and stuff. But then you might not get to know them, further aspects [...] When you're in a club, to keep the club going, people have to commit to showing up on a certain day of the week at a certain time of day. If you just have an Internet interest group, people can sign up, sign in and out, whenever they want. Both can work. But the second one doesn't require ... the specific, more specific commitments." It is probably too early to adjudicate between these two arguments. Tensions between "broadcasting" and "narrowcasting," promiscuousness and selectivity, and periodicity and pervasiveness will be fundamental features of community-making practices for the foreseeable future. But both tendencies are alive and well in the ways that mediated communication is being used to disseminate information and organize activities.

Yet, the advent of online communities has already re-shaped the imaginary of geek culture. Digital communication channels not only disseminate information but can also be communalized themselves. Wedge, for example, explained the Internet's role in compensating for nerds' introverted personalities and connecting interested but isolated individuals into an online community of practice: "I think the Internet is a big ... is like probably the biggest thing, is that you can always find somebody who likes to do what you want to do. So if I like ... I like painting miniatures, and there's nobody in my small town that likes painting miniatures, I can go online and find videos of somebody painting miniatures, and so then ... I'll do that because I *like* doing that. So then people tend to do things they like to do because they're no longer ostracized from – they may still be ostracized but they're not ... ostracized from *every*where. They have that connection and they can talk to somebody about it ... and enjoy it, and then that fosters that ... *growth* in *every*thing, basically." The Internet is a means for real communication, which is always (at least potentially) communalizing. Perhaps most importantly, online fan activity also leaves traces that can be followed. The Internet creates visible, searchable paths into geek culture for anyone who cares to look, regardless of their physical location, with much less time and effort than in the days of sending away for dittoed zines. As a result, the distinctive practices of geek culture are now more accessible than ever before.

MAINSTREAMING AND CHANGE

As I've noted, there is a widely held belief that geek culture and its place in the ecology of lifestyles is changing. When I began the research for this book, this was still, for many, an intuition or debatable proposition. People would ask *if* geek culture was becoming mainstream popular culture. Today, thanks to the prominence of the triumphal narrative, it goes without saying. Mainstreaming has been central to how we think about alternative forms of cultural expression since (at least) the work of the subcultures researchers associated with the University of Birmingham's Centre for Contemporary Cultural Studies (Hall and Jefferson 2006; Hebdige 1979). For the Birmingham School subculturalists, distinctive ("spectacular") youth cultures were a sign of inchoate political resistance, filtered through a generation's distinctive experience and displaced into the realm of style; but this oppositional impulse is inevitably appropriated by the dominant culture, not only becoming "diffused" into the mainstream but also "defused" of its dangerous potential energy. This view of a subculture's life cycle has migrated into common-sense understandings, as well: we all "know" that innovative fashions, aesthetics, and lifestyles come from the streets, borne out of the authentic experiences of marginalized populations, but these innovations are always taken up by outsiders, first as a mark of nonconformity and later as simply the latest trend. However, this familiar trajectory from the margins to the mainstream – and the negative judgments cast upon it – need to be re-evaluated in the case of geek culture. For fans, the availability of an ever-widening array of goods designed for their tastes is a positive outcome of "mainstreaming." But if a community necessarily requires an out-group, then what happens to the communities of geek culture when they are dissolved in the universal solvent of lifestyle trends?

We might begin by asking if nerds and geeks were ever really "marginalized" in any meaningful way, certainly in the ways that would lead us to anticipate some kind of politicized response *à la* Birmingham subculture theory. Perhaps this expectation is wrong-headed from the beginning. Many of my informants pointed to the commercial or critical success of cultural commodities they associated with geek culture as evidence of its improved status. However, Solo argued vigorously (and, in my view, rightly) that if this is how we wish to define geek culture, then we must admit that these properties have always been mass-market, commercial behemoths:

I mean, most of the fandom stuff, and even most of my nerdy stuff, I would argue it's more of a – especially the *Star Wars* connection? I mean, we were targeted and it worked. So, it's not really counter-culture at all. Like, people see me in a *Star Wars* hoodie, and they're like, "Wow! That's really nerdy!" And I'm like, "Are you kidding me? *Star Wars* is the most mass-merchandised entertainment item there is."

I see it in a lot of, a lot of – you know, outcast culture ... but where people are throwing themselves into the periphery by denying the fact that there's a mainstream for it. Like, anybody who holds onto their 'I'm a loner because I like comic books' is an idiot because comic books are incredibly cool right now, and you can be as cool as you want to be simply throwing those names around and being, you know, being a nerd is actually really, yeah, it's pretty hip right now. ((laughs)) So holding onto that sort of stuff is just, like, just doing it to yourself, and I have no sympathy. ((laughs)) No sympathy!

Having been associated with a particular taste culture, nerdy cultural texts could be described as having niche appeal, but niches of a globalized, capitalist mass-media system. Nonetheless, we should distinguish between *Star Wars* as a lucrative media franchise that has successfully appealed to a massive audience of cinema-goers, on the one hand, and the much less widely distributed practices of some of its viewers, on the other hand. The average audience member, for example, probably did not follow the Expanded Universe spin-off novels and fan fiction the way that Shiera did – nor did they collect *Star Wars* LEGO sets with Solo's dedication, for that matter. While objects of consumption (in particular, brands) were indeed always already mainstream, the manner in which they were taken up by geeky consumers was not.

So I am not so quick to discount the subjective experiences of marginalization that some people describe. The relatively narrow appeal of these particular modes of consumption is consistent with the narratives of stigma and recuperation frequently deployed by my interviewees:

MR FOX: Mostly it's different because ... I don't feel weird about it anymore. I don't get the sense of people judging me for my hobbies. It's no longer a step above being a dope fiend [...]
BEN: How much did that sense of, I guess, stigma –

MR FOX: How much did that affect me?

BEN: Yeah.

MR FOX: Quite a bit when I was back home. People thought I was … the strangest of guys because I liked to read comics and play games and such. They didn't understand how a guy who's nineteen, twenty could be interested in these things because it's all … kids' stuff.

These feelings of alienation from one's erstwhile peers and the subsequent, delighted discovery of a more receptive community are very real. Certainly, the persistence of accounts of geek-identified children being bullied or ostracized should lead us to take them seriously (Anderegg 2007; Bishop et al. 2014). Yet people may not be correct when they identify their geeky tastes as the cause of this perceived exclusion, nor do these facts give us good reason to attribute an inherent political substance to geek culture. Geek culture is a space that may furnish resources for political critique or action, but these are not determined by social structure in anything like the straightforward way proposed by subculture theory. Moreover, the politics of geek culture – including activism around the Stop Online Piracy Act, the various cases in which Anonymous has intervened, the charitable and advocacy campaigns mounted by the Harry Potter Alliance, and feminist criticism of comics and video games *as well as* the harassment of those critics (see ch. 8) – are ambivalent and arguably as likely to support dominant culture as to challenge it.

If the politicized narrative of subcultural incorporation does not have a lot of traction, mainstreaming nonetheless remains highly salient in members' own accounts. Compare, for instance, Mr Fox's previous comments about feelings of stigmatization with the following extract:

BEN: Right. So, because of that, I'd like to ask some questions about the changes in nerd culture and changes in the perception of nerd culture that maybe you've observed during your time.

MR FOX: It became cool.

BEN: Pardon?

MR FOX: It became cool.

BEN: Really?

MR FOX: Yeah. Or, at least, accepted. And that … that might just be my coming from a small town where … nerd culture was me. And then going to the city where I could safely say, "I'm a game design student," and have people say, "Aw, that's awesome, man," instead of, "Huh. Why you doin' that?"

This narrative of growing up and moving to the city to escape small-minded, small-town attitudes is highly conventionalized (for another example see sex columnist Dan Savage's "It Gets Better" campaign, targeted at LGBTQ youth; Majkowski 2011; Goltz 2013), but Mr Fox attributes it to changes in attitudes and values and not only his change of locale. So what do people really mean by "mainstreaming"? One major dimension is changing demographics that are gradually bringing (some) geek cultures more in line with the rest of society with the result that these communities no longer seem as set apart from the rest of the world as they once did. Informants almost universally affirmed a belief that geek culture's participant base is now more diverse than it was when they began. Although Diana, for example, still lamented a paucity of media representations of women geeks, she said that things had improved for women in real life: "I don't get the stares being a woman walking into a game shop [...] That's not as unusual as it once was." Solo suggested that the media oriented to young girls was tied into geek culture more now than for previous generations, comparing their experiences with the *Twilight* franchise to her own understanding of *Buffy the Vampire Slayer* as "the shoe for the foot in the door for a lot of nerdy culture." From the other side of the counter, retailers also reported more women participants. Gender was raised most frequently in these accounts, although it was not the only axis along which informants registered change. Mr Fox, for example, described increasing ethnic diversity in geek culture, although the lack of informants from racialized populations in this study undoubtedly produced a significant blindspot on this issue and these discussions were frustratingly vague.

However, demographic change was not always positive. While Mr Fox associated a rising average age among video gamers with increased "sophistication," Barry viewed aging as a threat to the sustainability of some communities. He noted that the new entrants to the field were largely ending up in newer communities within geek culture. More "traditional" fandoms, such as SF literature, were looking significantly grayer than when he started out, raising concerns about the future viability of these fandoms. Solo registered a similar generational tension between comic book and media fans at the San Diego Comic-Con, which she attended for the first time during the research period for this book: "Whereas the younger fans [...] were more into media, more into cartoons and television, less into comics. Like, it's weird because it's Comic-Con, so you feel like you're okay if you're a nerd, but you're still a nerd if you're into comics ((laughs))." These last comments suggest that geek culture's changing status is not as simple as "revenge" against an imagined mainstream. Far from triumphal media claims about geeks and geek culture, the changes my informants observed brought with them a mixture of positive and negative consequences and will impact different people and communities in very different ways. To borrow a phrase from cyberpunk novelist William Gibson, the triumph of the nerds may be here but it's not evenly distributed.

However it ultimately plays out, perceptions of new acceptability and even cachet are already changing the stories informants tell about themselves and their communities. Insofar as a shared perception of alienation from the majority of mass culture was a key component of the these stories, the phenomena we're calling "mainstreaming" may also result in a loss of group identity. As more diverse practices and an increasing number of ever more specific media sub-genres are brought inside the big tent of geek culture, the ability to believe in a mutual orientation of purpose, in shared experiences, and in the sense of community may be stretched. Definitions of geeks and geek culture have expanded in recent years, and traditionally "core" members inevitably have less power to define legitimate membership or correct practice than they once did. Another way of talking about mainstreaming, then, is as an erosion of boundaries or a loss of autonomy. What will it mean to be a nerd or geek in this context? Barry and Dianna offered two different pictures of a "post-fandom" world:

> If everybody became a fan? No, I don't think we're losing anything, unless it's displacing interests which are equally valid and important. I mean, I don't want our society to lose things. Most things. ((laughs)) None of us can do everything, and if something grows, something else must diminish in our lives. I would think. On the other hand, different aspects of our lives can enrich each other and can communicate to each other, so there might be enough overlap and ... anyway. (Barry)

> It loses its community. That's not necessarily a bad thing because, before, it was just a little tiny group of people who are geeks and they all interact, but it can be very insular. So now that there's

more people in it, it's a much more vibrant? Much more going on
kind of thing. But at the same time, it loses its community so it can
be stretched and pulled and changed in ways that it wouldn't necessarily have wanted to be. (Diana)

For Barry, negative consequences are individual problems of management, like those faced by all people, and fandom can – at least in theory – expand to embrace and thereby "enrich" anyone who should like
to join us. For Diana, however, expansion also meant the weakening of
community ties, which could signal either a fannish renaissance as old
gatekeepers and barriers are removed from the field or an end to the
community as a real entity beyond its dubious media representations.
There is no consensus about the impacts of the purported mainstreaming of geek culture – in part because this process is not yet run
its course. Certainly, either trajectory will present its own problems and
opportunities for the people who work and play in the geek culture
scene, but I find Patton Oswalt's pronouncement that geek culture is
coming to the end of its days unconvincing. There is no reason to assume the particular nerdy practices with which we are familiar will continue indefinitely, but, as long as the media continue to make objects
available to us, there will always be some people who engage with them
at a deeper level than the average consumer, who orient their lives towards some media object in a way that most of us do not: "I think there
will always be the core geeks, you know, core nerds in their *Star Trek*
uniforms ((laughs)) that when it stops being popular and it stops being
you know the in, hip thing and goes back to obscurity, they're still
gonna be there, you know" (Diana). Challenges will remain at the level
of institutionalization, but as long as there are people taking these
leisure activities "seriously," they can provide the basis for meaningful interaction and, therefore, for community.

Community is not a thing existing out there in the world but rather a
state of being. It describes a set of relations that must be maintained
on an ongoing basis. It is, in other words, a collective and ongoing social accomplishment. Zygmunt Bauman (2000, 169) is certainly correct
to say that community is a project, but it's not a do-it-yourself one. A
lone individual can play games, watch sci-fi movies, or read comics
(though where those products would come from or how she might

know about them without the labour of others is another question). A single, particularly motivated person can even do a lot of organizational work and stage an event – in the scene I studied, Logan was one such key individual, having been instrumental in the creation of both the City Gaming Network and Screens & Sorcery. But only a group of people can, by their mutual orientation to shared practices, make a community. This is why I am very suspicious of any definition of geek media cultures that would privilege the "media" over the "culture." Let me return to something that Kurt, an independent game designer and president of the City Gaming Network, said in our interview: "Basically, if we talk about geek culture, which is a thing that I think genuinely does exist, where does geek culture congregate and what does it congregate over? It congregates in stores and places of business, and it congregates over collections and collectibles and status that's driven by possessions and material goods." Kurt is offering a warranted, if somewhat cynical, view of geek culture as a materialistic and status-driven subculture of hardcore collectors – you may or may not agree with this assessment, but it follows logically from those perspectives that define geek culture in terms of its objects rather than the practices that come into focus around them. Reducing geek culture to the things around which it congregates is like reducing Christianity to Welch's grape juice and little cubes of bread or a university education to a PowerPoint slide. To turn Kurt's formulation around, the *congregation* – in both senses of the act of being collected together and the resulting body of people – is more important than where it happens.

As discussed at the beginning of this chapter, social critics across the ideological spectrum and in seemingly every age lament the loss of community. Since the turn of the millennium, Robert Putnam's (2000) influential book, *Bowling Alone: The Collapse and Revival of American Community*, has been a major resource for the communitarian critique. Like *Habits of the Heart* (Bellah et al. 1986) a generation before, *Bowling Alone* drew significant public attention to the changing qualities of American communities, in this case through the lens of social capital theory. Putnam takes pains to avoid charges of romanticism and distance himself from a simple "declensionist" narrative of a fall from grace (25), yet employing examples like bowling leagues, bridge clubs, and fraternal organizations inevitably evokes images of 1950s suburbia that are increasingly distant from how most people live today. To his credit, Putnam acknowledges this distance in some aspects of social life – in increasing inequality and lengthen-

ing commute times, for instance – but, as the book's critics have
noted, it remains unclear whether community is in decline or is simply expressed differently today.

For all his talk of "community involvement" and "community life,"
Putnam largely takes community itself for granted. It is never defined
beyond the truism that it "means different things to different people"
(Putnam 2000, 273). Throughout *Bowling Alone*, there is a persistent
slippage between communities as objects of analysis in themselves and
feelings or indicators of community. We are left to infer from his references to attending public meetings on town or school affairs, serving as an officer or on a committee for clubs and organizations, and
joining groups interested in better government that community is defined by some alloy of local scale and civic-political function. Thus,
the nostalgia of Putnam's "neo-Tocquevillean gaze" (Shapiro 2002, 108)
lies less in quaint examples of community involvement than his vague
conceptualization of community as a space apart from everyday life:
"If, instead of constructing civic engagement as a movement from neutral to political space, we recognize an aspect of civic engagement in
persistent struggles to maintain workable identities, it becomes difficult to quarantine the idea of political space within the boundaries of
particular assembly halls. We can think instead of civic engagement
as more pervasive and differentiated with respect to locale; it arises in
connection with many aspects of daily life, as part of differentiated
sets of social ontology" (110). Rather than looking at groups and organizations as indices of social capital or how participation in them
strengthens ties to communities – imagined as the settings in which
these entities exist – what the practices of geek culture suggest is that
we should think of groups and organizations, even loosely bound
ones, as themselves communalized social objects – that is to say,
as communities.

According to Putnam (2000, 49), "voluntary organizations may be
divided into three categories: community based, church based, and
work based." Where in this typology would the formal and informal
communities I have described fit? They're obviously not based in
church or, for most participants, work; under Putnam's implicit theorization of community, it's not clear that groups oriented to leisure are
"community based," either. The forms of association I have discussed in
this book are not new, even if some of the objects to which they are oriented are more recent, so why are media-oriented cultural practices –
other than book clubs (148–52) – absent from Putnam's account of

community life? Media in general play a relatively small role in *Bowling Alone*'s worldview, entertained only as potential causes or solutions to the problems of civic decay. Putnam makes reference to the idea that "virtual communities" could serve as substitutes for "the real communities in which we live" (172), but he pays significantly more attention to the idea that entertainment media may be a cause of the trends he observes with such anxiety. Harkening back to the Progressive Era, he approvingly cites John Dewey's belief that an "increase in the number, variety, and cheapness of amusements" had produced an earlier decline in civic life (378). It is further suggested that "television and its electronic cousins" (246) uniquely focus its heaviest viewers inwards, rendering them less likely to participate in activities outside the home. While other forms of media and social participation are positively correlated (237), "dependence on television for entertainment" is "the single most consistent predictor" of civic disengagement in Putnam's model (231). This is, nonetheless, part of a broader picture where individual consumption of commercial entertainment media displaces vernacular creativity and the collective production of culture, such as in community bands (216). Thus, when Putnam closes *Bowling Alone* by issuing a series of "challenges" to increase social capital and community, one is of particular relevance to this discussion: "Let us find ways to ensure that [...] significantly more Americans will participate in (not merely consume or 'appreciate') cultural activities from group dancing to songfests to community theater to rap festivals. Let us discover new ways to use the arts as a vehicle for convening diverse groups of fellow citizens" (411). What does it mean to participate in, rather than "merely" consume or appreciate, culture, particularly culture that is highly mediated? In a society of "cultural omnivores" (Peterson and Kern 1996), what does it mean to "convene" around the arts? Which arts? Putnam doesn't tell us, though one might reasonably extrapolate that it involves interacting with others in the place where we live, building relationships with one another, and mixing media consumption with robust participatory and creative activity. In other words, it might look a lot like geek culture.

Although the social worlds of geek culture are not much like the community organizations, parent-teacher associations, and megachurches that Putnam (2000) praises as generators of social capital, they are spaces of encounter that provide opportunities to "bond" and to "bridge." Like the "small groups" he discusses, they are "redefining community in a more fluid way" (149). Not strictly bound to (though in other ways reliant upon) localities like neighbourhood and town, geek culture scenes and the activity that takes place enable participants to find and make communities out of what mass culture gives them. In contexts like these, media and media-oriented practices are not distractions from but serve as the fundamental basis for meaningful, communalized social relationships.

6

Institutions

Building Worlds between Production and Consumption

"World building" numbers among the most important concepts in geek media cultures. It refers to the imaginative construction of a detailed, immersive, and logically consistent narrative context, whether in a science fiction movie, a high fantasy trilogy, or the backstory of a comic book or video game. The construction of imaginative worlds may be, as Mark J.P. Wolf (2012) suggests, a fundamental human activity, but it takes on a particular form in fiction, especially transmedia franchises. World building is to some degree a prerequisite of creative narratives, though it sometimes threatens to arrest narrative: authors are supposed to "show, not tell," but world building "results in data, exposition, and digressions" (29). Investment in world building is a key element of aesthetic tastes shaped by the scholastic disposition, and the relative quality of a story's world building is frequently referenced in reviews by subcultural media. But another kind of world building is even more important to the ongoing viability and vitality of geek media cultures.

The practices of geek culture are ambiguously located in the hierarchy of cultural activities and forms. They largely belong to commercial mass culture, yet many have only niche appeal and relatively small audiences. Few publicly funded cultural institutions and virtually no policy initiatives take any responsibility for supporting the practices associated with them.[1] In this atmosphere of relative neglect, geeks, nerds, and fans have created their own institutions. Indeed, Donald A. Wollheim memorably called the history of fandom a "struggle for organization" (quoted in Gardner 2012, 69), a struggle to build something that would last and that would enable their practices to not only endure but flourish. While most of the practices of geek culture can be pursued in private – whether by one's self or in the company of a small group of friends – they thrive when participants are able to share their

tastes and hobbies with others. Hence, this chapter will examine a handful of local institutions where people gather to communicate with one
another about – and thereby instantiate – geek culture.

ALL YOUR BASE ARE BELONG TO US: INFRASTRUCTURES AND INTERMEDIARIES

No practice can exist – at least, not for long – without the support of institutions. Indeed, one sign of a mature practice is the existence of distinctive, autonomous institutions. In MacIntyre's schema, the role of
institutions is to collect and redistribute external goods. One way to
talk about institutions' roles in the geek-culture scene is in terms of subcultural infrastructures, a term Hodkinson (2002) introduces in his
study of British goths. Thus, we might begin a consideration of subcultural institutions by asking what members need in order to participate in some practice. The "values" discussed in chapter 3 serve as a good
starting point for thinking through this problem.

In the city where I conducted fieldwork, a number of organizations,
groups, and clubs mount events for their members and the general public. These events range from small, relatively informal game nights to
periodic screenings of cult-classic films or children's cartoons to multi-
day conventions. Their partners or sponsors in many of these ventures
are specialty retail stores, which not only host and develop their own
events but are themselves meeting places for local participants. In addition to pursuing their own ends as not-for-profit societies or small
businesses, these institutions provide an economic and organizational
base for subcultural activities. They organize markets for commodities
(i.e., goods to be collected and about which aesthetic judgments are
made), act as venues for interaction (i.e., sites where people can showcase their familiarity with and mastery of relevant cultural references),
and connect participants to networks for communication (i.e., opportunities to exchange information and build expertise within and across
scenes). This is probably not an exhaustive list, but it provides a start
for analyzing how communities of practice are articulated together
by institutions.

Commodities and Markets

Participation in geek culture, like many leisure activities, presupposes
access to at least some material or cultural commodities. For example,

if you want to garden, you need seeds and tools; if you want to play music, you need instruments and perhaps sheet music; if you want to go bird-watching, you need a pair of binoculars (Keat 2000, 144). Russell Keat calls these objects "equipment-goods." They are commodities whose consumption enables the pursuit of some practice, rather than being a pleasurable end in itself. Cultural goods can also be considered equipment-goods for at least some of their consumers: comic book fans need comics and gamers need games, just like birdwatchers need their binoculars. In our society, the production and distribution of these goods are principally orchestrated through markets. Markets not only supply practitioners with needed equipment-goods but also generate a livelihood for the people who make and distribute them – after all, even the most committed individuals can only volunteer so much of their time and personal financial resources. Yet the interests of producers, intermediaries, and consumers do not always match.

On the one hand, local institutions are frequently enlisted to reach subcultural audiences, as when comic shops are given passes to a new film to distribute to a handful of lucky customers. However, they have little power relative to producers, who tend to download risks and upload benefits. One example of this tension was Screens & Sorcery's Saturday Morning Cartoon events, which usually comprised episodes of animated television shows, vintage commercials and public service announcements, and a feature film. Attendees were encouraged to wear pyjamas, and the concession stand sold sugary breakfast cereal. They were the group's most popular events, but organizers struggled to license series that members were requesting. According to Logan, "to license a twenty-minute cartoon is usually the same price as licensing a full-length movie"; moreover, they had difficulty identifying and contacting the rights holders of the most frequently requested cartoons. Discussing problems with licensing at a staff meeting, one organizer said that, while media companies know that nerds' tastes sometimes become popular, they do not really care about these audiences unless they can be exploited. Because these events did not directly lead to building "buzz" around new Hollywood productions, there was no real incentive for producers to cultivate this community. By the end of the research period, the group had redefined their events as "private exhibitions," thereby (in their understanding of copyright law) excluding them from requirements to acquire screening rights. Local intermediaries stabilize the field by consolidating hidden focal practices into a visible market, but they themselves are vulnerable to the effects of decisions made by large, corporate producers that may or may not include them in their calculations of enlightened self-interest and what's "good" for the industry.

On the other hand, while we might think of institutions as "serving" communities of practice, members of these communities can also represent a source of instability. Thinking in terms of markets positions participants as consumers rather than practitioners, and once interpellated as consumers, participants may attempt to maximize utility in ways that undermine the viability of institutions. Among my interviewees, the City Gaming Network's Kurt was most concerned that consumption was displacing creative social interaction among participants: "So, I noticed that a lot of – of the conversations that 'geeks' have with one another are over product releases. And if you go to, like, for example RPGnet or storygames.com, or any role-playing game fan sites or forums, you'll notice there's a huge amount of people talking about when is something being released, you know, who's doing the art, what product format is it going to come in. It's a really product-driven culture, which strikes me as absurd because the focus of the activity is generating our own media and yet the culture rallies around consuming media." People I spoke with frequently described local geeks as cheap, argumentative, and flaky. Stores struggled with customers who purchase very little and haggle over prices for what they do buy, while group organizers fretted over attendance rates. In stores, I frequently observed people "gleaning" entertainment. Haggling over prices and "gleaning" entertainment (e.g., reading comics in the store, using demonstration copies of games without purchase, or "pirating" copyrighted video; see ch. 7) maximize consumer utility without necessarily accounting for impacts on local institutions or cultural producers. "Customers are," according to Eastside's Scott, "fucking dicks."

Markets are moral economies that "embody norms and sentiments regarding the responsibilities and rights of individuals and institutions with respect to others" (Sayer 2000, 79). However, strategies for generating and expropriating value from fan practices can lead both producers and consumers to act in ways that have unintended negative consequences. If the economic foundations of subcultural practice are eroded so that creators, publishers, or retailers are no longer able to make a living, participants' ability to access needed equipment-goods will obviously suffer.

Interaction and Venues

Physical space is another basic infrastructure for most cultural practices. The space provided by events and retail stores facilitates access to and enjoyment of practices by bringing participants into contact with one another. Moreover, as public events and spaces – anyone who wishes may walk into a comic or game shop and all of the events hosted by studied organizations were open to the public, subject to modest admission fees – they also represent an interface between geek culture and the "mainstream." However, suitable venues at affordable rates were scarce in the city, and the availability of venues was the single main constraint on most organizations' activities, limiting the scale, frequency, and accessibility of their events.[2] In this context, businesses – especially, retail stores – became particularly important venues for interaction. Specialty retail stores serving the geek market are not merely links in a commodity chain between producer and consumer but are themselves social spaces.

This was perhaps clearest in the case of game stores, which typically scheduled periodic events for customers to play games in the shop. In some cases, organizations like City Gaming Network or producers like Wizards of the Coast co-sponsored these events. Retailers discussed in-store events in terms of "supporting" different products they sold. By providing space and time for a particular game, they brought potential customers into their store and articulated individual players who might otherwise have no way of meeting one another into a community. For example, I spoke to two *Dungeons & Dragons Miniatures* players at Plaza Games about their use of the store's space:

> BEN: Do you play this much outside of a store setting like this?
> GARY: I play it online, probably once or twice a week. And then here, we play once a month.
> DAVE: Yeah [...]
> GARY: If we didn't have this space, the game would have probably died.
> DAVE: Yeah.

Although players could access an online version of the game, monthly tournaments at Plaza Games are the primary opportunity for playing the game as it was designed – that is, using the figurines that they spent time and money collecting – and to be co-present with others who share this interest. The space and time game stores make available to interested participants involve retailers in their customers' lives in a way that goes beyond market transactions. As Scott said: "These aren't just customers, these aren't just gamers, these aren't just people that you spend some time with. These are people that you share a passion with."

The comic shops studied did not tend to have events of this type; rather, the experience of shopping for comics was itself understood as a social activity involving interaction with other customers and store staff. In Sean's words: "Definitely, it's a social activity. The conversation that they have with other customers and um and ourselves is, yeah, that's a big part of it." Similarly, King St's Warren contrasted the more solitary nature of actually reading comic books with the sociability that is expressed in the store:

> You know, as long as they're going to buy a couple of comic books, I don't mind if they want to hang out and chat. And I think it's actually really important that some of the … certain types of people actually get that opportunity to share their … you know, their love of the medium or even just, like, to get that social interaction because it seems like a lot of them probably don't get a lot of social interaction otherwise. Or, you know, say high school kids that are a little shy. They might not enjoy going to school, and they might not have someone at school that they can talk to about it, but when they go to the comic store, they know that they're in an environment where they're with people that will understand and share their interests. Yeah, there's definitely some interesting conversations ((laughs)) that take place in here. Some of them even go over my head.

Like Scott, this comic-shop owner used the discourse of consubstantiality (Burke 1969, 21) to describe interaction among his store's clientele. Doubtless, this rhetoric conceals much, but it expresses the ideal image of community through shared cultural practices that shapes their provision of space for interaction. For their part, retailers all expressed support for social uses of their stores. They believed in the long-term benefits of developing communities, even if it does not result in immediate sales, but this was largely a matter of intuition rather than informed strategy: "The point … again, because there's no direct … it's hard to connect directly, how much money did we make because we had game nights and what have you. We don't even think of it that way. It's fortunate that we don't have to think of it that way because we're doing well enough that we don't have to go, 'Oh, is it worth it to keep those tables at the back blah blah blah?' And we have the luxury of just feeling that the feeling we have about Friday night being good for business is right" (John, Westside Board Games). However, given low margins, high rents, and relatively inelastic demand, some retailers did entertain the possibility of reducing or even discontinuing these activities in favour of, for example, stocking additional inventory. Hank was in negotiations with the shopping mall to move to a larger unit (which he did eventually get), and he told me that if the deal didn't work out he would have to reduce the play space to put in more product. It was not his preferred outcome, but "I need to sell products in order to survive."

Communication and Networks

A third basic form of infrastructure is access to information. Communication involves exchanging news, gossip, opinion, and aesthetic sensibilities. Communicative networks help knit together a scene and, by circulating information between related scenes, help practitioners maintain a sense of their membership in the larger field. In many cases, trans-local communicative networks, such as amateur press associations (APAs), fanzines, niche magazines, and conventions, antedate the local institutions and have developed an independent role in the field. Studied groups and stores function less as networks than they do as markets and venues; nevertheless, local institutions are important sites for communication. Some of these networks are mediated. For example, a number of small circulation magazines for niche audiences such as toy collectors and Whovians were available for purchase at Downtown Comics & Collectibles. Other communication is interpersonal, and stores and group events provide occasions for participants to communicate their experiences – whether direct or second-hand – of developments in other scenes.

Today, web sites, forums, and blogs have supplemented or replaced older networks. The effects of these new networks are still unclear. E-commerce and digital distribution of cultural goods have the potential to disrupt the business models on which some local institutions are based, and online sources of information and opinion reduce the aura of authority and expertise vested in store employees and group organizers. More fundamentally, increased and increasingly immediate access to trans-local networks may divorce identification with "geek culture" from participation in any local scene. However, many groups and stores also make use of new media, in addition to more established forms of promotion, to communicate with members and patrons. Most organizations had their own websites and a Facebook page, which they used to advertise events, supplementing posters and word of mouth. Groups and stores alike made use of message boards and mailing lists, allowing for asynchronous interaction outside of the physical venues of nerd culture, and game stores' websites usually feature a calendar of events. Hodkinson (2006) has noted that the relationship between online and offline venues can be quite complex, and intermediaries' uses of social media and computer-mediated communication warrant further research that was outside the scope of this study.

By organizing markets, providing spaces of interaction, and linking participants with communicative networks, the stores and organizations I studied contributed to the maintenance of a social and cultural milieu, giving substance to the fuzzier qualities of subcultural identity and shaping the local scene's distinctive character. It was because of their critical role in provisioning these resources that I identified them as "nodes" in the network of geek culture and approached them for inclusion in the study in the first place. Although they all act out of their own investments and commitments to some practice or other, they are also constrained by the need to reproduce themselves. The people running these organizations are not only relatively well endowed with (sub)cultural and social capital but they are also deeply involved with the circulation of infrastructural resources. That is to say, these institutions act as "cultural intermediaries."

Pierre Bourdieu (2010) introduced this term to describe a new and ascendant occupational category cum class fraction in his classic study of French lifestyles. A component of the "new petite bourgeoisie," this group came "into its own in all the occupations involving presentation and representation (sales, marketing, advertising, public relations, fashion, decoration and so forth) and in all the institutions providing symbolic goods and services" (359). More recently, the term has been appropriated by cultural studies scholars interested in the "culturalization" of economic activity (du Gay and Pryke 2002; Nixon and du Gay 2002; Maguire and Matthews 2012). On this view, cultural intermediaries are concerned with circulation – of not only commodities but also discourses about their meaning – and there is a great deal of overlap with MacIntyre's conception of a practical institution. In what remains of this chapter, I want to focus on the immaterial and affective labour of these intermediaries.

A JOB YOU LOVE

In his seminal essay, "Subcultural Conflict and Working-Class Community," Phil Cohen (2005, 91) describes subcultural participation as a merely imaginary solution to structural contradictions that have only viable two exit strategies (i.e., either assimilation to work and family life or criminal deviance): "Although there is a certain amount of subcultural mobility [...] there are no career prospects!" Yet despite their associations with fleeting adolescent rebellion and the sphere of leisure, some subcultures have developed relatively durable institutions that do indeed offer career prospects to long-time participants.

The longest-standing such positions are probably those of cultural producers (e.g., comic book creators, game designers, or SF&F authors). However, over time subcultures may develop a variety of ancillary positions, many of which perform vital mediating functions, such as retailers, distributors, convention organizers, and members of a journalistic or critical specialty press. While participation in a leisure activity does not always lead to paid employment or even significant volunteer work, the opposite is even more rare: finding work related to a subculture typically presupposes some form of "career" in the sense described in chapter 4. In music scenes, for example, "spectators become fans, fans become musicians, musicians are always already fans" (Shank 1994, 131). The retailers I interviewed cited detailed knowledge of products as the principal prerequisite for success, and such knowledge is originally acquired through membership in relevant hobby communities or fandoms. In the case of non-profit organizations and clubs, the connection is even tighter, as organizers' unpaid labour is a direct expression of fan activity and has no significant financial incentives. Although more systematic analysis of career paths fell outside the scope of this project, some features of their careers were apparent in my interviews.

While many intermediaries operate on a for-profit basis (at however small a scale), all of them discussed their affective ties with the practice, which generally originate during childhood or adolescence. Retailers typically described opening their store as the apogee of their engagement. Several reported "always" wanting to be specialty retailers (John and Warren), while for others opening stores represented a way to turn their hobby into a livelihood when schooling or other work became unappealing (Hank, Eastside's Nathan, and Sean). The trajectories of organizers of non-profit groups seemed more varied. Logan and Peter created organizations to fill perceived gaps in the scene, while others, like Bobby and Kurt, joined existing organizations and eventually took on leadership roles.

Insofar as they are "always already fans," subcultural intermediaries both participate in and act upon the scene. Put another way, their work is embedded in the leisure practices of subcultural communities. The former relies on the knowledge, dispositions, and resources that these people acquired from their experiences with the latter. However, this embedding is not complete. By virtue of their positions as retailers and organizers, they are subject to a different set of problems from ordinary participants.

INTERMEDIARY ORIENTATIONS

Having observed two women at Plaza Games hesitantly wade through a gaggle of young, male CCG players to reach a shelf of jigsaw puzzles, I asked Hank about the relationship between the core community of gamers and his more casual customers. Although he believed the spectacle of in-store gaming events drew curious passersby into the shop, the rowdiness of the gamers – including occasional off-colour comments and personal-hygiene issues[3] – sometimes interfered with business. Pressed to define the relative importance of these two publics, he struggled to choose between them: "Unfortunately, they both come first, which is a contradiction. So, in other words, customers come first because I need to make money in order to sell things. However the tournament comes first because I create an event for them to come in here and play, so I will have the tables for them, I will do those pairings, I will do all of that, too [...] So, I know it's a contradiction, but I do my best to do both." This contradiction encapsulates the dilemma facing cultural intermediaries in relatively marginal cultural fields: Should they focus on the needs and desires of established and known publics, or risk alienating them by seeking new life and new civilizations? In the following sections, I want to explore two pairs of dispositions towards the fraught relationship between geek culture and the mainstream: (a) amateurism and professionalism and (b) introversion and extroversion.

Amateurism and Professionalism

In speaking of "amateurs" and "professionals," I do not mean intermediaries' occupational status (i.e., paid worker or volunteer); rather, I refer
to two contrasting ethical dispositions. Amateurs talk about their motivations principally in terms of intrinsic, immaterial satisfactions. For
example, Sean believes that his employees are over-qualified for their
jobs as comic-bookstore clerks but, like many others working (at whatever level) in the media and cultural industries, are motivated by their
love of a particular art form and accept the related opportunity costs of
not pursuing other, potentially more lucrative forms of employment
(McRobbie 2016; Tokumitsu 2014). Indeed, a number of people made
employment inquiries while I was observing Downtown Comics &
Collectibles, with one hopeful explicitly saying, as he handed his résumé to Sean, that working in a comic store was his "dream job."

In ordinary use, "amateurish" implies inferior quality. This is not
necessarily the case here, although organizers and participants do
sometimes use altruistic love of a practice to rationalize amateurish
execution: "I do find that a couple of people might show up and complain about a certain level of professionalism with our ticket handling
or whatever, but, really, we're not hiring people. It's just a group of
friends who are doing this. So I don't mind pissing a couple of strangers
off as long as all my friends have a good time" (Logan). Here, the two
senses of amateurism collude so that claims of authenticity ("just a
group of friends who are doing this") justify keeping costs low and volunteer labour to a minimum ("we're not hiring people"). Peter made a
similar distinction between comic conventions that have "heart" and
those that are merely "corporate." In contrast to corporate conventions,
King Con was kept small to simplify administration and allow him to
charge low rates. He also offered free admission for children and provided free exhibition space for local creators, arguing that these policies are good for the local comics community and for comic book
culture as a whole. However, groups dominated by an ethic of amateurism sometimes displayed a tendency towards cliquishness, as in the
above quote where Logan privileges his friends' enjoyment over that
of "strangers."

There is much to value in this approach to facilitating subcultural
practices. Nevertheless, the everyday demands of running a store or
group exert pressures towards an ethic of professionalism: "Well, I guess

a lot of people think it's sort of a … quaint little business that people sit around and talk about comics all day. And, certainly, we talk about comics a lot around here and, certainly, comic stores are little businesses […] but it's a huge amount of work […] With so many titles coming out, to do the job properly is very labour intensive" (Sean). Those I am calling professionals tended to de-emphasize the field's specificity, appealing to more generic frames of reference, such as "small-business owner," to describe their work. Professionals also made use of strategic planning to address vexing problems in a way seemingly foreign to the amateurs. For example, Kurt led an "appreciative inquiry" to develop a mission statement for City Gaming Network as part of a broader initiative to professionalize, clarify the organization's scope, and thereby reduce volunteer burnout from undertaking too many activities, and the Alternate Universe Club and Downtown Comics & Collectibles both ensured that women had visible roles as officers and staff, respectively, in order to combat the perception of their practices as essentially masculine and encourage further participation by women. Encouraging a long view, professionalization offers intermediaries more stability, but in re-framing subcultural institutions as generic organizations, it may also undermine their identity as part of a distinctive community.

Introversion and Extroversion

While the previous pair of values described interviewees' views of their own motivations, these keywords describe their strategic orientation to the mainstream. "Introverts" are indifferent or hostile to mainstream attention in favour of cultivating the existing community of practice. Explicitly rejecting the pursuit of more mainstream audiences, Logan best exemplified this orientation. Although he wanted to share his interests with others – as evidenced by his involvement in founding both Screens & Sorcery and City Gaming Network – he discussed this in terms of making "the weird, cool stuff that we do more viable," rather than pursuing a broader audience. While one might expect retailers to welcome any expansion of their business, some also shared the introvert orientation. Despite claiming "comics are for everybody," Warren did not believe advertising was a worthwhile investment "because people that are into comic books tend to seek them out. You know, it's not something you really need to tell people about." Introverts see their activities as principally oriented towards pre-existing, stable, and relatively inextensible audiences: comics are for comic-book people, games for gamers, and cult media for their fans. How people become interested in what they do is a black box, and intermediaries have a limited role, if any, to play beyond building it and letting them come.

"Extroverts," by contrast, embrace mainstream interest and may be willing to modify practices to make them more attractive to those outside the subculture. For example, referring to more introverted retailers, Scott said, "I think it's true that the hobby community is one where the hobbyists look for the stores and the stores can just sit there and wait [...] but I still think it's bullshit to sit on your laurels and just hope that that works for you." From the extroverts' perspective, their hobbies' growth and development have been constrained by an exclusive focus on already initiated participants. For example, Kurt, who is also an independent game designer, was very critical of aspects of geek culture that, he believed, limit the appeal of RPGs: "I think if you market towards social awkwardness, you get the appearance of social awkwardness. To give a counter-example, [I published a game] and when I was making the product, I was like, 'I'm going to make a gorgeous-looking product that when I tell sexy, intelligent women about it, they'll really want to see it, and when I show it to them, they'll really want to play it.' And so that was the goal, and when you create that goal, you see that result in the demographic. Like, the people who I end up playing [it] with most often are sexy, intelligent women. It strikes me as strange that we don't say, 'Role-playing games: These are things that sexy, creative people do because they don't like sitting around like couch potatoes.' Instead, we market them as, 'This is stuff for couch potatoes.'" Similarly, Hank expressed concerned that players at his weekly board game night were unrepresentative of the "real" players of board games, mainstream consumers like families, schools, and church groups.[4] Efforts to "re-brand" a practice (and thereby change the composition of the community) will obviously meet with varying degrees of success, but they can exacerbate tensions between those participants who prefer the status quo and those who, whether out of economic self-interest or a genuine desire to share their hobbies and interests, seek new audiences.

These values and strategies chart a range of orientations to the relationship between geek culture and the larger space of media-oriented practices in which it is situated. While all intermediaries have an interest in the reproduction of the practices they support and of geek culture more generally, their conceptions of what will secure these interests vary. Extroverted professionals will produce very different spaces and events from those run by introverted amateurs. In this, we may find an echo of the struggles over the relative autonomy or heteronomy of the field of cultural production (Bourdieu 1983, 319–26). Like those making up the literary field whose genesis Bourdieu analyzed, all agents in the field of geek culture are involved in activities that push its borders one way or the other. Some of these efforts are explicit, strategic, and accessible to discursive consciousness but many of them are only implicated in practice.

GATEKEEPING AND
THE REPRODUCTION OF SUBCULTURAL PRACTICES

One dimension of this practical process of definition and boundary maintenance is gatekeeping, a concept with a long history in communication studies. Pamela Shoemaker defines gatekeeping, a metaphor that can be traced to Kurt Lewin's (1943) studies of food habits, as "the process by which the billions of messages that are available in the world get cut down and transformed into the hundreds of messages that reach a given person on a given day." Control of information is not limited to selection but also includes "withholding, transmission, shaping, display, repetition, and timing of information as it goes from sender to receiver." (Shoemaker 1991, 1) Nonetheless, the image principally connotes holding back *information*. But while communication scholars have tended to focus on this kind of "editorial gatekeeping" in media organizations (Barzilai-Nahon 2008, 442), Lewin viewed gatekeeping as a generic feature of social life, equally applicable to how food ends up on our tables as how stories are chosen for the nightly news (Shoemaker 1991, 9).

Gatekeeping, like Foucault's conception of power, is not simply repressive but also productive. Cultural intermediaries enable practices, but they enable them in particular ways. For example, there is no necessary reason why comic books, collectible card games, and sports cards are frequently sold in the same stores. It might be argued that the common denominator is collecting, but this is hardly a sufficient criterion: we don't typically regard coin collecting or stamp collecting, for instance, as part of geek culture.[5] Rather, these products and their consumers seem to "fit" together within the field because they have been brought together by geek culture's intermediaries. These agents' work activities are informed by and expressive of existing interests and passions: knowledge, experience, and in some cases material goods acquired through participation in leisure (e.g., retailers' own collections) are leveraged as resources. My research suggests three significant forms of gatekeeping practiced by cultural intermediaries: curating the store or group's offerings; "educating" their patrons and members in order to shift their tastes and interests; and diversifying their core mission to appeal to multiple communities of practice.

Ultimately, what gatekeepers filter out may be less significant than the things they admit and the particular configurations into which they admit them. In this sense, gatekeeping resembles a process of curation. Curating denotes the selection of content available to participants – products in a store, vendors and exhibitors at a convention, or events and activities supported by a store or organization, and so on. To several of my retailer interviewees, running a shop was like having a gigantic collection to showcase their love of comics, games, and so on (see ch. 3). However, a potential contradiction between personal taste ("quality") and beliefs about the tastes of others ("demand") lies at the heart of the curation process. In the following extract, for example, Warren talks about how he selects products for the store: "I think everything definitely has a bit of my taste's influence in it. Like I said, I want to be surrounded by things that I like. I won't say that everything in the store is something that I like, but definitely if it's something that I believe in, I will invest heavier in it in hopes that other people will have similar taste. Mostly, that would probably be reflected in the toys more so than the comic books because ... the comics, I want to order what will sell regardless of whether I believe in it or whether I like it, but when it comes to things like action figures and statues and things like that, I definitely think my taste is reflected more in that department." Having begun their own careers as fans, intermediaries' conceptualizations of their audiences and customers – of what they like and dislike, and what they will or won't buy – are based on their own experiences in geek culture. Definitions of the field are normalized and often remain tacit until members or customers fail to respond in anticipated ways, bringing the quality–demand tension to the fore.

That is to say, despite their extensive expertise, retailers and other intermediaries will not necessarily succeed in providing what practitioners seek. Their tastes may not match participants' sufficiently. Retailers frequently described ordering inventory based on their own taste that then fails to sell: "Obviously, I'm trying to bring in what people want, and I have to remember that just because I think that something is good doesn't mean that other people will, and vice versa [...] I've brought in things that I thought would do well lots of times that people didn't find that interesting" (John). Hank mentioned that he finds selling children's games particularly challenging since he cannot rely on his own tastes to evaluate whether kids will have fun. These problems are not limited to retailers; group organizers also struggle with tensions between quality and demand when developing events. For example, I attended a Screens & Sorcery staff meeting where a great deal of time was devoted to trying to understand why a screening they organized was not as popular as they had hoped it would be.

Difficulties involved in anticipating participants' tastes and curating accordingly are clearly a source of stress for many intermediaries. Nathan at Eastside Games & Comics put it in particularly forceful terms: "Ordering *still* to this day is the worst process in the world [...] It's like playing the lottery every time you do it, and from day one it's been difficult." One significant exception was Downtown Comics & Collectibles' Sean, the most experienced and professionalized retailer included in the study. By this point in his career, he accepts that some mistakes are inevitable: "You're gonna get fooled sometimes because it's an especially good issue or [...] because it's an especially bad cover and you don't sell as many. That's gonna happen; you don't worry too much about that. But you can guess pretty accurately how many you're gonna sell. When a new book comes out [...] you don't really know how well it's gonna sell until you've ordered a few. And when it's selling really well, you're upset because you know you're not going to have enough of the next issue, and when it's selling really poorly, of course, you're upset because you know you're gonna be ((laughs)) stuck with a bunch." He de-emphasized the role of taste in ordering, instead emphasizing his method: "I just try and find similars – you know, if they're doing a new *Legion*[6] series, how well did the last *Legion* series do? Who's doing it? – and base it off that." However, the choice of meaningfully "similar" comparisons relies on shared frames of reference, and so even this seemingly objective process is embedded in shared experiences of participation.

Second, curation is constrained by intermediaries' limited agency within the trans-local geek subculture and associated cultural industries. Eileen Meehan (2005) has argued that the market for entertainment and cultural goods does not provide any forum for audiences to articulate their desires, and local intermediaries similarly have little influence upon production decisions. Stores can only stock products that are available to them, and we saw that Screens & Sorcery, for example, had difficulties obtaining exhibition rights for cartoons and films that its membership requested. When curating proves inadequate, more active interventions may be required.

One possible response to gaps between the tastes of intermediaries and those of consumers is for the former to attempt to "educate" their patrons. I frequently saw participants interact with store staff and key group organizers as if they were authoritative sources of information and opinion. Even so, influencing tastes is a difficult proposition. Nevertheless, stores such as Plaza Games and Eastside Games & Comics reported some success influencing buying habits as customers have come to trust the staff's judgment. This became apparent when the players at Plaza's board-game night could not agree on which game to play next: Hank had offered to teach us to play a game called *Wasabi*; one attendee, Michael, had brought his own game, while two others wanted to play *Small World*. Michael didn't want to play *Small World* but no one seemed very keen on his game, and so he resolved the impasse by suggesting that we try *Wasabi*, remarking that it was a good idea to take up Hank's offer, as he often picked fun games one might otherwise never try.

Trust in an intermediary's taste was also an explicit theme when Alex discussed the range of comics they sell at Eastside. In the context of a well-developed retailer–customer relationship, it is possible to shift consumption patterns: "It becomes a thing of where … there's a delicate balance. Some retailers can do it. I don't know how many actually try it, but there are ways you can sort of wean customers." These processes also take place outside of retail stores. At the semester's first meeting of Alternate Universe Club, many members introduced themselves with reference to the aspects of nerd culture that they liked (e.g., "I'm into anime and I play *Magic*"), with several saying they had originally joined to pursue one specific interest and gradually learned to appreciate others supported by the club. As Bobby said, "I find now in the club pretty much everybody is open to everything or was a fan of everything to begin with. I don't think it's really hard to convince gaming people to go to weeklies [i.e., their regular screenings] or anime people to go to gaming night." This is partially due to the club's "interdisciplinary" character and partially due to Bobby's intentionally educative stance. However, tastes often prove resistant or unpredictable, and the flip side of the internal diversity of tastes within this nexus of niches is a factionalism that separates fans into distinct communities. These divisions are sometimes turned into half-facetious rivalries (*Star Wars* versus *Star Trek*, Marvel versus DC) and occasionally they erupt into real conflict over the nature of the practice. But, more often, they co-exist as multiple solitudes sharing convention spaces and stores. For example, Warren of King St Comics described the split between fans of "mainstream" and "independent" comic books: Although the last several decades have seen significant rapprochement and increased crossover between these two sub-fields of the comics world,[7] "there's still obviously people that are only interested in superhero comics and that, when exposed to a book like [*Strange Tales*], might kind of flinch because it's not the superhero comics that they like. You know, they don't look like the right characters and that sort of thing because they're done in such a kind of extreme or abstract style that it turns them off." And while some partisans of alternative and independent comics might like to imagine themselves as more open-minded and sophisticated than superhero fanboys, Warren suggested they are "pickier," and might potentially view an independent creator crossing over to work on a Marvel or DC title as an instance of selling out. As a result, the total size of a store's clientele or an organization's membership is not a good indicator of the demand for a particular product or activity, and there simply may not be enough people with a set of tastes to ensure the survival of a store or organization.

Another common way of dealing with unpredictable or irregular demand among core participants is to broaden the product categories or types of events offered. Some intermediaries may seek new customers who do not identify as practitioners – as when Kurt experimented with holding gaming activities in cafés, a site he associates with social interaction and an "artsy, creative" clientele – but it is more common to attempt to consolidate existing niches within geek culture. Institutions whose particularistic commitments are already less clearly specified have more freedom to diversify. For example, although gaming and anime were the focus of the vast majority of its activity, Bobby resisted pigeonholing the Alternate Universe Club: "The club is definitely more successful when you promote it in a vague way rather than specifically as an anime club or a gaming club. That's when we've done the worst, when it's been tied down to being one or the other. And, yeah, I want to try and not only promote those activities to the community at large but sort of open people up to different types of things within that category."

Similarly, the range of different games allows some play in the City Gaming Network's focus. While most activities are primarily for RPG players, Kurt said: "We intentionally have a bit of a vague classification of what we mean by games because we want to be open and holistic and kind of a networking portal, rather than yet another small niche." This is not to say that only such loosely defined institutions can bridge multiple communities: Downtown, nominally a comic-bookstore, is perhaps the most diversified site studied, embracing comic readers and collectors more comprehensively than other stores and selling magazines, manga, anime DVDs, action figures and toys, statues, t-shirts, posters, RPG books, board games, picture postcards, celebrity photographs and film stills, movie and television scripts, and miscellaneous merchandise such as buttons and magnets. Robust conceptions of "genre" and "popular culture" provide the explicit justification for this diversity.

In some cases, the communities consolidated together are relatively contingent, such as the blend of various gaming activities, anime fandom, and, increasingly, viral videos and Internet memes supported by the AUC or the sometimes-idiosyncratic mix of films shown by Screens & Sorcery. In others, the combination of niches complement one another, as when stores such as Plaza and Eastside sell both board games (higher profit margin, less frequently purchased, more casual consumers) and collectible card games (low profit margin, consumed frequently, mostly regular customers). Expanding their offerings does, however, place obligations on intermediaries to become knowledgeable concerning new practices with which they may have less direct experience.

In the work of gatekeeping, local cultural intermediaries make their most significant contributions to the creation of geek culture as a scene. Their decisions concerning what products to stock, what events to host, what recommendations to make, what combination of communities to court, and so on, have a variety of intended and unintended effects on its composition. Practices of curation, education, and diversification shape the matrix within which cultural capital circulates and those key infrastructural resources are distributed, while their orientations toward the mainstream and attitudes towards their own practices shaped how geek culture evolved in this particular city.

***

Initial stages of research for this book involved hanging out in the spaces of geek culture, in specialty stores, at club meetings and conventions, and so on. Throughout, I was deeply impressed by geek culture's vitality and the depth of enthusiasm and commitment displayed by participants at every level. As Shank points out, one way to define a scene is as an "overproductive signifying community" (1994, 122), and the scene I studied certainly fit that bill. While much of its "effervescence" can be attributed to the activities of ordinary participants, we must also acknowledge those who work, whether for pay or not, to support these practices. Many accounts of media culture are overdetermined by the idea of the commodity chain. As Mark Deuze (2011, 138–9) argues, "the traditional biases and boundaries of (critical) communication and media studies" tend to "[reproduce] people and their media in terms of production, content, and reception [...] As a result, we are often stuck describing cultural activity in terms of production or consumption, work or leisure, sending or receiving." However, production, distribution, and reception are not discrete steps in single, linear process. The social life of media goods is more complex. All three "moments" emerge from a field of practices, a culturally constituted ground without which they would be unintelligible. Moreover, they feed back into one another. The relations between them run in multiple directions, and mediating work – work that adds meaning and enables connections – happens at every point along the way. To borrow a phrase from Obi-Wan Kenobi, the work of cultural intermediaries surrounds, penetrates, and binds geek culture together.

Whatever their occupational status within the scene, intermediaries and the institutions they operate are not simply economic agents. They are also participants, and their mediating labour may seem less like work and more like a calling. In a way, most of the intermediaries I studied had prepared for their roles since childhood. Years of experience as ordinary participants prior to taking up these more instrumental roles have generated a frame of reference that they share with customers and group members, allowing them to make judgments of quality and to anticipate demand – albeit imperfectly. This "feel for the game" (Bourdieu and Wacquant 1992, 128–9) also shapes responses to changes in the field, such as the entrance of new participants at a time of mainstreaming or the translation of practices to digital environments. The lesson to be drawn from these subcultural institutions is that personal, affective identification with the field and love for its practices are part of what doing such work is all about. It is only from this perspective within the practice that the possibility and capacity of running events or starting stores become thinkable, let alone actionable.

By the same token, the embedded character of cultural intermediaries' experience and judgment means that they are likely to reproduce the failings, blind spots, and prejudices that are also part of participants' common-sense views of their activities. Nonetheless, when cultural intermediaries do their job well (or, at least, well enough), they establish and maintain the physical and symbolic spaces where individuals can articulate themselves into collectivities and develop the resources of self- and group-identity through rich forms of participation. Without the material and organizational infrastructures described in this chapter – markets for equipment-goods, venues for interaction, and networks for communication – geek culture would be very different indeed. Perhaps some of the trans-local manifestations of geek media cultures would still exist: people might still make and sell the media forms we understand to be nerdy. But they would probably be organized very differently without local intermediaries having worked, over the decades, to build and sustain the communities in which these goods take up their meaning. Certainly, local scenes would be unrecognizable and individuals' experiences would be much impoverished without these spaces.

7

The Limits of Participation

Over the last several chapters, I have tried to build up an account of geek culture as a space where people do community-making, examining how individuals construct narratives of their own "careers" in these leisure practices, how they discursively and practically articulate themselves with groups, and finally how intermediary institutions keep these possibilities open within a given scene. Taking place in and around media, these communities are at some level imagined ones. In Benedict Anderson's (2006) usage, "imagined" is not strictly opposed to "actual." Nations are imagined communities but, as anyone on the business end of one could tell you, they are hardly imaginary. Despite the fact that most people will only ever personally know an infinitesimal proportion of their fellow citizens, "in the minds of each lives the image of their communion" (6). Because this communion is first imagined, it can be oriented to, performed, and enacted in everyday practice. I've already shown that maintaining these communities involves real (if frequently pleasurable) work on the part of ordinary members and cultural intermediaries. Even so, community-making isn't simply a matter of rolling up one's sleeves and getting on with things. However desirable its rewards may be, our desires for belonging may at times be frustrated by forces and circumstances beyond our control.

Part of taking a practice approach is, necessarily, giving some consideration to practices' conditions of possibility. People typically face constraints that limit or otherwise distort their ability to participate in the way that they would like. In some cases, there are adequate workarounds; in others, no straightforward solutions present themselves. When I asked them about the things that kept them from doing what they wanted, interviewees talked about four major limitations they have experienced:

money, physical space, time, and "real-life" commitments. The real, determining effects of these constraints need to be understood. More than large-scale cultural norms or ideologies, they shape the texture of geek culture as it is lived by its members. They are the horizon that limits the real possibilities for subcultural participation.

THE PRICE OF ADMISSION

As discussed last chapter, the practices of geek culture – like most practices – require at least some commodities, or "equipment-goods" (Keat 2000), which are acquired through markets. The marketization of a practice is not only an abstract or philosophical problem; it also imposes fundamental constraints on how and how much people can participate in these practices and the communities that have been built around them. Thus, it should come as no surprise that the financial cost of participating in geek culture was one of the most commonly cited constraints.

A number of the practices and hobbies I discussed with my interviewees could quite easily be done on the cheap. However, costs generally rise with greater participation and, particularly, with greater emotional investment in the signs of legitimate commitment:

BEN: Do you consider science-fiction fandom, is it in general an expensive hobby?
BARRY: It doesn't have to be, no … On the other hand, if you are buying all the DVDs, you know, of all the shows, it would probably add up pretty fast. Books – new books are pretty expensive these days, as well […] I mean, if one were a millionaire and didn't have to worry about … any of this stuff and spend 24 hours a day travelling to conventions around the world. So there will always be some kind of limitation … and it's actually best to make it a limitation or things can get out of control.

SCOTT: One question that I hope that you do ask is … um how I feel about people spending that kind of money.
BEN: How do you feel about people spending that kind of money?
SCOTT: ((laughs)) Well, I'm glad you asked. I feel really good about it, actually […] It's been a very positive way for me to express myself, to be creative, right? And to participate in a community and be competitive and have people to talk to about stuff. And the most

really important thing that I find is for people to have something to play with in their head, you know? That really has some depth. Like, I bet you could go up to this gentleman here ((gestures to a customer)) and you could say, "Okay, well, I'm looking for a deck that does blah." And I bet out of the back of his head, he'll have a hundred cards just start flipping into his mind, you know, saying, "Oh, this is a good card, this is a good card, this is a good card." He'll go through his collection and start pulling out this and this and this and this. All that information is in your head. All that information stays there, and you have access to it, and you use it all the time. It's a really wonderful mental tool.

Status within the scene is not based on crude "pecuniary strength," as Thorstein Veblen (1948) might put it, but opportunities certainly do abound for "invidious distinctions" to be made. There are forms of authentic participation and kinds of subcultural capital that are more easily attained if one is willing and able to devote financial resources to their cultivation:

> SHIERA: People devote a lot of time and an awful lot of money to … their focus […] Attending an [SCA] event is not a cheap thing. It's cheap entertainment compared to modern entertainment standards […] By modern standards, it's very cheap entertainment.
> BEN: I guess if the specific fee to attend something isn't very high, but the cost in terms of the amount of time it takes to prepare yourself and uh –
> SHIERA: If you're gonna be camping, you can do it the cheap, mundane way and hide away in a corner with your little dome tent and your little Coleman stove, or you can … go all out, buy the pavilion or build it yourself, or you know build the stove, build the – you know, learn all those things. There's an awful lot of investment into even just the camping in the SCA […] You'll see it if you go to one of those camping events – they don't camp light. They buy the big van so they can go to the big event with the big pavilion ((laughs)) which takes nine people to set up? And only two people sleep in it.

Moreover, there is apparently no upper limit to how much money could be devoted to equipment-goods and accessories, particularly if buying leisure time and travel is counted among the possible expenditures.

Comic books and miniatures gaming, by contrast, were described as particularly expensive practices:

BEN: How much money do you regularly spend on comics and comics-related things?
MR FOX: Seventy bucks a month, I guess. If it's like a bad month, yeah, seventy. A bad month meaning there's lots of good things coming out.

Mostly because I can't afford it. It was getting to be almost a hundred or a hundred fifty bucks a month, and it was just a little bit too much. So, I'm a little bit removed from the world of comics at the moment. (Solo)

Like, *Warhammer* is *crazy* expensive. (Mr Fox)

It should be noted, however, that these costs are not necessarily out of line with those of similar levels of involvement in the other practices noted above. How "expensive" something is is a situated judgment based on financial circumstances, perceived value for money, and (I think in these cases, in particular) a sense that the financial outlay is somehow compulsory. Following comics means following a series month by month – possibly following a particularly beloved character across however many series the publishers decide to feature it in. *Magic* and other collectible card games demand the periodic purchase of new packs of cards, both to stay competitive with other players and even to participate in certain formats of organized play within the community. *Warhammer* just isn't *Warhammer* without the miniatures produced by Games Workshop. In these practices, one seems trapped by a regular investment of money.

Diana, for one, made clear distinctions not only between seemingly compulsory and voluntary expenditures but also between geeky expenses that were small enough that they didn't really "count" and those that that had to appear as a line in the household budget. However much they might add up to as a category, the former were perceived as merely discretionary spending, or "coffee money":

BEN: How much money is involved in regularly, in participating in *World of Warcraft*?

DIANA: ((sighs)) More than I want. Because we have the two accounts, I think it's thirty bucks a month, which, again, isn't … isn't that much and doesn't, doesn't stretch our budget. But we did have to re-budget, we had to re-do our budget to get thirty bucks a month. I'm not going to say we had to take it out of our food budget ((laughs)) but we had to take it out of our food budget.

BEN: And … uh I guess when you say that it's more than you want, like, does that reflect that adding that second account … is there less value for money for you?

DIANA: Yeah, it was, you know. And it's also, like, as we said with like movies and TV and books, they're free. You know, like, we can buy books, but you don't have to buy books, you can get them from the library. They're free. And the same with D&D. Once you bought the books or we have one subscription, because we're able to have one subscription to Wizards of the Coast, it feels – you can do a lot with that one subscription, so it feels like it's free. But with this, it just – I don't know why, it just doesn't feel like it's free, you know? And certainly having to – to have the two accounts, like if we had the one account, eh, fifteen bucks. That's coffee money. You don't really think about it. But when it goes up to thirty, for some reason, that's not – that starts, as I said, that had to be a line item.

BEN: That's like, you know, *good* coffee money.

DIANA: That's good coffee money. ((laughs)) That had to be a line item on the budget, whereas fifteen bucks didn't. You know, fifteen bucks was, oh, that's just disposable, discretionary spending kind of thing, whereas – and I don't know why. Like, what's the difference between fifteen and thirty? Like, it's not that much. But for some reason that seems to be crossing a line. And it's like … it also feels like we didn't need to do that, you know? We were perfectly fine on the one account until we wanted to play together, and then suddenly it's each of us has fifteen bucks.

Again, part of the perception of "expensiveness" is based on perceived ubiquity and ease of access. When it comes to novels, TV, and (via the D&D Insider subscription service) role-playing game manuals, Diana *feels* as though she is in a situation of abundance. But there is only one purveyor of *WoW*, creating a sense of scarcity over this theoretically unlimited digital resource, as well as an imbalance between provider and player.

Diana had earlier described herself as middle class, arguing that a middle-class upbringing stayed with you and informed your "way of being in the world," no matter your current standard of living. That any category of spending can be regarded as below the threshold of budgeting is a good example of this. In contrast to the four informants who considered themselves, broadly, "middle class," Mr Fox and Shiera grew up in circumstances they described as poor. When I asked the others if they could ever felt like money kept them from participating, I usually received vague affirmations that they could have theoretically spent more or done more things if their priorities were different. Mr Fox's and Shiera's answers felt more immediate, though this could be due to my own knowledge of their circumstances:

> When I was poor … as a child. That inhibited my buying of video games immensely … When I was poor and a student. (Mr Fox)

> I don't spend much money because I don't have much money to spend. If I had more of a discretionary income, I would spend more on geeky things. Um. I see … books, I'd probably buy a lot more books if I had more money. ((laughs)) I go to the library once a week. I usually take out five to seven books from the library every week. I read voraciously. (Shiera)

Although Mr Fox said he now enjoyed a comfortable lifestyle (despite the somewhat precarious nature of his work as a freelance writer), Shiera still experienced significant economic constraint. Unable to work, she lived on a fixed income from disability benefits. Without much disposable income, being able to participate was, she said, "a question of budgeting. If you budget, you can go. It's just a question of knowing how much to budget." Like Diana, she played an MMORPG and enjoyed playing it with family members, and she developed a system of account rotation in order to keep the costs of play manageable while still meeting her in-game obligations:

> I have four accounts. Only one is up all the time. If I'm short on funds in a month, I'll let the other ones fade […] If an account is coming due that I don't want to have re-upped, I'll just move the money out of the account. That account will go dormant, then I'll put the money back in for the account that I need it to be there for. I generally try to have at least two accounts running […] But if my middle son has expressed that he wants to play, that account will be up. If my older son has expressed that he wants to play, I'll up

his account. If my younger son wants to play, then I re-up his account [...] Once my second computer's fixed, my youngest is gonna be playing pretty much constantly, so ... 'cause we'll both be able to play at the same time, we'll be able to play together. That's kind of why I do it. In that case, I'll have more than one account on the three-month-at-a-time. Then, we'll just cycle through [...] Because of the way citizenship works, I re-up each account at least every three months. So, there's always two accounts up. It just depends which month it is which two accounts.

Even the most creative budgeting can only accomplish so much. Because there are still some months when she is inevitably "short of funds," finances remain a significant obstacle. In response, people have developed a repertoire of tactics for accessing entertainment and fan practices under financial constraints. We might think of them as a kind of gleaning – the collecting of leftover, unharvested food from farmers' fields, which has been a historic right of widows, orphans, and other economically marginal members of society. These tactics enable participants to manage or avoid the costs of participation.

For SF fans, the most commonly mentioned way of reducing costs was using the public library. Buying used books, whether from local used bookstores or searching online for deals, was another common tactic. Although some interviewees (Solo and Wedge) expressed a marked preference for buying books over using the library, everyone also mentioned trading – both borrowing and lending – books, movies, and games with their friends. Shiera was part of an elaborate ring of book-lending amongst her circle of friends, and since Wedge and his friends usually played with one another anyway, they kept tabs on what board games they owned to avoid duplication. Swapping is a way not only to share costs but also to recommend and learn of new things. Networks of friends and acquaintances also featured as a resource for co-ordinating rides to events for Barry and Shiera, neither of whom owned a car. In these cases, social capital is not only mobilized as a resource, it is created and cemented through patterns of reciprocal exchange in a quasi-gift economy. Downloading movies, television shows, and other entertainment commodities was a somewhat more controversial activity. Some interviewees were opposed to such "piracy," due to its impact on cultural industries and their workers. Others had no such ethical quandaries and embraced downloading as a way of reducing costs. Finally, as Barry quipped, the most effective way to reduce costs is "simply staying away from the really expensive aspects of fandom." Since "expensiveness" is a subjective evaluation, we cannot be sure how much this will impoverish individual experience, but as long as the equipment-goods of geek culture are produced in a capitalist economy, literal economic costs are an inevitable, pragmatic problem, and these workarounds will remain only ad hoc tactics.

TIME ENOUGH AT LAST

Many of the available strategies for avoiding financial costs involve paying more in the coinage of one's time. But those lacking financial resources are not necessarily any richer in free time, and using these tactics leaves one perpetually behind new developments in the field. If you simply must read the next volume in your favourite fantasy series and can't justify the full price of a new copy, then you can camp out on the library hold list, scour used bookstores for a second-hand copy, or wait for a friend to finish and pass it along. However, all these solutions involve different rhythms of circulation from the "first-run" economy. This creates complex temporalities of access and circulation in geek culture, with many participants lagging behind others. Moreover, because the time someone devotes to a practice is taken as one of the principal indicators of engagement and commitment, struggling with these constraints is a fundamental feature of their experience of nerd culture:

> And then you have the casual gamer who just likes to come out for a ... a game every once in a while. They'll play a game when it's offered but not necessarily ... organize games or go out of their way to play games ... and they may be ... more interested in the social aspect or just hanging out, which ... I think *maybe* I am kind of a casual gamer? but I would play more games if I ... I kind of had the time because I really do ... enjoy ... doing it? (Wedge)

As I noted earlier, the problem of co-ordinating different people's (more or less) busy schedules is an important component of the time constraints faced by my informants:

> Time. Yeah. Just being able to find the time to do it, being able to find a night that works for everybody. (Diana)

> MR FOX: I have guys – I talk to my friends online about games and play together, that kinda thing. Throw down some ... *Left4Dead* or ... *Company of Heroes*, that kinda stuff.

BEN: About how often does that happen?

MR FOX: Two weeks or so, I guess? Depends when we have enough time to actually … play. I mean … for *Left4Dead*, you need four people. You need roughly four people for an hour and a half for one campaign, and rounding up *four* adults … who all have full-time jobs, it's not the easiest thing. It's why our D&D campaign is kinda waffling.

For participants who involve themselves in several different parts of the scene, there is the added complication of scheduling conflicts or poor co-ordination of events. This is possible even within one community, as Barry noted when two SCA events fell on the same weekend:

BARRY: It's too bad that they were going on at the same time. I don't know how that happened. Normally, nearby events, they try to have them on different dates so that everybody can go to each of them.

BEN: I guess the calendar – the calendar seems pretty full this summer. I don't know if that's unusual.

BARRY: Well, it's – they've actually pared it down?

But it's particularly acute when someone is involved in regions of the scene that don't habitually think of themselves as in "competition" for quite the same population of attendees.

Compared with financial costs, there are fewer tactics of avoidance for dealing with time constraints. After all, human beings can only be in one place at a time, multiple people and objects cannot occupy the same space simultaneously, and everything has a finite duration. Indeed, Anthony Giddens (1984, 111–12) suggests that these facts of time-geography should be axiomatic to any study of social phenomena. The one bright side has been the growth in time-shifting technologies that permit greater control over media consumption. Rather than having to fit one's schedule to those of the networks – especially if they are so foolish as to pit one fan-favourite show against another on the broadcast schedule – programs can be viewed when convenient to the viewer. Barry still made use of the grandfather of time-shifters, the VCR, to record shows off the air, and Solo spoke in glowing terms of "TV-DVD," by which she meant collections of TV series on home video: "That was nuts. I have a lot of TV-DVD. Well, that's not that much there. But TV-DVD was huge. I mean, I had *Buffy* on VHS as soon as it came out on VHS.

Like, I wanted it to be able to watch it at my own pleasure. I didn't want ads; I hate ads ... Yeah. That's probably the biggest thing I've noticed." Downloading audiovisual content also appeared as a tactical response to time pressures and not only (as it is often portrayed by industry lobby groups) as a way of avoiding paying for content. For Solo and her friends, it was now the preferred method of time-shifting TV shows. Importantly, however, she not only viewed time-shifting as a way to customize the schedule and avoid ads but also as a qualitatively superior, more immersive way of watching television: "I watch TV in *blocks*, like I don't watch it on TV anymore, it's different. And I go into what I call 'TV comas,' where just two weeks, I just watch one show for two weeks, and my brain is just melted by the end of it, but I just can't stop. And there's a lot – yeah, it just becomes *so* much content, though. Like, right now, it's *Mad Men*, but ... three weeks ago, it was *The Wire*." Wedge reported a similar dynamic with e-books, which he had recently started reading in odd moments on a new smartphone, and anticipated doing more reading as a result. But there are some practices that simply can't be time-shifted, particularly those that require the mutual co-presence of others, such as forms of tabletop gaming. In these cases, the "workaround" may be little more than a compensatory mechanism for being unable to play: "Well, you certainly have – like, even for me because I don't have time to play a lot, I'll read stuff online or ... participate in ... forum discussions or ... that sort of thing" (Wedge).

BIGGER ON THE INSIDE

There is a recurring fantasy in geeky media of objects that miraculously contain multitudes: from *Doctor Who*'s TARDIS to the D&D item known as a Bag of Holding, from *Star Trek*'s Holodeck (or *Community*'s Dreamatorium), which can conjure any environment in a small, grid-covered room, to an old armoire that contains a whole world of mythical beasts and talking animals. This trope can be read as a case of straightforward wish fulfillment, for if such things were real then one would never have to throw anything away. But physical space and the material nature of equipment-goods represent another pragmatic constraint on participation. It is not enough to scratch up the money to buy that book or statue or board game; you still have to find somewhere to put it.

Technically, the term "material culture" is redundant; there's no such thing as *im*material culture. Thoughts and ideas are created by brains and bodies and expressed through physical media. Similarly, cultural practices cannot be understood apart from their equipment-goods. In a real, immediate sense, they equip us to be participants. Even the relatively cerebral pleasures of narrative and character presuppose books to read them in or screens to watch them on. But, having devoted financial resources to acquire them, all these things must be cleaned, maintained, and organized. At the most basic level, they take up the limited space available in our homes.

Thus the external storage of objects, whether in rented storage spaces or a parental home, was a common theme. Some members of the university-based Alternate Universe Club complained over dinner after an anime screening that their *Magic* cards and *Warhammer* figurines were still at mom and dad's, and Diana's partner Steve, who had a home and family of his own, recalled the "whole whack of stuff" that still remained at his parents' house. But this was only a special case of the more general problem of moving collections. For example, although Wedge considered comic books the collectible par excellence, their material qualities made them difficult to keep in the long run: "I sold all of my comics, or most of my comics, when I moved […] because it was a lot of comics. I had 4,000 comics or something. Like, ten boxes, ten of those big long boxes. They're hard to move. They get wrecked when they get moved […] I still love the stories, and I still love the artwork, but I kind of quit cold turkey sort of. ((laughs)) Like it was costing a reasonable amount of money and taking up a lot of space and I was moving around for – I think I moved to university, which is probably when I ended up […] stopping." This sentiment was echoed by many other participants for whom the need to dispose of collections when moving – or moving in with a significant other – was proverbial. These accounts are a reminder that objects' useful or pleasurable qualities are "bundled" with other, less convenient ones such as extension, weight, and fragility (Keane, 2005).

Around the time I conducted fieldwork, a number of reality television shows about people whose lives are dominated by the junk they amassed were popular. As a result, "hoarder" was a ready-to-hand name for the "dark side" of collecting. Diana used it playfully to tease Steve about his attachment to games and books, but it represented a real fear for others. Shiera, for example, tried to be a ruthless curator due to family history ("My mom, I think, is on the verge of being a real hoarder, and I just never want to go through it.") and a more general tendency she observed among fans: "That's based on having visited a lot of fans' homes ... There's an aesthetic of messiness [...] Your average home, so-cial services would take those people's kids away! ((laughs)) They real-ly would! You have to maintain a certain amount – and I'm dusty ... and I'm messy, but I try to stay on top of it [...] I have lived with peo-ple who do that. I have to lock them out of my room, or they'd carry the entropy with them." I want to adopt Shiera's turn of phrase, drawing on anthropologist and material culture scholar Daniel Miller's (2008, 293) sense of an aesthetic as the "overall organisational principle" in people's lives. Of my informants, the "aesthetic of messiness" probably best de-scribes Barry.

Barry vocally espoused the virtues of simplicity and thrift. He cer-tainly didn't lack for possessions, but like a true *bricoleur* tried to econ-omize by making do with used goods whenever possible and designing his own improvised systems to meet needs. The lion's share of the ob-jects in his home were related to his fandoms: projects and awards from the SCA, VHS tapes, gaming trophies, and, most importantly, books. Vir-tually every wall – windows included – of his apartment was covered in shelves of reference books, RPG manuals, and science-fiction novels, and he had as many again in a storage unit. Warren, whose comic-bookstore evinced a similar accumulation of things (but whose home I never saw), said the physical premises at King St Comics were so full because "I've always enjoyed being surrounded by things that I like." This comment could be easily applied to Barry, and I think it's the best way to under-stand his aesthetic.

Miller (2010, 87) asserts that people with strong social relationships are more likely to have mastery over the object world, and vice versa. I don't know if I would describe Barry's apartment as "mastered" – dur-ing my visit, he kept pointing out objects he intended to organize bet-ter or get rid of. Given his frequent references to conflict arising from misunderstandings or unintentional slights, perhaps he hadn't mas-tered social relationships either (if such a thing is even possible). But his engagements with geek culture are certainly the key to the objects and relationships that were part of his life: Barry's fannish commitments could be read in the clutter of his home, while fan activities – from Tolkien meet-ups to local cons, from the SCA to an amateur writers' group – were also primary sources of social interaction. If Mary Douglas (2003, 44) is correct that "dirt" (or, in this case, "mess") is "matter out of place," then the aesthetic of messiness represents a refusal to separate leisure from other spheres of life. Rather than discriminate between them, Barry piled them on top of one another, allowing his fandom to

literally surround him waking and sleeping. Warren similarly conflated fannish and economic logics in his store, amassing products that he
personally "believed in," even when unsold stock strained the store's
available physical space to its limits.

Like Barry, Mr Fox and Solo lived alone. Shiera's children lived with
her part of the time, but she clearly made decisions about how things
were arranged in their apartment. Not everyone experienced the same
freedom to organize their space. Diana and Steve both identified as
geeks or nerds, while Wedge and his wife had different tastes. Despite
this difference, both homes ended up similarly "zoned," with certain
areas given over to the storage or display of fan-oriented objects. Zoning was a point of negotiation:

> I'm not a collector. Not at all [...] Pretty much if it's six months
> old, you're a hoarder. ((laughs)) Almost. Like, I just get rid of every-
> thing. (Diana)

> Basically, what happens is it just fills up and then I get more boxes
> and try to organize it and make it fit until Diana freaks out, and
> then we do a purge. (Steve)

> BEN: Seems like a lot of people have that cycle of gradually accu-
> mulating things, and then, as you say, a move or some other life cir-
> cumstance, or just a feeling that they're getting too much stuff –
> WEDGE: Sometimes predicated on … external forces, like a wife.
> ((laughs)) Yeah, 'cause I certainly wouldn't have got rid of as much
> stuff as I did. Any of the time, probably.

Zoning is all about maintaining boundaries, and thus, their homes did
not share in the aesthetic of messiness. With the exception of the computers on which they played *World of Warcraft* and a shared library of
novels, the geeky objects in Diana and Steve's home were relegated to
a space they jokingly referred to as "the man-closet." In Wedge's apartment, novels and board games were collected together on one shelf in
the living room, and the remainder of his gaming supplies – including
the character sheet and map from his very first D&D session as a child
– were filed by the computer of his home office; other objects were in
a rented storage space awaiting disposal. Things make demands on their
owners, and, one way or another, their presence in the home was a problem that had to be solved and re-solved. Thus, most people I spoke to

were perpetually in the middle of a cycle of bingeing and purging objects. Wedge tried to sell old things in order to free up money he could reinvest in the circuit of collecting, and other informants mentioned garage sales and used bookstores as places where they got rid of things. Mr Fox was turned onto comics while hospitalized as a child, and now donates comics and games he's done with to a children's hospital. And just as networks of peers and friends dominated accounts of acquisition, they were likely destinations for goods no longer wanted: "When the time comes for them to go on to their new homes, I have new homes for them because I have a lot of friends who are *Star Wars* fans who would love to have ... a collectible of ... Boba Fett. He's never been my favourite, so I'm not gonna ... hang onto that one too much, even though it's a gift and I'm re-gifting it, if it's taking up too much room on my shelf, if my shelf starts to get cluttered and I start wanting – no, then it goes" (Shiera).

At the best of times, purging is therapeutic – a chance to clear out some material and psychic clutter. As Shiera put it, echoing William Morris's dictum,[1] the things remaining in her home "are things I either use or like aesthetically." Nevertheless, purging is rarely done entirely whole-heartedly. The loss of goods can be a source of regret: "The most money I've ever spent on a comic was *Iron Fist* 14, which is the first appearance of Sabretooth. And I think I spent 150 bucks on that um ... and it took me ... that one took me three years to find a copy. Like, I hadn't found – I hadn't even seen a copy of it? Until I found that, and it was in really good condition and uh ... I ended up selling it, which was a big mistake, ((laughs)) to pay rent, probably" (Wedge). If Miller and others are correct about just how entwined our subjectivities are with the objects around us, such losses can be almost traumatic. Shiera, for instance, was still lamenting the loss of possessions from a flooded storage space eight years prior. When we get rid of certain things, related ways of being may no longer be available to us – as we are no longer equipped to participate in the relevant practices.

Digitization is frequently proposed as a solution to the problems of materiality. As Lisa Gitelman (2004, 200) notes, much ink has been spilt about how "digital technologies make the means of communication 'virtual,' freeing information from the limits of physicality, from tangible things like pages, books, and files." Several interviewees were optimistic about these possibilities, but dematerialization is more rhetoric than reality. "Paperless fandom" is only thinkable with respect to those equipment-goods that can be imagined as "content" alienable from its "medium," and re-mediating an activity or a text simply transforms it into a different object. For example, although Steve happily subscribed to the Dungeons & Dragons Insider service so that he didn't have to store all the rulebooks needed to run his campaign, he retained a strong emotional connection to his old print D&D manuals: "Just even to open the copy, it's the artwork, it's the feel of the book, the size, the shape, it's everything that goes along with it."

More often than not, digital technologies were auxiliaries to, not substitutes for, material practices. They supported the primary practice or generated new, spin-off activities, but their ability to enable communication and interaction with real people – albeit on distinctly mediated terms – was more important than their "virtuality." For example, Wedge played *Blood Bowl*, a miniatures game that mixes tropes from the *Warhammer Fantasy* universe with American football, in a local league. They met monthly in a hotel ballroom to play, but in between game days Wedge spent a lot of time on the league's website. On the site, members' win-loss records could be tracked and players could discuss their strategies on the attached forum. These were not a separate form of digital fandom but fed back directly into their monthly game days.

Moreover, material practices of acquisition and curation also apply to digital objects. Two of the portraits in Miller's (2008) *Comfort of Things*, for example, focus on organizing and sorting emails and media files, such as digital photos. Editing metadata, searching for downloads, and levelling up *World of Warcraft* characters require brains and hands in addition to computers. In point of fact, not even digital information is truly immaterial – although it may seem that way to those privileged with unlimited, high bandwidth Internet connections and cheap storage media. Digitization does not solve the problem of space; it only adds another layer.

MY SO-CALLED REAL LIFE

Balancing leisure pursuits with the demands of "so-called real life" (Barry's term) is another constraint every participant faces. To a certain extent, this is a simple function of the other constraints discussed above. Everyone has a limited supply of financial, temporal, and spatial resources. Individually, these scarcities limit participation, but they must be seen in the context of a participant's whole life where other important and meaningful commitments compete for their own share of money, time, and space. And the responsibilities that emerge from our necessary entanglements with other people, such as spouses, children, and friends carry their own complexities. That is to say, it's all fun and games until someone loses their job, ruins their marriage, or otherwise fails to make good on their commitments.

We've already seen the rhetorical power of appeals to "real life" in distinguishing normal from over-involved ("bad") participants. Moreover, fannish references to "mundanes" and "getting away from it all" (or, GAFIA) further speak to the significance of the symbolic opposition between real life and fantasy, which only re-expresses those between work/responsibility and leisure or constraint and freedom: "Gafiation is such a good word. Yes, and it is understood in the SCA and in fandom in general that real life comes first. That you need to … that you might have to pull out, and people shouldn't resent you for it and you shouldn't feel bad about it yourself beyond the fact that you know you're missing out on some of the fun" (Barry). Whereas mundanes might use the expression "getting away from it all" to describe a much-needed vacation from their responsibilities, fanspeak inverts its valence. As Sanders and brown (1994, 267) explain its origins, GAFIA was "originally used to mean turning away from the mundane world to join fandom," but fandom eventually becomes the "point of reference" rather than the escape. This suggests an ambivalent attitude to the relationship between "extracurricular" cultural practices and everyday responsibilities. On the one hand, most people recognize that real life is a source of rich, fulfilling experiences. On the other hand, it is the realm of necessity and can be experienced as a constraint on what "really" matters most to someone; indeed, it can completely prevent people from doing the things they find most enjoyable.

Given the ideological alignment of "free time" with freedom, its opposition to real life and responsibility is fundamental, and it appears in all of my interviews. However, I want to concentrate on Diana and Wedge. They were about the same age and both have a spouse and young child. But, as mentioned above, Diana and her partner Steve were (in her words) a "geek family," while Wedge's wife shared few of his nerdy interests. This point of comparison allows me to explore the ways that family life and adult responsibilities can limit participation.

Diana and Steve met while in university, and they later moved to the city when Diana pursued graduate studies. At the time of our interviews, she ran a small business and he worked as a software developer. When I talked with them about their library of SF&F novels, there was some lively back and forth about their different taste in books, but precisely the kind that is only possible when people agree on the broad contours of a field. They started playing D&D together seven years ago when invited by a friend who was starting up a group, and Steve now serves as their Dungeon Master. He is actually involved in a wider variety of nerdy practices than Diana – at one point, she said he is *"more of a geek"* than she is – but this doesn't involve any necessary conflict, since nerd culture is a space where they equally feel at home: "Every once in a while we'll hold a painting party because Steve paints miniatures and a couple of our friends paint miniatures. So I'll be there, but I don't paint miniatures, you know but I'll be there, probably playing *World of Warcraft* actually, but in the same room, so, you know, part of conversation."

The arrival of their first child introduced some new pressures into their life:

BEN: Are there any other factors that limit or constrain your ability to participate as much as you might like to?
DIANA: Baby. Baby. "Stupid baby, ((laughs)) taking me away from *World of Warcraft*" [...] So, yes, obviously the baby really, well, my whole life I guess limits what I can do, but other than that – sometimes Steve, ((laughs)) he's like, "You have to get off the computer so we can, I don't know, be social together." It's like, "Yeah, yeah, Steve."
BEN: "Get your laptop."
DIANA: ((laughs)) Exactly! "Grab the laptop, we'll play together!"

But this meant an evolution of her engagement with geek culture, not its decline. For example, it was only *after* having Donna that they were introduced to *World of Warcraft* by a friend, who gave them a trial subscription. Skeptical at first, she found the game well suited to her maternity-leave schedule, since it rewards time invested but doesn't necessarily require long sessions or (as she played it) co-ordination with other people. However, parental responsibilities introduced new dilemmas when it comes to scheduling face-to-face activities with other community members: "I feel much more connected to [a friend who is also a parent] because we have that. You know, because he's like, 'I can only game one night a week because I have these other responsibilities,' where so many of our friends are childless and are like, 'I don't know why! We should be able to game all the time!'"

Wedge would probably recognize this dilemma, too. He moved to the city a few years ago to be closer to his wife's family. His job had him commuting quite far, but he was able to work from home two days a week. Although his wife will play and enjoy some board games and they share some sections of their bookshelf, Wedge said they have quite different tastes in, for example, movies and television shows. But it was in the realm of tabletop gaming where tensions between fun and family were most keenly felt. In addition to playing board games socially, he was in two regular RPG campaigns (though he admitted one of them often devolved to just hanging out with friends), played in a *Blood Bowl* league, and was involved in running the City Gaming Network. Wedge sounded almost sheepish whenever he admitted to conflict between these priorities – and note that, where Diana would talk about "the baby," he almost always mentioned his wife rather than their daughter as the factor that limited his opportunities to participate in geek culture activities:

> In my marriage, the lack of … the lack of being able to game with my wife certainly divides our time […] because generally I like to get out and game once a week or something like that, and I would love for her to be able to be involved because it would mean we'd get together a little bit more often with other people and interact that way.

> Most people would play two [*Blood Bowl* games on the monthly game days], but in general I will probably play one because I'll normally – I like to spread mine out. I like to play … I'll play a game sometime during the week, and then play one game on a game day so that – I find sometimes getting in and playing the same game for … like, six or eight hours, and it also … it's a little bit hard for my wife, just because then I'm gone all day. And that's once a month, so … so it makes it a little hard, whereas if I'm just gone in the morning, come back, we have the afternoon to spend.

> I like conventions. I think if I had – if I had more time … or didn't have a wife ((laughs)) or something like that, I would go to conventions more often.

That is to say, his nerdy interests had to compete with family for his attention, while, for Diana and Steve, gaming or going to see the latest sci-fi blockbuster *was* family time.[2] I need to underscore that, although Wedge wished that his wife liked playing games more, he mentioned other interests that they shared, like hiking and going dancing. But, anecdotally, his situation is more common in the field than Diana and Steve's, a fact Diana herself noted: "Most of our geek friends, their wives aren't, so we don't see them because we, we game and we … you know, we do … even when you're doing the stuff that isn't directly gaming like miniature painting or Friday night fun night, they just don't come because they have, they do different things, you know?"

This split between participants who were relatively unencumbered by "real life" responsibilities (Barry, Mr Fox, and Solo) and those who had to juggle their fan activity with family and parenting (Diana, Shiera, and Wedge) exemplifies Hodkinson's (2012) arguments about aging in "youth" subcultures. However, the fact that Barry, the oldest of my interviewees, was in the former category also reminds us that "growing up" is only contingently related to growing older.

I have suggested that geek culture can be understood as an example of a "real utopia," in Erik Olin Wright's (2010) sense of an actually existing social arrangement that may nonetheless point towards a more just and humane future. The sense of community and meaningful engagement with the other that flourishes amidst nerds and geeks' media-oriented practices is one such index. These practices provide spaces and contexts for people to communicate about things that matter to them. That is to say, they enable people to articulate – whether implicitly or explicitly – ideas of the good life, of human flourishing. But even a real utopia still smuggles in More's double meaning – of *eutopia*, the good place, and *outopia*, no place.

Geek culture is routinely constructed as part of the world of leisure, and thus as a realm of freedom, an exception to the necessities and responsibilities of mundane life. The fantastical character of its symbolic contents no doubt reinforces this way of construing its practices: the comic-con as a carnivalesque suspension of mundane order, or the sense of wonder evoked by science fiction and fantasy literature as an escape into adventure. Yet the communities of geek culture belong to the real world and rely on a series of conditions of possibility in order for their practices to come off. Not only must the problems of institutionalization be resolved so that these activities remain available in the scene, but individuals must also cope with a number of problems in their own lives before they can get out and access them.

It should be noted that none of these limitations is unique to geek culture. They are generic problems that likely perform similar regulative functions for any practice, though the workarounds people develop will obviously respond to the substance of the activity in question. But neither are they *natural* problems. They are generated or exacerbated by features of the way we organize our lives under given social relations. For example, while it is indeed fundamental to the human condition that we have only a finite amount of time on earth, how we are obligated to spend that time – working, commuting, running errands, and so on – is the result of a series of collective choices. The particular way that capitalist societies institutionalize time sets up the division between freedom and necessity in the first place and results in an uneven distribution of agency. As Michel de Certeau (2011) famously asserted, popular culture can be thought of as an art of "making do" in everyday life. The body of cultural studies research shows the extraordinary power of "vernacular creativity" (Burgess 2006) to generate meaning on the margins of "official culture" or out of its leavings. The practices of geek culture are a good example, as media that had exhausted their lifecycle in the cultural marketplace or never found a mass audience in the first place became the basis for a set of cultural practices and, ultimately, for human connection in vibrant communities.

But if this is what people can accomplish under conditions of constraint, then what else could they (and others, participating in other practical communities) create without them? What new ways of meaningfully inhabiting the world could be devised? It is in this sense that everyday life and the identities built within it contain a hidden utopian impulse – but this ordinary utopianism is always hedged in by externally imposed constraints.

The Geek, the Bad, and the Ugly

In January 2011, Jared Lee Loughner, then twenty-two years of age, attempted to assassinate US Representative Gabrielle Giffords at a meet-and-greet with her constituents. Giffords survived, but six people died that day in a supermarket parking lot. A few days afterwards, Matt Feeney wrote an essay for *Slate* about Loughner and his favourite author, Friedrich Nietzsche (about which more below), under the headline "Angry Nerds." While Loughner's specific motivations apparently emerged from a miasma of untreated mental illness, his crime also fit into a pattern of violence perpetrated by young, mostly white, and mostly middle-class men and boys. As Michael Kimmel (2010, 134) notes, they were "mercilessly and constantly teased, picked on, and threatened" for being different from their peers: "shy, bookish, an honor student, artistic, musical, theatrical, non-athletic, a 'geek,' or weird." We know that such students are more likely to be harassed and bullied, particularly when they attend schools that value athletics and popularity more than academics and that implicitly tolerate the treatment kids labelled as geeks and nerds receive (Kimmel 2010; Bishop et al. 2004). In a handful of cases – Montreal, Columbine, Virginia Tech, Tucson, and Isla Vista, to name a few – these unhappy, alienated young men try to inflict the pain they feel onto others.

My account of geek culture as a "real utopia" (Wright 2010), as a space of shared commitments and everyday moral reflection, will undoubtedly ring hollow to some. Obliquely referencing Obsession_inc's (2009) distinction between affirmational and transformational modes of fandom, Kristina Busse (2015, 114) describes a "new geek hierarchy" that elevates "white, straight, male, intellectual [and] apolitical" fan identities over those of "person of color, female, queer, embodied [and] political" ones. The assumption that "affirmational" male fans are apolitical has obviously not aged well. As the "alt-right" style[1] jumped from the geekier edges of the entertainment industries to the centre of political discourse and political culture in the wake of the November 2016 US presidential election, some journalists suggested that geek culture has become a site where young men are radicalized into a particularly toxic form of misogynist and racist masculinity (Walter 2016; Wilkinson 2016). While I am by no means setting out to explain these tragic and horrific acts of violence or the less spectacular forms of harassment, intimidation, and violence now regularly visited upon women, people of colour, and their perceived allies, I couldn't avoid some discussion of the darker side of geek culture in this book. The ability to imagine this subculture as a space of possibility and freedom is a privilege that is not equally distributed. Even as the triumphal narrative loudly proclaimed that everyone is a geek and geek culture is for everyone, a backlash was brewing. Today, the face of geek culture is not only fan communities sharing their enthusiasms together: it's also a comment thread troll; it's a Twitter egg threatening rape and death; it's Loughner's crooked grin. In this context, Charles J. Sykes's advice to "be nice to nerds" takes on much more sinister overtones. But it wasn't so long ago that geek culture promised something different – a different, perhaps better way of being a man. How did we get from "sensitive new age geeks" to "angry young nerds"?

This trajectory mirrors the broader history of "men's movements" that followed in the wake of feminism. Kimmel (1987) categorizes them as "masculinist," "antifeminist," or "profeminist," while Messner (1998, 12) positions them in a "terrain" defined by their orientation to "men's institutionalized privileges," "the costs attached to adherence to narrow conceptions of masculinity," and "differences and inequalities among men." Between these approaches, we have a matrix of potential responses to feminist critiques of unequal gender relations. The point of departure for contemporary politics of masculinity was the "male liberation movement" that sprung up, largely in intellectual circles, in the 1970s. Books like Warren Farrell's (1975) *The Liberated Man* and Herb Goldberg's (1979) *The New Male* argued that men needed to be freed from restrictive sex roles as much as women did. This movement was oriented to the "costs of masculinity" pole and was, at least initially, profeminist. As depicted in advertising, the press, and self-help literature, the liberated "new man" was supposed to be more egalitarian in his relationships with women and more emotionally available to himself and others (Gill 2003; Elliott, Eccles, and Hodgson 1993). Raewyn Connell (1993, 610) describes this as a struggle *for* hegemony *between* masculinities, one based on physical dominance and one based on professional expertise. The latter – stereotyped as intellectual, effete or both, and represented in popular discourse by celebrities like Alan Alda and Dustin Hoffman – was sometimes equated with the existing social type of the nerd on the basis of their shared deviance from traditional masculine norms. This comparison could cut both ways: either elevating nerds as exemplars of enlightened gender roles or tarring any man supporting feminism as a pencil-neck geek of suspect virility.

However, as Connell (2005, 79) usefully suggests, we should not take every non-hegemonic masculinity as a challenge to patriarchy. There is a world of difference between identities that are complicit in oppressive gender relations and those that offer genuine liberation. The enemy of women's enemy is not necessarily a friend to women. The early men's movement was grounded in an internally incoherent theory of symmetrical sex roles, and their allyship was contingent upon the benefits that new gender relations could have for men. Foregrounding men's feelings of frustration and powerlessness set the stage for a "conceptual framework in which a man may blame women for his own lack of freedom." Farrell, Goldberg, and others began to articulate an anti-feminist "men's rights" discourse that posited liberation as a zero-sum game (Messner 1998, 262, 266). Whether geek culture will cultivate alternative but ultimately complicit masculinities or furnish resources for constructing truly oppositional identities remains, for the moment, an unresolved question.

MEN OF RESSENTIMENT

When Disney and Lucasfilm announced their intentions to restart the *Star Wars* franchise with a seventh instalment, fans were obviously anxious – particularly after the last attempt to add onto the much beloved trilogy. While *The Force Awakens* (J.J. Abrams 2015) would include many cast members from the original films reprising their roles, it would also pass the torch to a new trio of heroes: the force-sensitive scavenger Rey, rogue stormtrooper Finn, and Resistance pilot Poe Dameron, played by a woman (Daisy Ridley), a black man (John Boyega), and a Latino man (Oscar Isaac), respectively. It also featured a notably more diverse secondary cast than many films, a trend that continued with the casting of Gareth Edwards's *Rogue One*, the first of the "*Star Wars* anthology" films spun off from the main series. Episode VII was the midpoint in a year –

beginning with *Mad Max: Fury Road* (George Miller 2015) and ending with *Ghostbusters* (Paul Feig 2016) – that put women and people of colour at the centre of franchises previously dominated by white, male bodies. There is some textual evidence to support the notion that the filmmakers knew exactly what they were doing. Given the scarred visage revealed when Darth Vader's mask was finally removed in *Return of the Jedi*, for instance, audiences perhaps expected another example of the Evil Makes You Ugly trope with *Force Awakens* antagonist Kylo Ren. But when he finally removes his mask halfway through the film, we instead see the perfectly ordinary, even bland, face of Adam Driver underneath. The popular parody Twitter account Emo Kylo Ren (@KyloR3n), which re-imagined the character as an exaggeratedly angsty teenager perpetually embarrassed by his father, suggests at least some viewers picked up on the Driver's portrayal of troubled, maladjusted masculinity. Similarly, the villains of both *Fury Road* and Paul Feig's genderswapped *Ghostbusters* are marked as white men, with Immortan Joe representing a toxic, domineering "alpha" masculinity, and Rowan the misanthropy of the embittered "beta," respectively. These films seem to indicate a shift from more conservative strategies where franchise owners attempted to discretely serve different audiences "through a logic of multiplied cultural production" (Johnson 2013, 6): "With production crossing multiple markets, media franchising can just as feasibly enable one branded property to reach *different* audiences as it can encourage a *single* audience to consume in multiple ways. These differentiations can turn on gender or other markers of difference, with new productions geared toward audiences and/or characters defined by specific identity categories" (2014, 898). As Derek Johnson (2014, 900) suggests, "iterative franchised production and marketing [had] cast *Star Wars* as *almost always* for boys yet *sometimes* for girls." Notwithstanding a controversy over the lack of toys and merchandise featuring Rey, which Scott (2017) observes both welcomed in and ultimately denied female fans, Disney used *The Force Awakens* to break down walls between audiences/markets it had previously attempted to hold at arm's length from one another – thereby making the existence of those other fans undeniable.

While some welcomed the increased visibility of women and people of colour in and around geeky blockbusters, a segment of fandom decried these films as evidence of an agenda to politicize simple entertainment and take cherished properties away from their "real" fans. Some fans even went so far as to call for boycotts of these films as "anti-white" and/or as feminist "propaganda" (Bui 2015; de Coning 2016).

Others suggested that any positive review of *Ghostbusters* must have been the product of a conspiracy (Carbone 2016). Media that responded to industrial and audience activism and dallied with diversity faced similarly hyperbolic criticism from some people calling themselves fans. Such reactionary perspectives have routinely been accompanied by campaigns of online intimidation and threats of violence, such as those aimed against novelist N.K. Jemisin and facilitated by people connected with the then-leadership of the Science Fiction Writers of America (Huang 2013; Jemisin 2014), against critic and former comic-book editor Janelle Asselin (Asselin 2014; Moosa 2014), and against vlogger Anita Sarkeesian, developer Zoë Quinn, and numerous other women by the Gamergate movement (Chess and Shaw 2015), to name only a few examples. These attacks are contested, often at great personal risk, but they seem to show many nerds' own self-understanding of their communities as places that welcome outsiders and the marginalized to be in bad faith.

Geek culture has long been imagined as a space principally, if not exclusively, for straight white men. The reality was always much more complicated (see also Eglash 2002; Stanfill 2011; Scott 2012; Wanzo 2015), but this stereotype enabled labels like "geek," "nerd," and "gamer" to form the basis of an ersatz identity politics for certain members of these communities, who imagined themselves to be the field's rightful occupants. For instance, while Gamergate became best known for its "ethics in games journalism" slogan, early on it drew as much of its animus from a series of editorials declaring the "death of the gamer." The phrase was meant to refer to the end of the young, white, heterosexual, and cisgender male player of AAA games as the primary audience of an increasingly diverse video game culture. However, as Mizuko Ito et al. (2010) suggest in line with my discussion in chapter 1, "producing particular forms of gamer identities is a form of 'boundary work'" (228), and these identities regulate access to certain gaming activities that, in turn, "provide an accessible entry point into geek identities and practices that are tied to technical expertise and media literacy" (240; see also Eglash 2002). In response to progressive developers and critics signalling an open door policy, Gamergate supporters appropriated the rhetorical tropes of progressive identity politics and turned them back against those critics and journalists who were attempting to envision a "post-gamer" culture: "Although their movement targets women specifically, #Gamergaters insist they speak for a victimized 'demographic,' and that anyone who opposes misogyny while making generalizations about gamers must be a hypocrite" (Hathaway 2014, under "What about the 'death of the gamer' stuff?"). To people invested in particular gendered, racialized, and heteronormative conceptions of geek identity, attempts to represent the interests of the existing women, visible minority, and queer fans who felt underserved by their own culture or – heaven forbid – to actively appeal to new audiences that come along as part and parcel of the "triumph" of geek culture could only be understood as a betrayal. In the most charitable light, their concern represents a lay version of the cultural studies model of subcultural incorporation: subcultural formations like geek culture are inevitably repackaged by commercial interests in such a way as to negate their original, authentic essence (see Clarke 2006). Yet this interpretation would problematically align "authenticity" with one group of members (defined, inter alia, by their race, gender identity, and sexuality), and it doesn't really account for the *virulence* of the misanthropy and misogyny that has been evident in recent years.

Reflecting on the fact that school shooters are almost exclusively nerdy young men, Michael Kimmel (2010, 125) identifies the emotional pain of marginalization, "a fusion of that humiliating loss of manhood and the moral obligation and entitlement to get it back," as the motive force behind these acts. He calls it "aggrieved entitlement" and notes that it is a specifically "gendered emotion," one that is sometimes, if statistically rarely, translated into violent action. I find Kimmel's effort to locate the *emotional* substance of reactionary masculinity highly suggestive, if only because it cuts against the insistent attempts to align geek culture and identity with rationality. In chapter 3, I discussed the "scholastic disposition" that enabled knowledge and expertise to be recognized as a specific form of symbolic capital by my interviewees. Reason and rationality functioned as discursive frames employed to characterize themselves, their actions, and their communities. While irrepressible enthusiasm is a hallmark of geek culture (Hills 2002; Reagle 2015), emotion also figures as a source of trouble and conflict:

Especially if – if let's say things get emotional, then the original point can be completely lost. (Barry)

I need to be able to trust their opinion when I say, "Am I way off base?" and they'll say, ((laughs)) "Yes you are. You are reacting emotionally to something that needs to be, you know, not emotional, so get your head out of your ass." And I need that, too. (Shiera)

Such rhetorical renunciations of emotion are even more pronounced among the partisans of reactionary geek identity politics. For instance, Milo Yiannopoulos – an active player in Gamergate, as well as technology editor for Breitbart News and thus a more or less direct line between geek culture and the alt-right – insists that he and his compatriots are for *facts*, while their political nemeses (e.g., "social justice warriors, hand-wringers, feminists, Black Lives Matter [activists]") are motivated by *feelings*.[2] Indeed, they delight in offending people precisely because it produces affective responses in their targets, thus reinforcing their own position as unmoved movers. So, a focus on the emotional contours of toxic masculinity not only represents an effort to understand some of its root causes but may also undercut one of its most powerful rhetorical appeals.

In his essay on Loughner, Matt Feeney tries to pick apart "the nexus of Nietzsche and troubled young manhood" (2011, ¶2). "If we never discovered that Jared Lee Loughner honed his murderous outlook while sitting alone in his bedroom, reading Nietzsche and thinking about nihilism," Feeney writes, "*that* would have been real news" (¶1, original emphasis). Mark Kingwell (2004) has also suggested Nietzsche's appeal lies in his stylistic and rhetorical gifts, his way of welcoming the reader into the position of the superior "master moralist." Yet the aggrieved entitlement that typifies reactionary geeks sounds much more like what Nietzsche calls *ressentiment* than like any noble qualities.[3] In *On the Genealogy of Morals*, Nietzsche (1989) contrasts the "noble man" and the "man of ressentiment." Indeed, ressentiment is the motive force of "slave morality," behind which (Nietzsche asserts) lurks a will to power that is frustrated and therefore necessarily disguised: "The slave revolt in morality begins when ressentiment itself becomes creative and gives birth to values: the ressentiment of natures that are denied the true reaction, that of deeds, and compensate themselves with an imaginary revenge. While every noble morality develops from a triumphant affirmation of itself, slave morality from the outset says No to what is 'outside,' what is 'different,' what is 'not itself'; and *this* No is its creative deed. This inversion of the value-positing eye – this need to direct one's view outward instead of back to oneself – is of the essence of ressentiment" (Nietzsche 1989, 36–7). Nietzsche's attempts to historicize and racialize these concepts are not compelling. Nonetheless, as Reginster (1997) argues, Nietzsche's account of ressentiment captures a very specific emotional state, and thus should be regarded as a real contribution to moral psychology.[4]

In Reginster's reading, ressentiment is the distinctive experience of someone caught between two value systems, one they believe in but can't attain and another, opposing set of values they can attain but don't really believe in. The "man of ressentiment" knows he cannot beat the "noble man" at his own game, and so he plays a different game and invests instead in an alternative set of values. Similarly, conventional discourses have constructed geek culture as an Island of Misfit Boys, a refuge for men who cannot compete by the standards of hegemonic masculinity: they are physically too small, too thin or too heavy, uncoordinated, introverted or awkward, brainy, bookish, or just plain "weird." But they haven't necessarily surrendered their claims to that game's stakes. In *Revenge of the Nerds* (Jeff Kanew 1984), Lewis goes so far as to impersonate jock Stan in order to sleep with his girlfriend, the cheerleader Betty. From today's vantage point, this is a shocking violation, but Betty takes it in stride and, by the sequels, they are happily married. The same double standard persists in contemporary "men's rights" discourses, such as the manifesto of Isla Vista shooter Elliot Rodger who complained endlessly of women choosing to give their attention to other men he viewed as less deserving (Myketiak 2016). In a reversal of Kimmel's definition of aggrieved entitlement, where the sense of entitlement is to *redress* their humiliation, I would suggest they experience ordinary life as humiliating *because* they feel entitled to material and sexual rewards.

REAL UTOPIAS, REAL DYSTOPIAS

In *After Virtue*, Alasdair MacIntyre attempts to rescue a teleological model of ethics by grounding what is right and good in particular social practices. This seems to neatly evade the problems presented by historical change and contemporary pluralism. There's no need to continue to seek a universally valid conception of the good for a human life, only the good for particular lives engaged in particular social practices. But almost immediately after introducing his sociologically grounded version of virtue ethics, MacIntyre raises a potential objection: "surely, it may be suggested, some practices [...] are evil" (2007, 199), and if a practice were evil, how could we call the dispositions that sustain it virtues?

MacIntyre does not entirely rule out the possibility of an evil practice, citing torture and "sado-masochistic sexuality" as potential examples (2007, 200). However, he is not convinced that they would meet the criteria set out in his definition of a practice. Not every form of activity constitutes a practice in this specific sense. In any case, despite the intimate connection proposed between practices and virtues, MacIntyre denies that his theory entails that anything done in the name of a practice is therefore good. Rather, his moral theory is "a sociology which aspires to lay bare the empirical, causal connection between virtues, practices and institutions" (196). MacIntyre invites a conjunctural analysis that investigates how these elements interact in real social situations, and this strikes me as a more fruitful direction than speculating about the existence of practices that are vicious a priori.

So, how do good practices turn bad – or at least produce bad behaviour and bad outcomes? Where do the anxieties and fears underlying nerdy ressentiment come from, and why does a portion of the audience react to them in these aggressive ways? I can't answer these questions with any kind of psychological or sociological precision – demonstrating an empirical, causal relationship is more difficult than MacIntyre intimates, and in any case my interviewees simply weren't those people (or at least didn't talk about perpetrating or experiencing these phenomena in our interviews). In his review of MacIntyre's theory of practice, Kelvin Knight (2008a, 44) speaks of "a teleological ordering of social relations" where the pursuit of goods and the needs of institutions are subordinated to the substantive rationality of practices. This implies the existence of disordered practices and further suggests that the same forces, the very same understandings, values, and beliefs, can produce quite different outcomes. In what remains of this chapter, I want to discuss three discursive and practical orientations: lay theories, namely, of authorship and the self-professed authority to speak on creators' behalf; of gender and the alignment of femininity with constraint; and of play and the dissociation of actions from consequence. Each is ambivalent, simultaneously pointing towards geek culture's "utopian" and "dystopian" possibilities.

Authorship: Not Dead, but Dreaming

If, as Barthes would have it, the author is dead, someone forgot to tell geeks – who continue to make (at least some) cultural producers into objects of veneration. Indeed, the controversies discussed above were fuelled, in part, because the fans who objected to these new remakes and sequels had arrogated to themselves the "author-function" (Foucault 1977), the authority to circumscribe what *Star Wars*, *Ghostbusters*, and *Mad Max* can mean and for whom. Similarly, struggles to define the true meaning of and true audience for video games, comic books, and science fiction are frequently waged on behalf of the imagined wishes of cultural producers – and, just as often, against others.

In *Popular Culture and High Culture*, Herbert Gans (1999) argues that the creators and users composing every taste public have fundamentally distinct orientations to culture – distinct not only from those of other taste publics but also from one another. Yet he notes that a substantial proportion of the "users" of high culture routinely adopt the perspectives of artists, authors, and other cultural producers. What Gans calls "creator-oriented consumption" is defined as the more or less exclusive property of elite taste cultures. While "high culture is creator-oriented and its aesthetics and its principles of criticism are based on this orientation," popular culture remains, "on the whole, user-oriented and [exists] to satisfy audience values and wishes" (62). Such formulations have the air of common sense because they largely coincide with long-standing discourses about cultural consumption. The audiences of prestigious art forms "appreciate," rather than "consume," culture; they seek to be "enlightened" or "challenged," rather than merely "entertained" or "pleased"; they value formal innovation over formulaic content; and so on. Meanwhile, popular culture is generally constructed around opposing values (Bourdieu 2010; Holt 2000). In this, at least, Gans implicitly reproduces the mass culture critique he explicitly rejects.

In geek culture, however, we find audiences that apply creator-oriented standards to the products of pop culture. For example, in the following extract Diana responds to a question about how she might describe a novel that fails to live up to her expectations: "The friend that I was talking about earlier, she'll often pass on [i.e., lend] books that aren't great. Like, the writing might not be great or the characters might not be great, but the idea that the author's trying to play with is a good idea, is one that she really liked, so that, you know, if it's a good idea or it has a really good – I want to say 'hook,' but even if it doesn't work, even if the idea is, I don't like the way that they've done it, but if it's like, 'Oh, this! If they'd just done this,' or you know, 'This is a great idea but they did it wrong.' Something that you can wrap your head around, that doesn't just go in one ear and out the other, but it's like, it makes you think." She offered this as an example of typical evaluative talk, but I find it very telling. In this quotation, Diana not only expresses her opinion that the book wasn't very good but she further implies that she knows how to fix it. She can take enjoyment from a book like this – a bad book that nonetheless "makes you think" – because the pleasure she derives from reading it is the pleasure of *re-writing* it, at least in her imagination. While an initial glance at fan studies accounts of audience creativity as "poaching" (Jenkins 2013), "appropriative writing" (Black 2009; Leavenworth 2015), and even "theft" (Lothian 2009) might suggest that fans hold authors and the author-function in low regard, there is no necessary contradiction between "world-based" and "auteur-based" fandom (Hills 2015). Creators like Gene Roddenberry, George Lucas, and J.K. Rowling may be lionized for their "vision" as creators of immersive, engaging worlds for their fans to embroider as much as for the quality of individual works. Fandom and authorship are complexly intertwined. Audiences are encouraged to develop intense investments in the products of the media industry and in their producers, but a corollary to these investments is a sense of ownership that may also destabilize professional media producers and rightsholders' ability to exercise authority over them. In a suggestive paper on fans' responses to authors' statements about fan fiction, Judith Fathallah (2016) describes fans who remain invested in the "*concept* of the Author" (474; original emphasis) but may withhold legitimating a given author depending on factors such as their embodied identity, their perceived skill or quality, and their political positions. Or, as Fiske (1992b, 40) puts it, "the reverence, even adoration, fans feel for their object of fandom sits surprisingly easily with the contradictory feeling that they also 'possess' that object."

My interviewees not only aligned themselves with creators – as when Shiera expressed her admiration for the actor and digital content creator Felicia Day by saying that "I think she'd be a really fascinating person to work with" – but also conceptualized some form of creative production as the natural outcome of fannish engagements with media. That is to say, it is a relatively short move from imaginatively re-writing to just plain writing. At one level, participants identified with creators as a source of distinction from "recreational" writers (Barry), "wannabes" (Shiera), and "naïve" or "entitled" fans (Mr Fox) – that is, from those who, by comparison, don't take popular culture seriously enough. At another, it formed one plank of what Henry Jenkins refers to as fandom's moral economy. In other words, people used their orientation to creators as part of a process of ethical reasoning. Mr Fox's comments about the ethics of downloading copyrighted entertainment, for instance, were grounded in an empathetic identification with cultural workers: "Well, it's stealing. I mean, if someone downloaded a story I wrote off the Internet or a game I made and played it for free, I'd be like, 'That's kind of a dick move! I worked really *hard* on that.' Or, at least, as hard as someone who does my job for a living works. I deserve, you know, recompense for that!"[5] These two levels are sometimes blurred, as when Solo offered a distinctly moral evaluation of other fans' behaviour that simultaneously distinguished her as a true, serious fan: "Like, the girls that went to – ugh, there were these two girls that went to England? For the premiere. Not to watch the movie, just to get signed by J.K. Rowling, and they got autographed and then they tattooed them. They got it tattooed to them. And I was like, 'What is that?' What does that do to you as an author? Like, I would be like, 'So … what are you going to do with this? No.' Oy."

Not all participants are necessarily attuned to the creative labour behind their consumption objects, yet the *idea* of creators and creativity can be rhetorically powerful. Indeed, when some readers criticized a variant cover for *Batgirl* 41 (DC Comics 2015) for dabbling with imagery of sexualized violence on a book that was then being marketed to young women readers, others cried political correctness run amok, despite the creative team's expressed support for the critics (see, e.g., McDonald 2015; Young 2015). In a press release announcing that they would not run the variant cover (at the request of artist Rafael Albuquerque), DC Entertainment referenced "threats of violence and harassment" that were levelled against the cover's critics online: "Regardless if fans like Rafael Albuquerque's homage to Alan Moore's THE KILLING JOKE graphic novel from 25 years ago, or find it inconsistent with the current tonality of the Batgirl books – threats of violence and harassment are wrong and have no place in comics or society" (DC Entertainment quoted in Ching 2015). Imagining themselves to be the true fans, these self-appointed inquisitors of geek orthodoxy felt emboldened to defend the faith by any means necessary. However, creator-orientation does not alone account for the fact that women experience more and much harsher criticism for supposedly heterodox views about movies, comics, video games, and so on. Today, to be a woman with an opinion – no matter how well founded – seemingly invites an unending barrage of invective and abuse from your "fellow" participants. For a subcultural community that has often explicitly prized knowledge and rationality, this is very curious indeed, and it raises serious questions about the gendered politics of participation in geek media cultures.

Gender: A Sad Garden

Some of the most uncomfortable situations during my research occurred when I asked people about their perceptions of geek culture's demographic composition. I never got very satisfying or candid answers. In retrospect, my questions were probably awkward because people were aware of the stereotyped white, male nerd and of how outsiders are likely to view homosocial and racially homogenous enclaves. At the same time, many people outside activist and academic circles are unpractised at talking about race, gender, and sexuality but know that one may be censured for "politically incorrect" speech. Consequently, they may have been afraid of saying the wrong thing and inviting criticism on themselves or the fandoms for which they acted as de facto representatives. Questions about race and ethnicity turned out to be a dead end; interviewees repeatedly asserted that geek culture was representative of the city's population as a whole, though I remain somewhat skeptical of these claims based on my own observations. By contrast, people had a story to tell about gender, one that, at the time, looked like it might have a happy ending.

When I asked people to talk about women in geek culture, most said that the number of women participating actively in their fan communities was on the rise – dramatically so, according to some. While Barry pointed out that "there were women involved in science-fiction" as long as he could remember, other corners of geek culture were notably homosocial. Diana observed, for instance, that she had no female nerd "role models," as popular media representations of the geeks and nerds were overwhelmingly male. Nonetheless, she said she no longer received "stares" when she went into the game shop: "When Steve and I first started playing, you know, I'd walk into Westside Games or, you know, a gaming shop and it would be like, ((panicked whisper)) 'There's a woman in the shop!' You know? And I'd be like the only girl, like, looking around kind of thing" (Diana). Yet as Suzanne Scott (2013b; 2017) suggests, women in conventionally masculinized fandoms are caught up in a politics of visibility: on the one hand, they are often forced to prove that their participation is legitimate lest they be entirely erased from the subcultural imaginary; on the other hand, they may be subjected to a kind of fetishistic hypervisibility. Both sides of this dilemma are encapsulated by the "Fake Geek Girl" discourse, which pop culture critic Alyssa Rosenberg describes as "one of the most hilarious and self-defeating memes to emerge" from the churn of male Internet outrage. This bogeywoman, as she emerged in online commentary, is supposedly engaged in some kind of long con, merely simulating "an interest in geek culture for the purpose of attracting men who like comics, science fiction, fantasy, superhero movies, etc., in order to later emotionally mutilate them" (Rosenberg 2013, ¶1). Interpreting this kerfuffle through the lens of cultural capital, Joseph Reagle (2015, 2863) argues that "the policing of fake geek girls can be understood as a conflict over what is attended to (knowledge or attractiveness), by whom (geekdom or mainstream), and the meaning of received attention (as empowering or objectifying)." The weakness of cultural capital is that it must be recognized by others in order to realize its value.

The falseness of the Fake Geek Girl discourse plays into a longer standing incredulity amongst certain male fans that women would – or indeed could – participate with them, as well as the resulting gendered gatekeeping that is a staple of many women's narratives about their experiences of participation. That is, some women entering comic shops, game stores, conventions, and other spaces (including workplaces; see Eglash 2002) associated with geek culture report being required to authenticate their membership in ways that men, generally speaking, are not.[6] What continues to be withheld is the right to be an unremarkable or "normal" member: "If the goal is for female comic creators and fans to become more than an industrial niche or surplus audience, to become invisible (read: accepted) members of that culture, increased visibility will be necessary to encourage that shift" (Scott 2013b, ¶3.6). If they are not taken as Fake Geek Girls, they were likely to be miscategorized as the girlfriend, wife, or mother of a male participant who has somehow dragged them there.

Many people I spoke with would speak of "guys" who had to sell off their collections or stop playing games with their friends because they'd married and of "bored girlfriends" being dragged along to conventions. As Hank put it, "A role-playing game is so much time to invest [...] *Wives* don't like that." Meanwhile, Mr Fox described a gaming session cancelled because one of the players had to celebrate his "year-and-a-half anniversary," which Mr Fox described as a pseudo-event and the "girlfriend's idea." Indeed, jokes about "wives and girlfriends" that would have been tired in 1950s sitcoms were still current features of conversation in comic shops and at game days while I was conducting field research. When I was interviewing Scott at Eastside Games & Comics, we started talking about age differences and life stages among gamers and comic fans. He cracked a joke, which led to a riff between him and two customers who were hanging around at the time:

SCOTT: Nerds start when they're kids, and they end when they die.
BEN: Okay. Um –
SCOTT: Or when they get married.
DOUG: Yeah.
SAM: And have to sell their collections because their wife doesn't like looking at the miniatures.
DOUG: No, that's true.
SAM: ((shrill voice)) "You spent how much money on these!?"
SCOTT: So, like, the marriage age is the time that you start having ... Like, you have a little garden of nerds. They start [as] little children, and then women come in and they kill lots of them. And some of them keep growing into big nerds, but many of them are taken away and re-planted in the married-with-kids garden.
SAM: It's a sad garden.
SCOTT: It's a ((laughs)) fucking sad garden.
SAM: Full of wilted flowers.
SCOTT: Full of wilted flowers that are stomped on by little children who don't care.

Along with the assumption that the default geek is male, this idea that women "spoil the fun" is one of the most basic and pervasive forms of sexism I observed in geek culture. The women of this discourse are not actually existing women, only stand-ins upon which male geeks project their ambivalence towards adulthood's responsibilities, but the discursive alignment of women with the "real life" responsibilities that constrain participation (ch. 7) is troubling. This framing of women participants not only tends to produce condescension towards them but also aids and abets harassment by excluding them a priori as legitimate members of the community of practice and attributing ulterior motives to them. Certainly, the ease with which Gamergaters and others have been able to portray women, people of colour, and sexual minorities as outsiders trying to meddle with or impose some nefarious "agenda" on geek culture owes something to this rhetorical tradition.

Play: It's All Fun and Games Until ...

From message board trolls to comment section flame wars, it has long been common to attribute the vitriolic nature of much online interaction to the anonymity that the medium affords its users. This explanation, favoured by scholars, journalists, and laypeople alike, was infamously expressed as an arithmetic formula in a *Penny Arcade* comic strip, where a "normal person" given an audience to perform in front of from behind a screen of anonymity results in a "total fuckwad" (Krahulik and Holkins 2004). While anonymity may be a necessary condition, it is hardly sufficient to explain the periodic eruptions of bile and spleen to which the Internet is subject. On the one hand, early theorists of online interaction believed that, under different circumstances, the anonymity of the computer-mediated communication could open up to progressive possibilities for identity construction. On the other hand, more people are using their real names on the web than ever before without a notable impact on the quality of digital discourse. Something else is missing from "John Gabriel's Greater Internet Fuckwad Theory," namely, the "play element" of online culture (Huizinga 1949).

Play, in order to be play, requires the creation of a special space. Johan Huizinga (1949, 10) called it a "magic circle." On the playground, like any other consecrated space, the rules of "so-called real life" are displaced by the rules of a game, even one as simple as "let's pretend." The boxing ring, for example, establishes a magic circle within which it is not only acceptable but desirable and laudable to punch someone (77). The double vision of play, what Michael Saler (2004) calls an "ironic imagination," is central to the intellectual enjoyment of geek culture's immersive narrative worlds. But as Elizabeth Losh (2016) argues, the magic circle must be defended from reality. For instance, when debating the rules of a tabletop wargame, one customer at began to justify his argument with an appeal to realism, to which another customer responded by crying out, "Don't bring reality in!"[7] Similarly, the threatening and harassing behaviour associated with Gamergate and other more or less organized groups of Internet trolls can be understood as attempts to defend gaming as a "zone of exception," a space that is perceived to be free of politics: "Social justice warriors must be treated as aggressors to be repulsed by Gamergaters from the magic circles of game worlds in order to reclaim these spaces and return them to their proper exceptional status and thus maintain their security from real-world incursions" (Losh 2016).

However, it is not only that video games (or comic books or cinematic properties like *Star Wars* and *Ghostbusters* or others) represent, as immersive and enchanting worlds, a magic circle but also that the acts of harassment themselves may constitute a perverse form of play. Psychologist John Suler (2004) speculates that one factor (among several) contributing to the "online disinhibition effect" is the dissociation of "virtual" acts from "real" consequences: "Consciously or unconsciously, people may feel that the imaginary characters they 'created' exist in a different space, that one's online persona along with the online others live in a make-believe dimension, separate and apart from the demands and responsibilities of the real world. They split or dissociate online fiction from offline fact" (323). Or, as Whitney Phillips (2015, 34) argues based on interviews with participants in "troll" culture: "The vast majority of trolls I've worked with […] insist that their troll selves and their offline ('real') selves are subject to totally different sets of rules." That is to say, trolling behaviour is real, but it is not indicative of their *real self*. It is, rather, a kind of avatar or character taken up within the "play frame" Phillips refers to as the "troll mask."

Take, for instance, the statements about "wives and girlfriends" quoted above. When asked explicitly to talk about gender and geek identity, people typically gave much more "politically correct" responses. Retailers, in particular, were usually careful to emphasize that geek culture was for everyone – it was, after all, in their material interest to do so. In retrospect, they might well be horrified with what they said. Yet within a joking "play frame" – the joke as a language-game unfolding within magical, ironizing quotation marks that set it apart from discourse that expresses their real self – they took up a normatively male avatar and were willing to express sentiments that seem, with the benefit of hindsight, quite sexist. Games are, at base, technologies that configure agency. Adopting a play frame is a way of displacing the ordinary rules of everyday life, which offer certain, circumscribed possibilities for agency, with another set, which offer different possibilities. To describe trolling, harassment, and other antisocial features of contemporary geek culture as a kind of game is by no means to excuse or trivialize it – these are, after all, people who take games very seriously – but it helps us to understand how investments in fantasy and play can have very real effects.

I was in grade 10 the year of the Columbine massacre. I remember how my school's own small "trench coat mafia" suddenly went from being mostly ignored to the subject of intense scrutiny from administration. The way they dressed, the music they listened to, and the video games they played were enough to make them seem dangerous, and some of them expressed themselves in ways that flirted with a "militarized masculinity" (Kline, Dyer-Witheford, and de Peuter 2003) familiar from, for instance, the fictionalized portrayal of the Columbine shooters in *Elephant* (Gus Van Sant 2003). Because I played *Dungeons & Dragons* with a couple of guys in that group, I often ate lunch with them, though I rarely socialized outside of school with the rest. I didn't share their taste for military fatigues or their interest in guns. I was more of a classic nerd, highly invested in academics and formal extracurricular activities (the only time I wore a trench coat was playing a detective in the school play). What we shared was a feeling of alienation from a school culture that prized sports and displays of piety that seemed to us – with all of our teenaged insight into the human condition – hypocritical and insincere. However different we may have been from one another, we were united by our felt experience of difference from the normative high school student of our teachers, administrators, and peers – Burke's (1969) doctrine of consubstantiality in practice.

The vagaries of (micro)politics continue to make strange bedfellows. On 23 October, 2016, as America's attention was split between a spate of athletes refusing to stand during "The Star-Spangled Banner" in solidarity with the Black Lives Matter movement, on the one hand, and the eruption into mainstream political discourse of a new strain of far-right ideologies incubated in the dankest recesses of Reddit and 4chan, on the other hand, R.S. Benedict (@RS_Benedict) tweeted a wry rejoinder to the conventional wisdom of the triumphant narrative of geek culture:

> football jocks: peacefully protesting against racism
> nerds: becoming internet nazis
> teen movies were wrong
> nerds are garbage
> jocks are good

But, taken as an essentializing statement, this is as problematic as naïve narratives of geeky underdogs getting their revenge. It is more complicated than either scenario. There is, not to put too fine a point on it, a battle going on for the soul of geek culture.

It is in the nature of social groups to erect boundaries – the "figure" of the in-group requires the "ground" of an out-group – and this goes double for the groups we have conventionally labelled subcultures, which may be united by nothing but a culturally arbitrary boundary with a so-called mainstream (Thornton 1996; Muggleton 2000). As I argued of the shifting referents of "nerd" and "geek" (ch. 1), such boundaries are contextual and even tactical. The object of "classification struggle" (Bourdieu 2010), they may be adjusted so as to embrace new "members" when situations demand particular alliances, or they can be defensive and reactionary (ch. 6). Indeed, "geekdom is actually constituted by these ongoing struggles," struggles between a conception of geekiness as an exclusive "category based on one's knowledge of trivia or rejection of the mainstream" or an inclusive one "based on a love of sharing" (Reagle 2015, 2874, 2873). I have suggested that the distinctive subcultural form of geek culture – the particular configuration of goods, values, people, and institutions that makes it *geek* culture – is a container for the true substance of every subculture: communication and community-making (Woo 2015; see also Pilkington and Omel'chenko 2013). Yet it seems just as obvious that, for some who identify with the conventionalized representations of geeks as straight, white, heterosexual men who are good with computers, obsessive about pop culture, and awkward around girls, geek culture has become little more than a vehicle for their ressentiment. At one level, this seems like the classic Manichean choice between good and evil, between the light and dark sides of the Force.

I know who I want to win. An open, inclusive version of geek culture that makes space for and celebrates difference strikes me as infinitely preferable to a narrow, backward-looking, angry and resentful one. But my mind also turns back to my lunch crowd in high school. I've lost touch with them and wouldn't want to presume anything about the paths their lives have taken since then, but back then they might have sympathized with the Gamergaters and anti-SJW arguments – as might I. To an extent, that's what gives me hope. Practice theory is necessarily anti-essentialist, and it follows from my account that geek culture isn't any one thing. It's neither the seething stew of sociopathy nor the waypoint en route to an enlightened future that it has, at various times, been imagined to be. As a scene of practice, geek culture is perpetually reproduced and remade: just as fans' creator-oriented consumption can result in thrilling forms of vernacular creativity *or* witch-hunts against perceived desecrators of canon; just as the "backstage" camaraderie of the game shop or comic store can be extended to welcome new participants *or* turned into a clubhouse for the same old cohort of aging fanboys; and just as playfulness and imagination can enchant our experience of everyday life through immersive fantasies *or* dissociate us from the consequences of our actions towards vulnerable people and communities, we ought not to give up on geek culture.   .

Conclusion

Lock your windows! Bolt your doors! Guard your children! Anything can happen when these four youths come together! For they are – The Eltingville Comic Book, Science-Fiction, Fantasy, Horror, and Role-Playing Club!

These words introduce the first of Evan Dorkin's Eltingville Club comic strips, which appeared sporadically over a dozen years in anthologies like *Instant Piano* and Dorkin's own *Dork*, as well as a limited series, and were eventually collected into a single volume by Dark Horse Comics (Dorkin 2016). The eponymous club, which comprised four officers but no other members, was fractious and vulgar. They fought constantly in public, and they tormented one another in secret. Everything became a competition, and their macho posturing over trivia and collectibles did nothing to cover up the stew of adolescent sexual frustration that defined their young lives. Wherever they went, their uncontrollable enthusiasm resulted in property damage and horrific injury. Dorkin is a devotee of Will Elder's "chicken fat" school of cartooning (see Dorkin 2008), and he fills the backgrounds of his panels in much the same way his characters lard their dialogue with references to cult media. But in Dorkin's hands the chicken fat has gone rancid: rendered in all their pimply, scabrous glory by his scratchy, aggressive line and gift for exaggerated facial expressions and body language, there is something primally repellant about them and the world they inhabit. As Dorkin himself suggests in the collection's afterword, the socially, sexually, and morally retarded members of the Eltingville Club represent the very worst features of a specific version of fandom: "*Eltingville* was about the shitty fans [...] Endlessly irritated, incredibly obnoxious, masters of trivia no one else gave a shit about, members of a special club of know-it-all nimrods who bitched about why so many people disregarded fandom as silly, stupid, and immature, all while doing everything they could to make fandom look silly, stupid, and immature" (2016, 124). Many details from the strips are drawn from real life, and the characters themselves are "composites" of Dorkin's boyhood friends. "The arguments, the pettiness, the obsessiveness, the fighting – that's all based on us and our idiocy," just turned up to eleven (124).

However, Dorkin (2016, 124) wants to establish a red line between his own adolescent "idiocy," which never extended to hate mail or harassment, and contemporary online fandom. Explaining why the collection represents the end of the Eltingville Club in his afterword, Dorkin writes: "Geek culture has exploded in the years since the first Eltingville Club meeting was called to order, and unfortunately, so has the outrageous behavior *Eltingville* made fun of." The comic was "not born out of love, but of anger" (123), and the strips become increasingly bleak over time. One gets the sense that Dorkin is just exhausted and depressed by the real-life material he would be required to satirize in order to continue it. Yet his cynicism owes something to the eternal present he has enforced on his strip. For instance, the series conclusion, "Lo, There Shall Be an Epilogue!" sees the Eltingville Club reunite after ten years at the San Diego Comic-Con with inevitably disastrous results, but both the sides of the time skip are full of contemporary cultural references. The characters never change, even as the real-life reference points of fandom change around them. It's absolutely true that Bill, Josh, Pete, and Jerry seem likely candidates for the kind of ressentiment-driven identity politics discussed in chapter 8, but we never see the other, increasingly diverse face of fandom in the world of the Eltingville Club. And I think that if the strips merely aired the worst behaviour of the worst fans, they would not have had the success they did (i.e., enough to last twelve years, have a pilot for an animated series produced, and finally be collected in a hardback volume). There is, despite Dorkin's manifest intentions, still something oddly endearing about the Eltingville Club.

In one strip, "The Intervention," President and Secretary of Comic Books Bill Dickey is kidnapped by two men his mother hired to "save him from fandom" (Dorkin 2016, 48). Tied to a chair in his own basement, Bill ends up in a tense psychological standoff with his captors and would-be saviours, Steve and Jeffrey. They are themselves ex-fans who got rid of their collectibles, started working out, grew ponytails, and made "the journey from fandom – to what we like to call – mandom" (50), and their appeal to Bill is to shed the stigma of geek culture:

Figure 4   "What do *I* say?" In "The Intervention," Eltingville Club president Bill Dickey rejects the efforts of fandom de-programmers Scott and Jeffrey (Dorkin 2016, 55).

"I know, Bill. We both know. It's not much fun being the local 'comic book geek,' is it? The '*Star Trek* nerd'? The 'role-playing game loser'? Do you know why you role-play, Bill? Because you don't like yourself [...] That's why you need your little dice and your little lead figures and your little online games – so you can become someone you do like, someone who goes places, does things, dates!" (55). Yet Bill refuses to yield to their various deprogramming strategies, using pop culture quotes and singing cartoon theme songs to resist. In the end, he wears them down, and in their moment of weakness reminds them that, while "real life is pain and sadness," geek culture offers an alternative:

> But fandom is whatever you want it to be! It's unity! Community! And above all, it's a team, like the Justice League or the Avengers! And when Hawkeye quits the team like an asshole, the Avengers always take him back because deep down he's one of them! And you're one of us! Yes, beneath the muscles and bullshit you're still fans!! [...] So what do you say, effendi? Captain America – or Nomad? Will you face front and live long and prosper, or cover your eyes with the vale of fucking tears known as a "normal life"! Just say the magic word, brothers! Say the word with me!! Excelsior! (57)

Although Bill is often portrayed as the worst of the four club members, this speech provides the comic strip's strongest, most unequivocal argument for the positive benefits of participating in fandom. In his own way, Bill is making much the same argument that I have in this book. In the final instance geek culture isn't about the comics, the games, the costumes or the toys; it isn't about the trivia or pop culture references; it's about finding and making a community. Of course, no good deed goes unpunished: after Bill welcomes Steve and Jeffrey back into the warm embrace of fandom, they leave him tied up and loot his collection to start rebuilding their own.

They say that living well is the best revenge, and notwithstanding Dorkin's protests, there has probably never been a better time to be a geek. The media system whose products we spent so much time and energy obsessing over is now returning the favour. Whereas "cult" media once had to be rescued from the dustbin of popular culture, today the themes and tropes of geek culture – space opera, high fantasy, robots, psychics, and zombies – are all over mainstream mass media, and high-gloss remakes or continuations of cult classics are a dime a dozen. Arguably, the entertainment industries in general have become reliant on fan communities for support, as they once provided support for more marginal, geeky properties like *Star Trek* (Meehan 2000). As a result, more resources are being deployed to understand and appeal to fannish audiences (see, e.g., Kohnen 2014), and more of the cultural industries' outputs are being oriented to properties with an already proven base of enthusiastic and dedicated fans – that is, to geek culture. Some of today's most prominent media brands and franchises have been left in the care of "fanboy auteurs" (Scott 2013a), and the performance of authentic appreciation, if not outright fandom, by on-camera talent is increasingly the rule rather than the exception. Having drafted this reserve army of audience labour, these brands have gone on to conquer a wider range of media, being exploited simultaneously in film and TV, as tie-in novels and comic books, as analogue and digital games, and as t-shirts, action figures, and every sort of licensed product.

At the same time, the condition that Patton Oswalt (2010) christened ETEWAF (or, "Everything That Ever Was, Available Forever") has created a playground for the cultish media consumer. Virtually any cultural good you could ever desire can be looked up on Wikipedia, ordered from Amazon, streamed on YouTube or Netflix, or if all else fails, torrented. In the rare case that something is truly inaccessible, you can probably find a forum of likeminded folks with whom you can sing its praises. The ability to cut popular culture into ever finer categories and nonetheless connect with other aficionados online or at one of the many specialized conventions that have popped up across North America means that no one has to feel like a weird loner – or at least not all the time.

For the dedicated subcultural consumer of science fiction, comics books, games, and other geeky media, this is undoubtedly the best of all possible worlds. But perhaps more significantly, people outside of geek culture seem newly interested in it as a socio-cultural phenomenon. As their cities are subjected to annual invasions by cosplayers during convention season, their multiplexes are overrun with heroes in skin-tight uniforms and CGI superpowers, and new cultural idioms are dredged up from the depths of Tumblr and 4chan like bizarre denizens of the aphotic zone, people have been confronted by something in need of explanation – hence, all the "triumph of the nerds" trendpieces. In the absence of a single, simple, and compelling explanation of geek culture (if such a thing could ever exist), it has functioned as mirror and screen for mainstream publics. Lurking behind much of the popular discourse about geeks and nerds is an intuition that they represent something important about life in our society today, about the kinds of people we are becoming in a media-saturated, hyper-connected, and thoroughly commodified culture. Geek culture has become a subject of significant public interest precisely because it can be made to serve as a focal point for a series of key tensions in contemporary culture.

One set of such tensions use geeks and nerds to contrast utopian and dystopian interpretations of contemporary media practices: as media fans, are they affirmational or transformative? As dwellers in the world of things, are they consumers or makers? And, as users of networked communication technologies, do they constitute a culture of democratic participation or a digital mob of trolls and harassers? An important recent development in fan studies has been the distinction, first introduced within fan communities themselves (Obsession_inc 2009), between affirmational and transformational fandom. In many ways, this parallels and updates a much older debate about the nature of media audiences – are we dupes who passively receive media messages, or are we active and even resistive makers of meaning? But whereas the earlier version took fandom as the model for a pop-culture heterotopia where media texts and social norms were negotiated, challenged, and reconfigured (see, e.g., Fiske 1992b; Jenkins 1988, 2013), the more recent incarnation recognizes that not all fan activity is created equal and that there are competing interests at play in defining who is a "good" fan. The transformational fan is the one we all know and love: the oppositional reader, the media audience's organic intellectual, the cultural studies scholar in the wild. The affirmational fan, by contrast, is a repository of many of the "pathological" behaviours or stereotypes that fan studies has worked hard to deny: compulsive consumption, slavish devotion to authorial intention, and obsessive cataloguing of trivia, Easter eggs, and goofs (see Geraghty 2014; Hills 2014a). This kind of fan activity, it is argued, aligns with the interests of media companies and tends to be encouraged by them, while transformational fans are policed in order to maintain authorial/corporate control over the media brand. The metastasis of what Matt Hills (2005, 45) has called "new hegemonic fandom" throughout our culture – that is, the juxtaposition of an expectation that everyone is geeky about something alongside the persistent suspicion of immersive, obsessive relationships with media – raises the question of what kind of fans we will be. Talk about geek culture, about "nice nerds" and "troglodytes," is one way that this question can be addressed. And, insofar as the speakers are not themselves members of geek culture as traditionally conceived (though they may be wine or finance geeks; Smith 2007), this subculture can serve as an alter ego, an "anti-them" through which they can explore questions of identity "without directly discussing any sense of self" (Hills 2005, 40). Admiration and disdain for the cultural practices of geeks and nerds and the symbolic boundaries that these emotional responses create index the aspirations and anxieties with which media consumption, more broadly, is saddled.

The oppositions between activity and passivity or conformity and rebelliousness that shape views of geek culture as a site of media fandom are paralleled in terms of members' relationship to the material world. On the one hand, nerds represent the ideal consumer: early adopters of consumer technologies while they're still buggy and expensive; dedicated audience members who will proselytize on behalf of a media franchise, follow it across platforms, and stick with it through all its iterations, no matter how terrible; enthusiasts willing to spend their own time and resources to add value to brands; and collectors who will absorb the supply of licensed merchandise. But, on the other hand, geek culture has been persistently associated with tinkerers, crafters, and makers, from ham radio and model rocket enthusiasts to early war and role-playing game players, from the hobbyists that made up the Homebrew Computer Club to the cosplayers that display their creations at comic-book and anime conventions around the world. The desire to take something apart, see how it works, and adapt it to new purposes – to hack both material and symbolic goods – runs deep in many geek culture communities. As a result, geek culture seems to offer a bridge between the romantic, anti-capitalist traditions of craft and vernacular creativity – a tradition with roots in Morris, John Ruskin, and the Arts and Crafts Movement, as well as the 1960s back-to-the-land counterculture (see, e.g., Gauntlett 2011) – and our own, high-tech age. Filtered through Silicon-Valley discourses of entrepreneurialism, disruption, and the like, there is no necessary contradiction between following your bliss and following the money. Performances of nerdiness are not only a gateway into technology careers, as Ron Eglash (2002) would have it, but also an alibi for the concentration of obscene profits in this sector of the economy. The framing of figures like Bill Gates, Steve Wozniak, and Mark Zuckerberg as nerds enables us to imagine them as "accidental billionaires," to borrow the title of Ben Mezrich's (2009) book on the founding of Facebook. Unlike the rapacious robber barons and fat-cat capitalists of the old economy, they simply indulged their passion for technology and only "accidentally" accrued vast fortunes.

There are also significant questions about the kind of activity that will characterize the network society. Will the emergent cultures of the Internet and social media be utopias of democratic participation and cooperation or anarchic dystopias of harassment and violence? For scholars of new media practices, such as Henry Jenkins (2006, 2008), Mizuko Ito (Ito et al. 2010), and Clay Shirky (2010), networked communities of fans, gamers, and the geeks who brought us lolcats have provided windows into the emerging genres of participation that could reshape our society. Jenkins's conceptions of "participatory culture" (2013) and "convergence culture" (2008) have been particularly influential in this respect, and they bear the inescapable imprint of geek culture. Active, enthusiastic media fans have long stood as both a limit case of and a normative ideal for media consumers in general, though the extent to which most audience members engage in similar practices has always been questionable. Indeed, I would question whether the "core media literacy skills" identified as necessary prerequisites for life in the culture of new media (Jenkins et al. 2009) can be taught or learned outside of the situated social practices that make them meaningful and the communities like gaming guilds, *Survivor* spoilers, and the Harry Potter Alliance that value them as internal goods. Yet there is also the dark side of new media practices that must be reckoned with. The same technologies around which new participatory cultures are emerging also facilitate a host of anti-social behaviours. When largely contained within particular forums, online communities and game environments, these activities are described with terms like "flaming," "griefing," and "trolling," though they have recently shown a stubborn tendency to escape from these spaces. As Anita Sarkeesian put it in an interview with Jessica Valenti (2015) in the *Guardian*, "I don't like the words 'troll' and 'bully' – it feels too childish. This is harassment and abuse." Digital networked technologies may unlock a new "cognitive surplus" (Shirky 2010) or "collective intelligence" (Levy 1997; Jenkins 2008), but how these new intellectual resources will be mobilized – to give voice or to silence, to include or to exclude – remains an unanswered question.

Another tension or contradiction surrounding geek culture hinges on the future and the past. Geeks and nerds are often imagined as sources of new things – of new technologies and new ideas. There is, for instance, a recurring narrative about scientists trying to make real what sci-fi authors have imagined – a future of space exploration, of self-driving or flying cars, of intelligent computers that can understand our speech, gestures, and desires and that can be carried around in our pockets. In a somewhat different way, the recent vogue for wonkish policy journalism and complex statistical modelling in election coverage, striving as they do towards the ideals of Isaac Asimov's fictional social science of psychohistory, suggests that sufficiently sober, objective analysis of available data can use what we know of the past to help us tame the future (especially if formatted in cool infographics). This is rivalled only by the use of science fiction thinking – in some cases by actual science fiction writers (Schroeder 2011) – as a planning tool in business and policy development under the guise of another "SF," strategic foresight. There is something about the combination of rigorous, logical thinking and unbound imagination that provides fertile ground for such forays into anticipating the future.

But while they are associated with the future, geeks are also defined by a particular relationship with the past – in particular, with their own pasts. On this view, far from a resource for the future, geek culture is a kind of time trap. The remakes and adaptations that dominate film and television today are not only products of an industrial strategy to leverage audiences' familiarity with these brands and properties but are, for already dedicated fans, also evidence of an overwhelming nostalgia for childhood. The problematic dimensions of this obsession with the past is underscored in an insightful review of Ernest Cline's novel *Armada* by the games and comics journalist Laura Hudson (2015). *Armada*, like Cline's previous novel, *Ready Player One*, is erected on top of a network of intertextual references that will be familiar to nerds of a certain vintage: "Barely a page goes by without a reference to *Star Wars*, *Dungeons & Dragons*, *Flight of the Navigator*, *Transformers*, *Starfox*, *Space Invaders*, *Zero Wing*, *Iron Eagle*, *Star Trek*, and on and on and on [...] *Armada* is a book designed entirely around getting the reference – high-fiving the readers who recognize its shoutouts while leaving everyone else trapped behind a nerd-culture velvet rope of catchphrases and codes." While I have discussed referencing as a game that enables its players to demonstrate their subcultural capital, it may also play a more personal function, indexing the speakers' biographies as much as a textual system. To Hudson, wallowing in the past like this results in "boring, self-indulgent, and regressive" art. As Adorno says of the emptiness of value judgments about music: "The familiarity of the piece is a surrogate for the quality ascribed to it. To like it is almost the same thing as to recognize it" (2001, 30). Redirected into an endless cycle of nostalgia and self-congratulation, the reference becomes a dead end rather than an entrée to active, creative engagement with media: "It's a valuable question for gaming culture – and 'nerd culture' more generally – to ask itself: Do we want to tell stories that make sense of the things we used to love, that help us remember the reasons we were so drawn to them, and create new works that inspire that level of devotion? Or do we simply want to hear the litany of our childhood repeated back to us like an endless lullaby for the rest of our lives?" (Hudson 2015). On this view, geek culture possesses not the wide-eyed innocence of youth but a wilful infantilism. Thus, its prominence in social commentary today has a connection with hand-wringing discourses of arrested development, prolonged adolescence, and merely "emerging" adulthood (Arnett 2000), a tradition of thinking that reaches back to Postman's (1994) arguments about the end of childhood – and therefore also of adulthood – as a distinct life stage. To mainstream commentators and many social scientists, geeks may be emblematic of postmodern anomie and narcissism, of the retreat into narrow enclaves based on lifestyles and hobbies – sad little men in their parents' basements obsessing over, in Hank's words, "the most useless trivia out there."

Over the last decade, the social type of the geek or nerd was cata-
pulted to new prominence because it could perform a certain kind
of work. Talk about nerds and geeks opened up a discursive space
where anxieties and hopes about media consumption, technology,
and society could be ranged against one another and resolved, if only
ever "magically" (Cohen 2005). While I detected echoes of these discourses during the research for this book – my informants are, after
all, also participants in the broader public sphere where these tensions are being aired – my findings provide few answers about these
concerns. That's because, in a very real sense, much of the contemporary interest in geek culture isn't really about geeks at all; it's about
everyone else.

Consequently, this book has attempted to get beyond the superficial
accounts associated with the "revenge of the nerds" and "geek chic" discourses. Instead, I wanted to build a new account of geek culture that
would also address how (some) ordinary people relate to media and
cultural goods today. In order to do this, I started locally, identifying
the spaces and institutions associated with nerds and geeks in one city.
These spaces played host to a tremendous amount of activity. In unas-
suming storefronts behind sun-bleached promotional posters, in hotel
ballrooms set up with gaming tables, in convention centres packed to
the rafters with amateur artists and costumed fans, and in small groups
of friends meeting in living rooms across the city to talk and play, I
found an awful lot going on.

While in some ways examples of "ethereal cultures" (Kinkade and Katovich 2009), they also evinced high levels of commitment and engagement. People had to organize and marshal resources to make these
activities available, and most events had their regulars and habitués as
well as one-off attendees. Tracing the connections between these institutions and the people who circulated between them around the city, I
found myself looking at a network of cultural activity that expressed the
dynamic, effervescent sociality associated with scenes (Straw 1991;
Shank 1994; Blum 2001; Woo, Poyntz, and Rennie 2016). Participants
took these activities very seriously. More than mere recreation, serious
leisure offers a kind of *re-creation* through which participants cultivate an
identity and ethos (Stebbins 1982, 257). Indeed, as Alasdair MacIntyre
(2007) argues, social practices like these are the fundamental frameworks
in which we articulate conceptions of the good and develop the dispositions that will help us to achieve them. As such, they are intimately
connected with processes of valuation and connect their participants to

one another in communalized social relationships. For many, these are not passing fancies but represent investments of care and limited resources in people and communities that unfold over years and even decades.

"Get a life."

Typing these words, my lip almost involuntarily curls into a sneer. It's that kind of a phrase. The *Oxford English Dictionary* defines the slang construction "to get a life" as "to adopt a more worthwhile and meaningful lifestyle, especially by making new acquaintances or developing new interests, or by abandoning pointless or solitary pursuits" ("life, n." 2009) Implicitly, then, the subject to whom it is addressed leads a worthless and meaningless existence, his enchantment with pointless and solitary pursuits leaving him sad and alone. In the imperative, it functions as a command to "stop being so boring, conventional, old-fashioned, etc.; start living a fuller or more interesting existence."

The basic sentiment should be familiar to anyone who is invested in something that other people just don't get. But thanks in part to William Shatner's 1986 appearance on *Saturday Night Live* – and, for audience and fan studies scholars, to Henry Jenkins's (2013) discussion of the same in *Textual Poachers* – the imperative "get a life" does not address just any "pointless" pursuit. Rather, it has become indelibly associated with science-fiction fans, gamers, comic-book collectors, techies, and those who care deeply about the minutiae of popular culture. It is something that gets said to the people we call geeks and nerds. This is the same argument Steve and Jeffrey put to Bill Dickey in "The Intervention" (Dorkin 2016, 55): "It's not much fun being the local 'comic book geek,' is it? The '*Star Trek* nerd?' The 'role-playing game loser?'" Wouldn't you rather be "someone who goes places, does things, dates?"

Yet the judgment this statement entails is profoundly unjust. Spending time at stores like King St Comics and Plaza Games and events organized by Screens & Sorcery and the Alternate Universe Club, observing how people used these spaces, and talking with people like Barry and Shiera, Diana and Wedge, Solo and Mr Fox about what their fandom has meant to them, I saw firsthand just how wrong it is. Geeks are not compensating for some absence of meaning at the heart of modern life, and geek culture is not a substitute for "a fuller or more interesting existence." On the contrary, they were making meaning in, through, and around their relationships with media and cultural goods – if anything, the contemporary excitement for all things geeky and the appropriation of the term outside of traditionally nerdy practices demonstrates that they're on to something special.

Geeks don't need to get a life. They already have one.

Participant Profiles

This appendix contains brief profiles of study participants and research sites. These are intended to act as a reference for the reader and to provide additional, contextual information for the extracts used elsewhere. Participants were given an opportunity to review their profile for factual accuracy, though not all responded.

The first phase of research included four organizations and five retail stores. Primary informants, site type, year of founding or establishment, location type, and key activities of all nine sites are summarized more schematically in Table 1 (21). In the project's second phase, I worked with six main informants. All names are pseudonyms; some participants selected their own code name, while others expressed no preference. They are listed here in alphabetical order. Key information is summarized in Table 2 (23).

PHASE 1: ORGANIZATIONS AND RETAIL STORES

Screens & Sorcery

Screens & Sorcery was a registered non-profit society that produced events for local geeks. At the time of data collection, most events were built around screenings and augmented with live performances and participatory activities of various types. They included *Star Trek* and *Ghostbusters* mini-conventions, a festival of Hayao Miyazaki films, a science documentary, and a popular series of screenings where attendees watch old cartoons in their pyjamas.

The group's president, Logan, and two friends originally came together in 2008 to organize an event with horror writer H.P. Lovecraft's "Cthulhu mythos" as its theme. Afterwards, the three organizers decided to form a more permanent group. As Logan said in an interview, "I just like getting people together for nerdy stuff. I feel like [sports fans] have their playoffs and they have their venues […] so I guess I kind of felt there was this hole that needed to be filled for getting nerds together." The original organizers recruited a group of officers, volunteers were also recruited for help with promotion and running larger events, and the group was eventually registered as a non-profit society. This suggests a level of professionalization that – while pursued in order to reduce the officers' workload – was not routinely attained. Staff meetings had an informal and chummy tone and were frequently interrupted for unrelated conversation. Furthermore, in interview, Logan espoused values of amateurism ("I do find that a couple of people might show up and complain about a certain level of professionalism with our ticket handling or whatever, but, really, we're not hiring people. It's just a group of friends who are doing this") and indicated that tasks were delegated on a relatively ad hoc basis ("If a person's really busy, then they're not going to be able to do the stuff that needs to get done for that responsibility, so we just kind of hash it out").

Although the group has faced numerous constraints, it successfully combined audiences from a number of different constituent communities. This is most evident in the sponsorship and cross-promotional agreements the group secured with a variety of subcultural businesses and organizations, both locally and outside of the local scene, including comic book and game stores, conventions, role-playing and video game developers and publishers, a local chapter of an international computer graphics society, and the National Film Board of Canada. Although these partnerships represented the considerable social capital of group organizers, they also suggest that media fandom – most especially for texts that evoke nostalgia – provides a point of articulation for participants in the relatively diverse and independent communities that are associated with nerd culture. Screens & Sorcery used various means to promote its events. It was heavily reliant on social media, such as Facebook, and hired a postering service for major events. Volunteers also distributed flyers to subcultural businesses as well as cafés.

Events were initially all held at a small commercial movie theatre, for which one of the group's founding members works. However, renting the theatre proved too expensive in the long run for a venue with a much larger capacity than actually needed for most events. More recently, the cartoon screenings have taken place at an artist-run centre focusing on video art. These screenings have also become members-only in an effort to circumvent licensing requirements and provide access to the most popular vintage cartoons, many of which are not currently available commercially.

Alternate Universe Club

The Alternate Universe Club was a university club primarily focussed on anime fandom and gaming activities. During the period of data collection, regular activities included weekly screenings that were frequently followed by a social activity (e.g., dinner at a restaurant, bowling, laser tag, or karaoke); weekly gaming nights; and cosplay workshops that culminated in photo shoots of completed costumes. The primary informant, Bobby, was club president during data collection but subsequently resigned the office upon graduation.

Due to the high turnover inherent in university organizations, the club's history is not entirely clear. Anecdotal evidence suggested, however, that it began in the mid- or late 1970s as a gaming club. At some point in the mid- or late 1980s, the club began to embrace anime fans, though it is not clear whether members began to incorporate it into club activities or if there was a separate anime club that eventually merged with Alternate Universe Club. The emphasis between these two primary components of the club's "mandate" has shifted back and forth over time, but Bobby reported that "pretty much everybody is open to everything or was a fan of everything to begin with." As a university club, the ages of participants were relatively delimited. Many members either exhibited a shy and reserved interpersonal style or were effusive and acted out in a way reminiscent of a class-clown type. Meetings and events were always punctuated by shouted comments, often making media references.

The club's demographics were noteworthy in one respect: Bobby estimated that approximately 50 per cent of the club's members were women, and when he first joined the club had more female than male members. At early meetings I attended, the gender composition was less obvious – Bobby made an announcement at the year's first meeting to assure newcomers that "there are more girls in the club" – but over time, the gender ratio of attendees evened out. Bobby was concerned to portray it as a safe space for women fans and "not just composed of a bunch of creepy guys who just kind of sit around in a dark room all day." Women appeared active in all the major club activities, and several served as officers in the club executive. However, they tended to be quieter and were often overshadowed by louder, attention-seeking male members.

Club events and activities closely mirrored the articulation of interests common on nerdy web sites, and group members' interactions were funded by references to popular Internet memes. Bobby said: "If there's any alienating aspect to our club maybe it's the appreciation for Internet memes and Internet humour and keeping up with all the jokes related to that." In between officially programmed selections at the weekly screenings, members suggest short, humorous videos from YouTube. There was an aura of one-upmanship to the process, and suggestions were often preceded by the question, "Has anyone seen *x* yet?" – implying that members were connected to similar sources of information but that status came from being the first to find a particularly funny or interesting video.

It should also be noted that Anime Con, the city's anime and manga convention, began as an Alternate Universe Club event. Indeed, Bobby suggested that there was a period when the club's activities were primarily oriented towards mounting the convention. It has since operated as an almost entirely separate entity but had, until very recently, continued to use its connections with Alternate Universe Club to book space and audiovisual equipment from the University. The two groups had a falling out over finances, and Anime Con has moved on to other venues, though individual members still attend the con. Other than this, there were no formal links with other groups or agents in the local geek-culture scene.

King Con

King Con was a bimonthly, vendor-oriented comic convention held in a small community hall on a commercial high street. The building is owned by the city and has an exhibition space of approximately 3,000 sq. ft. Although there was a core of regular dealers, the number of exhibitors varied between conventions. Some were local comic-book stores liquidating excess inventory, some semi-professional dealers, and some just individuals selling off their collection. Although Peter will coach first-time exhibitors and "will happily discourage people from doing the show if [he doesn't] think they're going to make any money or if [he doesn't] think they've got product that people are going to want," he did not strictly curate the convention. Besides comic-book dealers, exhibitors at conventions I attended included a restaurant-review web site, a model-making club, and someone selling used records, DVDs, and sets of trading cards.

A high-school English teacher, Peter has been organizing these conventions since 1989. He said he made "a couple hundred bucks a show at the end of the year" from admission and exhibitors' fees, but he did not charge children for admission and always reserved an allotment of free tables for local artists – gestures that he saw as "ultimately good for comics." He also sold comics at his conventions, focusing on comics and graphic novels that appealed more to the casual attendee or new comic-book reader rather than to dedicated collectors of superhero comics. As a youth, Peter was a member of a comic-book club organized through a community centre. Club members began holding collectors' swap meets in the early to mid-1980s and eventually attempted to mount a larger convention, which was a financial failure. Under financial pressure, the group of enthusiasts "sort of imploded," but many of them remained in social contact. During the late 1980s and early 90s, comic books and trading cards were perceived as investments, and new shows were organized locally to take advantage of the "speculator boom." Peter described this as a time when "it became all about money and just how can you fuck people over for money," and he decided – "reluctantly" – to return to organizing conventions in order to provide something that was more oriented the needs of comic-book aficionados as well as more accessible to young fans.

Peter's business model relied on the conventions' small scale and high frequency, which reduce overhead costs. In addition to giving local creators an opportunity to promote their work, Peter booked established comic-book creators as guests to attract attendees. He was proud of the variety and importance of the guests that he has been able to host in the convention's twenty-year history, giving him the opportunity to meet and interact with creators he personally admired and to facilitate contact between local creators and established industry figures. Despite occasional pressure from exhibitors and members of the local comics community to expand or diversify the convention, Peter maintained its size and its focus on comic books, resisting, for example, overtures from TV and film actors that now make a living off the convention circuit. Shortly before the interview, he was approached by Conventions, Inc., a company that franchises comic-book conventions across the United States and Canada. It proposed to buy King Con and the rights to its name, retaining Peter as organizer for at least three years. He was, however, skeptical of Conventions, Inc., its "corporate" approach, and the impact of his decision on the dealers and creators with whom he had ongoing relationships.

King Con also hosts an annual convention for independent or alternative comics. The decision to create a differently branded convention for cartoonists working outside mainstream genre comics came after Peter experimented with booking small-press cartoonists for regular conventions and subsequently recognized that he was dealing with two relatively distinct segments within the local comics community. At the time of data collection, the small-press convention had been running for ten years with this artist-centric model, and Peter had produced two promotional comic books for it.

City Gaming Network

In a city where many game stores offer playing space and numerous groups organize events and conventions for gamers, City Gaming Network offered a way of networking local gamers, keeping them informed, and helping them to organize opportunities to play. The group originally began as Yahoo! Groups mailing list. Logan, a previous City Gaming Network board member, created the list in 1996 as a way of connecting with local gamers when he first moved to the city. The mailing list was initially advertised on notice boards in comic and game shops, which traditionally fulfilled the same role in the gaming community.

According to the group's president, Kurt, its "mission is to network people who play games in [the city] and area," and it did this by means of "a web site which offers people the ability to find other gamers [...] and meet up with them, as well as a kind of on-line marketplace allowing stores to post events and allowing us to talk about conventions." This forum was a later addition to the original mailing list. The group also hosted events: at their height, four conventions a year; at the time of data collection, conventions were held less regularly but periodic game days were held in several local game shops as well as a café. Network members also helped run gaming programming at other local conventions. Organizing these events relied on a loose body of volunteers who committed to helping with particular projects as they are interested. The group focused on tabletop role-playing games, but other forms of gaming were included in events to the extent that volunteers were willing to support them.

One distinctive aspect of City Gaming Network was the steps that had been taken to professionalize the group. In 2008, it was incorporated as a non-profit society, which obliged officers to hold annual general meetings, file annual reports, and follow various regulations concerning the group's finances. Additionally, Kurt facilitated an "appreciative inquiry visioning session" during their presidency: "One thing that I brought up is the need to have a definite vision and mission statement and a plan for how to actually achieve those things beyond just trusting that it would work out, which is how a lot of [...] clubs and organizations, especially hobby-related ones, seem to operate. It seems to be common-sense operations and not a lot of definite planning." This attempt to make the group's objectives explicit may also help it deal with what Kurt saw as a significant change in the gaming scene. City Gaming Network was created to help individuals find their way in local gaming communities when social media tools were still quite new, whereas at the time we spoke Kurt was concerned about the over-abundance of channels. So, they saw the Network's role as "connecting groups rather than trying to build up our own audience [...] I think that [there are] a lot of isolated niche groups and that working to support them and interconnect them would be really great." These comments suggested that City Gaming Network was entering a transition period that will force its organizers and members to re-evaluate its place in a more diverse scene. Although gamers' concrete practices – playing games with friends at home, in game stores, and at conventions – seem little changed, these activities could now be organized and facilitated in many different ways.

Westside Board Games

When we first spoke, John said to me, "Yeah, I'm a gamer. I mean, all gamers want to open a game store." He and his wife opened their game store in 2002. Westside Board Games quickly became one of the best-known game retailers in the area. The store was located on a quiet stretch of a well-known commercial high street in a relatively affluent neighbourhood. While it carried a range of traditional games, role-playing games, and collectible card games, the store's primary focus was on German- or European-style board games. A second location in a suburban community was opened in 2006.

John stressed that most Canadians have some exposure to games in childhood, and so he considered "normal" people to be potential gamers. Westside Board Games was intended to be a comfortable environment for casual, walk-in customers who may not be familiar with the various forms of hobby gaming. This emphasis was evident in the design and organization of the store. Its interior was divided into front and back by a small step down. The front area was organized around an "island" of games displayed on an Art Deco chest of drawers. The games shelved in this area were mostly the German-style board games that have become increasingly prominent in North American game stores in the last decade; some familiar, American-style games were in this area as well, and CCGs were shelved behind the counter.

The remaining components of Westside Board Games's product mix – RPG books, jigsaw puzzles, traditional games (chess, checkers, cribbage, and poker sets), and some board and card games that have a more niche appeal – were downstairs. The back area also featured several restaurant-style booths and a bookcase of board games that customers were encouraged to play. This space could be used by customers whenever the store was open, but Westside Board Games did not formally organize events for other kinds of games on a regular basis. Others occasionally make use of store space with the management's blessing (e.g., City Gaming Network sometimes ran game days here, and a group of teenagers were playing RPGs in a back room during participant-observation), but a weekly board game night was Westside Board Games's only regularly scheduled event.

These weekly game nights were well attended. They represented an opportunity to play a wide variety of board games with a pool of players for free and without obligation to buy. Groups of players tended to congregate around particular games and then recruit others to fill open seats (cf. Plaza Games, below). Although John did not have any direct evidence of a positive economic benefit from hosting these events, he said "it would be dumb to get rid of the tables to put more stock in," and one of his managers reported that he thought the events did result in sales. John has a group of friends who attended and with whom he often played. The store was open late and, after the paid staff members go off the clock, he would run things himself for the rest of the night, attending to customers between his own turns. The manager I spoke with estimated that 75 per cent of players any given week were regular participants and suggested that it was rare for newcomers not to become regulars ("So, you might not see them for a couple of weeks, but they'll be back"). Players often greeted one another by name, and I found it easier to gain access to games the second week that I attended.

Plaza Games

Unlike other retailers interviewed, Hank did not aspire to enter the games industry. However, upon visiting a shopping mall in the core of a growing suburban community, he began to consider going into business for himself. He said the mall lacked "a game store, a place for people to hang out," so Hank tapped into his experiences as a dedicated gamer with a personal collection of over 500 board games and opened Plaza Games in 2003 with "bringing back social interaction through board games and card games" as his mission statement.

According to Hank, Plaza Games was the largest board-game store in the province. He stocked newer, more specialist games as well as more familiar games from major North American publishers and a selection of "party" games. Plaza Games, like other game stores studied, provided space and open copies of games for patrons to try out prior to purchase. In addition, games could be "rented" by placing a down payment on the game, which would subsequently be deducted from the price of a new copy should the customer decide they liked it well enough to buy it. Collectible card games represented roughly 30 per cent of the store's revenue. Hank was initially reluctant to sell collectible games, which he called "paper crack" and "plastic crack," but eventually bent to customer demand. The store also carried smaller selections of role-playing game books and miniatures game accessories and a large stock of jigsaw puzzles. Sports cards, action figures, and miscellaneous small toys, games, and candies made up the rest of the store's inventory. All of these contributed an estimated 20 per cent of revenue.

Hank said the mall was missing "a place for people to hang out," and Plaza Games was an exceptionally sociable space. Although quiet during weekdays, the store hosted numerous events on evenings and weekends, including card game tournaments and release events as well as scheduled, drop-in sessions for board games, collectible miniatures games, and RPGs. The store's full schedule of events may introduce a tension between serving customers who are simply shopping (especially those unfamiliar with the hobby) and serving patrons who are participating in tournaments and game nights: "Unfortunately, they both come first, which is a contradiction. So, in other words, customers come first because I need to make money in order to sell things; *however*, the tournament comes first because I create an event for them to come in here and play, so I *will* have tables for them, I *will* do those pairings, I will do all that, too."

As long as high volume and overcrowding didn't become obstacles to routine business, Hank believed that boisterous groups of gamers visibly having fun created a spectacle that could draw foot traffic into the store. This may be attributable to its shopping-mall location, which was more open and visible to passersby than a standalone storefront. The mall also presented Hank with challenges, however, as when it arbitrarily moved the store across the mall and refused to post notices of its new location. At the time of data collection, Hank was anticipating being moved by mall management again. It was his hope that this would work to his advantage, allowing him a bigger space to expand his inventory, since he feared having to remove the play space in lieu of additional product if he was unable to grow. When I returned to Plaza Games a year later to drop off some recruiting materials for the second phase of the study, I found that the shop had indeed moved across the mall. The new space was larger, allowing Hank to keep table space for in-store events and expand his inventory. He mentioned that he now shelved games by publisher, rather than trying to group similar games together as he had previously done.

King St Comics

In many ways, King St Comics looked like a stereotypical comic book store: located on a commercial high street, the windows of its narrow storefront were papered over with superhero posters, and every inch of available space inside was filled with comic books, action figures, vinyl toys, art books, and t-shirts. Nevertheless, Warren did not consider his store a typical comic shop. Indeed, he contrasted it with Downtown Comics & Collectibles, which he believed served more traditional comic-book collectors: "There's a different vibe in a store like that. They're definitely more focussed on the hobby itself than they are on just, like, you know, people enjoying what they're reading and that kind of thing."

Warren described his career as a comic-book retailer as a "natural progression" and a "life-long dream." After gaining experience working in another comic shop, he opened King St Comics in 2002, using his own collection as the store's starting inventory. New, periodical comic books were ordered on the basis of anticipated demand and subscriptions; on the whole, however, inventory was selected on the basis of two principles, taste and variety. First, Warren's own taste helped him select products within the range of goods offered by Diamond Comic Distributors. Second, he hoped that maintaining a broad range of products ensured that "anybody that walks into the store, there's going to be something for *anybody*": "I guess I would just say that … as broad a selection of comic book or comic book related merchandise and uh … I guess not all of the action figures could be considered comic book related but, you know, that genre at least – science-fiction, fantasy. And, yeah, we just try to have as wide a variety as we possibly can." Indeed, the sign above the store described its wares as "comics, toys, and stuff" (somewhat unusually, King St did not participate in the gaming market to any significant degree). However, despite efforts to diversify his clientele by investing in action figures and t-shirts, regular purchasers of periodical comic books remained the staple of the business: "Well, I guess Wednesdays, obviously, we see the nerdier side, if you will. The hardcore comic-book fans […] Obviously, my bread and butter are the hardcore fans, so I much prefer days when my store is full of people who are more likely to actually *buy* something than a day when they're just kind of in here because they're curious about what's in here and they just wanted to check it out."

King St Comics was located in a rapidly gentrifying neighbourhood and surrounded by hip cafés and boutiques. It was thus well placed to benefit from the current mainstreaming of geek culture – and especially of pop-culture nostalgia – among young, media-savvy urbanites. Nevertheless, King St Comics faced both the typical challenges of a small business owner and the particular challenges associated with the comic-book industry's "direct marketing" model.

Eastside Games & Comics

Eastside Games & Comics originated with a game store located across town. In late 2007, Scott was recruited to work in a new location in the city's east end, having been recommended by the manager of another store where he frequently played games. This second location was in a basement suite below a comic book store; according to Scott, that shop's owners wished to enter the gaming market but lacked the capital and so invited Eastside's owner to rent the space below them. The two businesses later moved into a shared space and began to integrate their operations as Eastside Games & Comics, though the relationship between the two sides of the business – and their respective clienteles – was still a work in progress.

The location studied was nestled among a cluster of retail stores and fast-food restaurants between a residential neighbourhood and a light-industrial area. It was accessible by rapid transit and within walking distance of a college. Scott managed the gaming side of the business as well as the general operations of the store, while Alex managed the comic books and performed more clerk and cashier roles. Nathan, a co-owner of the comic-book side of the business, now managed the other location but still put shifts in at Eastside.

Like other game retailers interviewed, Scott's was committed to providing space for playing games. The store was neatly organized and uncluttered, and additional tables could be set up if needed. Scott's primary experiences as a gamer had been with miniatures games, and this was the genre in which the store most heavily invested. In addition to the miniatures themselves, building and painting supplies, and rule books for sale, plywood boards and pieces of model terrain were kept in the shop for game days. The store also sold and scheduled events for several collectible card games, including *Legend of the Five Rings*, which was less widely supported within the scene than other CCGs. Eastside also carried role-playing games, and Scott had plans to expand its range of board games in order to "increase the amount of casual customers" who lacked the "commitment" to other kinds of gaming. Contribution to revenue was inversely related to the amount of space occupied – for example, CCGs require the least amount of physical space but provide the "bulk" of revenue, while RPGs are relatively unprofitable given the amount of space they occupy. However, Scott stressed that a game store cannot rationalize its product range, as this will alienate customers who expect stores to carry the products they need to participate in their particular gaming practices.

Comic books take up less physical space in the store. Although the bulk of comics sold are published by either DC or Marvel Comics, the store had cultivated a customer base that shared its staff's taste, including an openness to some independent titles, through discussion as well as signage singling out "picks of the week" and staff recommendations. Signs also reminded customers of the subscription service, and encouraged them to request re-orders of sold-out comics – features of comics retailing that are often opaque to new readers.

While Scott felt uncomfortable estimating the gender distribution of customers – leaving it at "more than 60 per cent" male – he did note that female customers tended to buy RPGs and board games. During participant-observation, most of the girls and women observed in the store were shopping for comic books, though this was likely exaggerated by the Free Comic Book Day promotion in which Eastside Games & Comics was participating. Scott said he tried to do what he could to make the store more accessible to girls and women, but believed that as a store manager he had little capacity to affect how the gaming community welcomed them.

Downtown Comics & Collectibles

Downtown Comics & Collectibles was the longest established business included in this study, having been located on a major downtown street since 1979. Although this had been at times considered a "rougher area," owner Sean viewed proximity to several nearby movie theatres as an advantage, and the busy street ensured a level of foot traffic past the store as late as 9 p.m.

Sean began reading and collecting comic books as a child in the 1960s. Participating in comics fandom as a serious collector involved buying, selling, and trading old comic books and corresponding with other collectors by mail. After high school, he opened a comics shop in a neighbouring municipality, eventually quitting university to devote himself to his business and relocating downtown. Although Sean had visited early comic stores in California and elsewhere in Canada, the closest model for his own business was a store owned by an American friend. The stores shared the same name, each owning the trademark in their respective countries, and they have at times shared the expense of printing promotional items.

Downtown Comics & Collectibles was also the biggest store studied, which allowed it to maintain a large inventory. New graphic novels and trade paperbacks were organized in two distinct ways. In one section of the store, they were shelved by creator, with high-profile writers being the focus. In the other, the books were organized alphabetically by title. Some works appeared in both locations. Downtown Comics & Collectibles also dealt in the collectors' market to a greater degree than other comic-book stores studied. This included back issues of contemporary series for completist collectors as well as rarer and more valuable vintage comics. Sean admitted that these sales contributed relatively little to overall revenue, but it was his "favourite part of the business." Like many other comics retailers, however, Downtown had diversified their product range beyond comic books. As Sean put it: "You can't just depend on comics, you've got to have a lot of other things." The store's product range included comics and graphic novels, comic-book collectors' supplies, magazines, manga, anime DVDs, action figures and toys, statues, t-shirts, posters, RPG books, board games, picture postcards, celebrity photographs and film stills, movie and television scripts, and miscellaneous merchandise such as buttons and magnets. During the peak of their popularity, sports cards contributed as much as half of the store's revenue, although this market was "more or less dead." Despite all this diversity, Sean still saw comics as providing the store's "focus." Besides dedicated comics readers and collectors, the store pulled in a high volume of foot traffic from passersby. Casual customers were frequently attracted to the store by the large glass display cases that flanked the entrance, featuring a mix of comic books and popular-cultural merchandise.

Given its longevity, size, and relatively large staff (at least three employees were always on duty during participant-observation), it is unsurprising that Downtown Comics & Collectibles was among the most professionalized of all the stores and groups studied. Sean said his reference group was other businesses in his neighbourhood, not other comic shops, and that his challenges were those typical of small businesses. While other interviewed comics retailers found the process of ordering comics particularly fraught, Sean was more confident. Similarly, he approached the problems of diversity within comics fandom in a straightforward manner: "I remember a conversation I had with a guy in the [...] bar where I used to drink when I was a young man. This would have been at least in the 1980s. And it was at the time when [a local] hotel became a gay hotel. And I remember saying to the bartender, 'Well, how does a hotel turn gay?' And he said, 'Well, it's easy. They just hire gay staff.' And it sort of dawned on me. Well, duh. You know, if I want girls to come in the store, I should hire some girls. Or, women [...] By exercising common sense and having a mix of gender in the store you sort of take away from that sort of frat club atmosphere that develops when just guys are working together. And so it's good for the store and it definitely makes it a lot more accessible … for women."

In conclusion, although Sean typified his main successes as "normal business success," he remained convinced that "nobody could run a comic-book store successfully if they don't really enjoy comic books."

PHASE 2: SUBCULTURAL PARTICIPANTS

Barry

I met Barry after someone forwarded my call for participants to the mailing list of the local Society for Creative Anachronism chapter. He wrote to me saying:

> Possibly I can be of assistance in your study. I've been a science-fiction fan since my teens, and am now 53, and a research scientist. I'm still moderately active in fan activities, and have had regular to occasional contact with the Society for Creative Anachronism (SCA), the Christian Fandom email-list, Westernesse (the local branch of the Tolkien Society), computer games, SF&F Con, Anime Con, various long-term or weekend Role-Playing activities, a local LARP group, and lots of reading.

I couldn't resist a résumé like that. Barry was the first person I interviewed for the second phase of the project, and he allowed me to tag along with him for the most number and widest variety of activities. We met at a coffee shop near his home regularly for a few months, and I came with him to an SCA event, a local writers' group meeting, a Westernesse meetup, and I played in his Arthurian Britain role-playing game.

Physically, Barry is a slight, spry man. He cuts his salt-and-pepper hair himself, dresses simply, and sometimes wears safety glasses when he is out and about. He has a puckish smirk that makes you want to re-examine whatever he's just said for references and puns, and nods enthusiastically when you catch them. During interviews, he would frequently ask me to let him think, and then turn his body to the side, looking down to the floor or up to the ceiling, carefully considering his response before answering a question. Sometimes, rather than venturing an opinion on some topic, he would call for more systematic research to be done.

As a boy, he was involved in scholarly and scientific pursuits, including a field naturalists' club for youth and a computer club that gave members access to the local university's computers. He was raised Roman Catholic and remains observant. He studied chemistry in university, eventually receiving a doctorate in that field, and taught at a major research university before moving to the city to take a job in the private sector. When we spoke, he was an independent consultant. A bachelor, he lived and worked in a crowded basement apartment in a nearby suburb where he covered every available wall with bookshelves that are stacked at least two rows deep. It was full of mementoes of his time in fandom, as well as the detritus of various projects. When he took me around his apartment, he repeatedly explained his habits in terms of systems. These ranged from making the same meal of rice and split peas day in and day out (he says he worked out the amounts of nutrients he needs, and none of the ingredients spoil so he can shop for groceries as infrequently as possible), making hot cocoa (using vanilla to reduce the bitterness, as the Aztecs did, instead of sugar), and even drinking water ("What I do is I fill a pitcher, and then I let it stand until the chlorine's gone from it [...] I fill a bottle, and then I take it here and I put it here, and when I thirst, I reach over, drink, and put it back. When that's empty, I refill it. When that's empty, I fill it from the – so, that's the story of water").

Barry discovered organized science-fiction fandom after seeing a flyer for an area fan club in the library. He attended a meeting and remembers "a debate on the merits of Ray Bradbury, and a song broke out – ((sings)) 'Oh, how we hate Ray Bradbury.' I didn't especially hate Ray Bradbury, but I thought it was kind of a capsule of what fandom was about ... they have their opinions, and they kind of play with them." The shelves in his apartment (which contain only part of his library; the rest is in storage) attested to his continued interest in SF&F literature, but he admitted he has fallen behind, partly because he enjoyed revisiting favourite authors like J.R.R. Tolkien, G.K. Chesterton, Jack Vance, and Gene Wolfe and partly because he preferred buying used books. More recently, his interest in SF had led him to a new avocation as an aspiring writer. His in-progress novel drew on stories and ideas that he had in mind for years. He wanted it to be "diamond-hard" sci-fi, and so it represented another opportunity to draw on his scientific expertise, collection of reference books, and broad general knowledge. He began attending meetings to give readings of his work to other amateur writers and participated in a workshop at SF&F Con.

Another relatively recent development was his involvement with the Society for Creative Anachronism. He recalls encountering the SCA through a demonstration they put on while he was in university. He enjoyed himself but never pursued it. But a few years ago, after attending a medieval-themed banquet put on by the Knights of Columbus, he decided to look them up again and get involved. As he explained it, "I was um ... looking for something to do with my spare time. Getting together with people about interesting stuff. The science-fiction ... groups were not very organized [...] Besides the conventions, which are like once a year, there were not a lot of get-togethers." While many SCA members are drawn by the martial arts, "Doctor Mercurius" was mostly interested in the arts and sciences competitions and, more specifically, in recreating the science and technology of the period. He also appreciated the opportunities that SCA events provide for camping and being out of doors. Moreover, he identified with the chivalric values that the SCA idealizes.

Diana

Diana was in her late 30s when we were meeting. She wore her hair short and had two piercings in her left brow. She described her ethnic background as "white" and "slightly Ukrainian." Diana's answers were often succinct and to the point, but she could also become excited explaining her points, and we joked around quite a bit during our interviews. When she first wrote to me to volunteer for the study, she said she played *Dungeons & Dragons* and *World of Warcraft*, knew a bit about comics, and had previously participated in several TV fandoms. She also described herself as part of a "nerd family." She and Steve met in university and had been together for twenty years at the time of our interviews. He was also a gamer (and the DM of their regular campaign). They had recently had their first child, and Diana was taking time off from her small business to care for her. She explained that they already involved her in the game – "she likes the dice" – and planned to introduce her to gaming when she got old enough.

Diana was an avid consumer of science-fiction literature and media. She described herself as an "advanced reader, like, right from a really young age," and said she couldn't "ever remember not reading it, so [she] must have been reading it forever." Her father, who was trained as a scientist and worked in administration at a college, was a science fiction fan, too, and she vividly recalled him reading to her as a child. He continued to recommend books and authors to her as she grew up. This developed into a taste for "media science-fiction, so like TV and movies – *Star Trek*, *Fringe*, *X-Files*, all that kind of stuff." Interestingly, Diana de-emphasized SF's intellectual uniqueness: "Like, you could say, 'Oh, it's the re-envisioning or the envisioning of what the future could be.' But it's not because that's not – I mean, you can tell by golden age [science fiction], like they got it *so* wrong, so you know that anything written now is going to be so wrong in the future. So, it's not re-envisioning. That's not why I read it. I just, a good writer is a good writer, it doesn't matter what they're writing. Sorry." On the hard–soft continuum, she expressed a preference for "the Connie Willis style of science-fiction, which is the more – which I'm (really liking) – the more feminine base. You know, like, yeah sure we're on a different planet, but really it's about relationships, it's about people kind of thing."

She and Steve moved to the city twelve years ago so she could pursue a master's degree in women's studies. Her thesis was on women writers of fan fiction. This background led to interesting discussions about gender and geek culture. Although she felt that she received fewer "stares" when going into a game shop now, she noted that media representations of women involved in nerdy practices were still relatively rare. We also debated whether fandom *per se* should be considered part of geek culture since, in her experience and based on her research, media fandoms are spaces with "women's rules": "Fandom to me is women's space. It's not geek space. It's a way of women connecting. And it kind of goes back to my 'women aren't nerds,' you know? [...] For me, the emphasis is that [media fandom is] women's space, and that's different from geek space or nerd space [...] If you're in, you know, science-fiction fandom, certainly in the old days, you went by *men's* rules or you didn't do it, right? If women stood up and tried to do differently, they were told they were doing it wrong." She acknowledged some overlap, but her primary associations with "nerd" and "geek" had to do with gaming cultures, such as *Dungeons & Dragons* or *World of Warcraft*, which were also her heaviest investments at the time of the interviews, rather than fandom.

Diana first played *Dungeons & Dragons* as a child. She didn't remember very much about those early campaigns and didn't play again until fairly recently when a friend of hers, who had met Logan at a convention, expressed interest and recruited her and Steve for a campaign. As gaming groups often do, this one split, reformed, and shuffled its members several times over the years. Eventually, Steve ended up in DM's chair, and that, combined with their need to watch over Donna, meant they hosted the gaming sessions in their home. When asked to describe role-playing games, Diana emphasized the collective exercise of imagination and the emotional rewards that come from it:

> DIANA: I think I would say that it's ... it's collective storytelling. You're ... playing characters with somebody, with the Dungeon

Master, who's the overall storyteller, and you're playing within his story. And there's swords.

BEN: And is that what you like about it most? The storytelling aspect?

DIANA: Yeah, I like that. And sometimes, when you've had a really bad day, sometimes it's nice to just … sit down and – I know you're just rolling dice, but it's nice to just hack and slash. You know, to just beat the snot out of something.

Although *World of Warcraft* lacked, for her, this dimension of collective participation ("I don't do a lot of really social things with it"), it offered a flexible form of leisure that she could engage in while her daughter was sleeping. It was also something she could share with Steve, though that required them to maintain two accounts. During our early interviews, the game was clearly at the top of her mind: she had only started playing in the last few months and was devoting quite a lot of time to it (several hours a day), and it frequently came up when she was looking for an example to illustrate some point about gamers or geek culture in general. However, by the end of the data collection period, her engagement with *WoW* had tapered off, as she had reached a point where the game had become less rewarding and Donna required attention for a greater proportion of the day.

Mr Fox

I first saw Mr Fox from across a public plaza. I was sitting in the window of the coffee shop where we had agreed to meet and looked up just as he dramatically threw open a pair of doors and rolled on through in his wheelchair. He had noticed a poster calling for participants in his regular comic shop (Downtown) and wrote to volunteer. In addition to being a comic book fan, he was a gamer, an SF&F reader, and a "movie geek." His self-presentation in conversation oscillated between the sardonic and the sincere – he might shrug off one question with a wry comment, while another would elicit a touching personal story. He had a hyperbolic style of humour, and we often ended up riffing on one another's jokes.

Mr Fox was raised in a small, rural town. His parents farmed, and he bussed into a regional hub for school. As a result of the lengthy trip there and back, he never got involved in extracurricular activities. He was something of a loner, though by the end of high school he hung out with a crowd he described as "the nerds" who played *Magic: The Gathering* together at lunch. One of the school's math teachers ("the best teacher I ever had") ran a course in science-fiction appreciation. He also mentioned writing "terrible science-fiction and fantasy stories" and "*terrible* fan-fiction" in his leisure time. An English teacher "inspired [him] to do things properly when writing."

Gaming was a major part of Mr Fox's life. When I asked him about his earliest recollections of playing video games, he told a story of playing a neighbour's console:

> MR FOX: Uh … TurboGrafx 16. My neighbour had a kid who *had* one, and I loved it. You'd play uh … it had cards? They were like a cross between a … cartridge and a floppy disk? *Splatter House*. That game is *the devil* because it gets … just randomly hard all of the sudden.
> BEN: But you say that with a smile on your face.
> MR FOX: Oh yeah because it was ((laughs)) awesome. It's just like, all right, duck! Jump! Two-by-four! Two-by-four! Duck! Jump! Two-by-four! There's this one level where there's these little weird amoebas floating towards ya? but at *random*? so you couldn't memorize a *pattern*, so you were just like ((sighs)).

His family's income level "inhibited [his] buying of video games immensely." Nonetheless, he got deeper into games at the same time as his ambitions as a writer were growing. In a moment of insight, he realized that people must write video games, and so perhaps could he.

In 2007 Mr Fox moved to the city to pursue a course in game design. In his home town, he felt people considered his hobbies and interests "weird," but in game school "everyone's a goddamn nerd." After graduating, he began working half-time as a writer and project manager at an independent game developer. Most of his co-workers also went through the same program, and the company was still indie enough that they didn't have an office. Mr Fox worked from home, co-ordinating with his team over the Internet. He also picked up freelance writing projects of various kinds to make ends meet.

Being immersed in a milieu of "goddamn nerds" at school also got Mr Fox involved in other kinds of gaming. Some of his friends and classmates were into *Warhammer 40,000*, a sci-fi/horror themed miniatures game, and joining them had become part of his "hang-out-with-the-guys weekend routine." Around the time we started meeting together, the group was transitioning to role-playing games:

> MR FOX: Yeah. Well, it's a … it's a D&D campaign set in the *Warhammer* universe. So. God, that was *so* dorky to say out loud. ((laughs)) Oh, well.
> BEN: It is what it is.
> MR FOX: Yeah. Whatever. I drove a truck off a building while shooting a gun at another truck last week, so really I've got nothing to be ashamed of. I killed the driver, and they *crashed* and they exploded in an alleyway. And I landed the truck, jumped out … and walked away just fine, so … good times [...] We had the *Lupin III* chase music playing and everything. We even had little models [...] We even grabbed some of the *40K* models? And put 'em on the table and shook 'em back and forth like we were actually in a chase scene. Yes. We are *huge* nerds.

However, by the end of the interview period their GM was moving away and the future of the group's activities were unclear.

Although he actually preferred to come into the store on Thursdays, when the aisles were less crowded, Mr Fox was the kind of customer Sean called a "Wednesday warrior" – i.e., he came in every week to pick up his new comics and chat with the staff. He mentioned having good relationships with a few of the longer-serving clerks. One of them was also a writer, and they would sometimes talk about their craft (i.e., "writer stuff"). However, Mr Fox denied being a comic *collector*. He would buy good story arcs or miniseries in trade paperback form, but when he was done reading floppies he donated them to the library or a children's hospital, which is particularly fitting since he first started reading comics when hospitalized as a child.

Shiera

Like Barry, Shiera responded to a call for participation posted on the local Society for Creative Anachronism mailing list, on which she lurked but was not an active participant. In addition to being a reader of "speculative fiction" and a former SCA member, she identified herself as a fan of the TV series *Doctor Who* and a player of the massively multiplayer online role-playing game *Star Wars Galaxies* (SWG). When we arranged to meet the first time, she said I would recognize her as a "heavy short lady [...] with a cane." She was a crocheter, often arriving to interviews wearing some of her own handiwork, and she took her coffee with a lot of sugar. Our interviews were quite a bit longer than average: Shiera had a lot to say and could effortlessly launch into discourses on virtually any topic – perhaps a legacy of her theatrical background.

Shiera was raised in the semi-rural communities surrounding the city. She describes her family as "the lowest rung on the socio-economic ladder" and, more cheekily, as "Po' ... white. ((laughs)) I won't go so far as to say trash because we're not, but very poor." As a girl and adolescent, she was an equestrian and a thespian. She entered the workforce after high school, although she audited some university classes and pursued her intellectual interests independently. She continued to work with horses and later in retail until her arthritis made her unable to work. She moved back to one of the city's suburbs a few years ago, where she lived with her youngest son, who was twelve at the time of our interviews; her two older sons lived in the area and stayed with her "every second weekend or so."

She was raised as an avid reader. Her earliest memory of reading sci-fi was discovering the novelization of *Star Wars* in her school library: "I've been a *Star Wars* fan since I was twelve and read the books when I was in middle school um and I didn't see the movies. Everyone else around me saw the movies. Everyone else had the merchandise. Where we grew up *extremely* poor, so I never saw the movies in the theatre until I was an adult. What I did do was read the books, and I *loved* the books. I thought the books were marvelous. It was a really great story, it left a whole bunch of things open, and my-my brain went tickety-tack." She immediately shared it with a friend and they wrote fan fiction together. Friends continue to give her *Star Wars* collectibles for holidays and special occasions – she had a number of expensive statuettes in her home, which were presents from a friend who salvaged them from a closing comic-bookstore. It was also responsible for what was, at the time of the interviews, her major geek culture activity.

Shiera didn't consider herself a gamer because she had never really been interested in video games until friends started recommending that she try out *Star Wars Galaxies*. She resisted at first because out of concern she would become addicted, but she was "hooked" nonetheless. The *Star Wars* setting drew her to the game, but she came to appreciate the kinds of skills it required and the rewards it offered. Although the game has numerous components and allows players to maintain multiple characters (or "toons"), Shiera's primary involvement related to "beastmastery" – that is, the skill that allows a character to use a trained animal (or "pet"). Some beastmasters were involved in breeding these pets using various in-game resources, and the community was trying to work out the algorithms that determine how the pets turn out. Coordinating this exercise of players' collective intelligence was a major task, and Shiera was heavily involved as a leader of the community.

When Shiera was a teenager, her next-door neighbour was a member of the Society for Creative Anachronism and hired her, Shiera, to look after her kids while at SCA events: "So, I'm at this event, I'm wearing thrown-together thrift-store garb, and I'm having a great time. And it became very quickly a big part. And then my family got involved, my mom and my stepfather and my sisters, we all started going to events as a whole group, as a household. As soon as I was old enough to get involved in the combat, I got involved in the combat." Performing traditional Irish music, however, was her main avocation in the Society, though she also eventually became involved in administration. When we were talking, she was wary of being drawn back into the interpersonal politics but spoke fondly of her experiences and rattled off people she missed spending time with. She indicated she would like to start attending events again, but even local events were difficult for her to travel to.

Because of her mobility issues, at the time of our interviews together, Shiera's average day revolved around the home. After breakfast and getting her son ready for school (including co-viewing an episode of *Pokémon* with him), she typically watched an episode of *Doctor Who* in re-runs on the Space Channel, possibly while crocheting. One of her sons encountered the series at a convention and recommended it to her; it started out as an opportunity to spend time and bond with him, but grew on her. Much of her day revolved around some combination of playing SWG or working on her writing projects (she blogged and was always working on stories and novels), but it was shot through with digitally mediated communication. Despite being somewhat restricted to her home, she kept in touch (by Ventrillo voice chat, instant messaging, and email) with fellow SWG gamers, SCAers, fan-fic writers, and professional authors. These networks provided emotional support, in addition to keeping her involved with new developments related to her interests.

Solo

Solo was in her early twenties and a student at Cross-Town University. She was a comics fan whose comic-book reading habit was dormant, and personally engaged with (although not involved in organized fandom for) media franchises like *Star Wars*, *Harry Potter*, and *Buffy the Vampire Slayer*. Moreover, she identified strongly with the *idea* of geek culture: "I don't play D&D, first person shooters, or *WoW* [...] Despite this, I would associate more closely with geek/nerd culture than other 'cliques' or social spheres." Peter, who had been her high school English teacher, recommended her to the study.

Solo comes from a professional family. Her father was an engineer, and in early childhood the family moved about internationally as he worked on various projects. They settled in the city when she was eight years old. They lived in a traditionally working-class part of the city, but maintained a "high standard of living." When we started interviewing, she had just moved into her first apartment downtown, which was decorated with toys, superhero posters, and her collection of *Star Wars* Lego sets.

She thinks that she first saw *Star Wars* on VHS when she was four. It's the first film she remembers seeing: "I remember watching it and being absolutely terrified when Luke ... *Empire Strikes Back*? When Luke gets his hand cut off, and the poles? And the (tube)? Just absolutely mortified ... like, I could not watch that scene after [...] I really like Luke. Luke was the first boy I had a crush on when I was, like, eleven. No, it must have been earlier than eleven. It was the first, like, the first ... thing I can ... the first moment I can recall looking at a boy and being like, 'Hey, he's really, he's yeah! All right." As her chosen pseudonym suggests, however, she later came to prefer Han Solo. She was ten when the prequels started coming out, and she was "indoctrinated." She saw *Revenge of the Sith* eight times in theatres and said she "cried buckets."

As a child, the only books that interested her were by Roald Dahl. Her mother, concerned that she wasn't reading enough, went to a bookstore where a clerk recommended *Harry Potter and the Philosopher's Stone* – she thinks largely because the cover blurb compared it to Dahl's work (which strikes me as a rather inapt comparison, at least after Harry is rescued from the Dursleys). She devoured it and followed the series. She remembers dressing as Harry Potter for Halloween one year well before the film adaptations and hype began, and no one recognized her costume. When the film *Harry Potter and the Deathly Hallows, Part 2* was released, she described experiencing the opening-night line-up as the end of her childhood. Alongside and after the *Harry Potter* books, she read other fantasy novels. Solo's media consumption in general had a kind of compulsive quality: she always wanted to have a book series (or a TV series) underway, and when it ended she had to find another. She said she didn't like to read science-fiction novels, but preferred SF-themed movies and television to cinematic attempts at the fantasy genre.

Her first exposure to the TV series *Buffy the Vampire Slayer* came through an interpersonal connection: "my brother had a friend who was really, really into it, so then I started watching it and then I got into it." At that point, the show was already halfway through its run, and she caught up with VHS "best-of" compilations from each season. A *Buffy* poster in her school locker was the catalyst for her peer group in high school, and she still considered the show a major influence on her life: "I mean, it was really instrumental in a lot of ways, in terms of, like … like, adolescence, I guess. Like, there's a lot of things where I think, 'Ah! Stupid *Buffy*, teaching me the wrong lessons!'" Like *Harry Potter* and *Star Wars*, *Buffy* was mostly dormant as a fandom (for her) because there weren't new instalments of the story coming out. Yet at the time of the interviews she was regularly getting together with a friend to work their way through the series on DVD. She still spoke admiringly of the show's creator, Joss Whedon, though her feelings about his post-*Buffy* projects were all over the map.

Solo's interest in comics had its roots in a childhood spent with superheroes and was initially nurtured by movies, TV, and video games. She saw *Batman Forever* very young, and she remembered fighting with her brother over *Mighty Morphin' Power Rangers* action figures. But she didn't actually start reading comics until she was in grade 12. Between a boyfriend and a friend of her parents who were both lapsed fans, she had sources of information who helped her fill in the backstories of the characters she had first encountered in their licensed adaptations. She started attending King Cons and buying bundles of back issues put together by local dealers. This led her to start a subscription account at a comic shop. At the peak of her reading habit, she spent somewhere in the neighbourhood of $150–200 a month, which she described as a source of guilt. When her comic book store closed, she got out of the habit. She would still occasionally drop by a mass-market bookstore and purchase a graphic novel or trade paperback and retained strong opinions about the DC Comics universe; when I mentioned the publisher's 2011 line-wide relaunch, she seemed intrigued and started making tentative comments about maybe getting back into comics.

Wedge

Wedge was connected to the study in two ways: he was involved with the City Gaming Network and, like many local geeks, was friends with Logan. When we arranged to meet at a coffee shop for our first meeting, he told me that he looks "like a gamer and [has] a scruffy beard, shouldn't be too hard to spot." What this turned out to mean was that he came wearing cargo shorts and a graphic t-shirt. Wedge was easygoing and quick to laugh.

Wedge was a software developer and project manager. He played board games, role-playing games, and a fantasy- and football-themed miniatures game called *Blood Bowl*. He also mentioned that he had once been an avid comic-book collector and was a member of the Society for Creative Anachronism as a teenager. He made sure to point out, however, that he was a well-rounded individual; in addition to his geeky hobbies, he enjoyed hiking and dancing and was interested in natural building, permaculture, and community gardens. At the time of the interviews, Wedge and his wife had lived in the city for two years, but they had been in the area for five years in total, having moved to be closer to her family. Like Solo, he took his code name from his favourite *Star Wars* character, Wedge Antilles (who I embarrassingly confused with Biggs Darklighter).

Wedge's earliest memory associated with geek culture was throwing up while watching *Alien* on laserdisc at age six. Thankfully, he wasn't permanently scarred by that experience. In fact, he described the media landscape of his youth as particularly accommodating to someone with his tastes:

> WEDGE: I can remember that time period when I grew up ... there was a fair number of like fantasy movies and like ... *Dragonslayer* and uh *Beast Master* and ... um ... not-not-not *great* –
> BEN: The kind of post-*Conan* fantasy wave?
> WEDGE: Yeah, post-*Conan* exactly, yeah. Like a lot of not necessarily *great* movies, but really fun and uh that genre really ... that was kind of a period when they were quite prominent?

His father was a plumber and at some point did work for the owner of a local video store who paid in kind, giving Wedge free access to the entire catalogue. The film adaptation of *Dune* got him interested in reading sci-fi literature, and the genre was still important to him. His favourite books were George R.R. Martin's *Song of Ice and Fire* novels, but he said he doesn't get as much time to read as he'd like and that he'd watch more movies if he and his wife had more similar taste in films.

Another early involvement with geek culture was learning to play D&D when he was eight years old. A friend of Wedge's father ran a game for the family, including both parents and his sister. In a sense, this is the wellspring of much of his geeky interests: "I know it made a huge impact on me. I can remember – and I have a really bad memory and I've always had a really bad memory, and so I only (have) very, very, like very singular memories of when I was a kid, and this one – like I can remember my character. I played like a barbarian guy with an axe. And I can remember pieces of the adventure. I know we were travelling through a dungeon trying to rescue a princess. And I can remember parts of the map because I still have the map. I still have the original map that my mom drew from that." After it was over, the friend left a copy of the rule book behind. Wedge then got some of his friends involved, and gaming became a major part of their lives. In university (he studied computer science), he joined a club that held regular drop-in gaming sessions. He started out playing *Magic: The Gathering*, but eventually drifted into the *Warhammer*/football miniatures game, *Blood Bowl*. At the time we were speaking, he still played *Blood Bowl* in a local league. He was also involved in two RPG campaigns, one in the traditional D&D mold (although set in the Asian-themed campaign setting, *Legend of the Five Rings*) and a more free-form game called *Over the Edge*, which he compared to the William S. Burroughs novel *Naked Lunch*. Wedge said gaming was "more about the story than necessarily the mechanics," but he also appreciated the nuance that well-designed game mechanics bring: "I find they, for me, they add a lot to the game, but the story is certainly the focus in a lot of my games or intentions." This was reflected in the variety of gaming styles represented by *Blood Bowl*, L5R, and *Over the Edge*.

Notes

INTRODUCTION

1 *Id est*, "turd."
2 What distinguishes these exemplars from equally bookish or "quirky" teens who *don't* grow up to be wildly successful is never quite accounted for.
3 According to Sanders and brown's (1994, 268) "Glossary of Fanspeak": "From an adjective meaning 'commonplace and routine,' this has become a fannish noun describing the majority of the human race that is content with familiar types of literature and thinking. Frequently used with disdain to describe people who denigrate fandom because it differs from the mainstream."
4 Extensive literatures do exist on both sports and music fans. However, these fans have not typically been allowed to serve as paradigmatic of fandom in the way that "media fans" do.
5 There is a weaker relationship with other fandoms. Consider, for example, the paradoxical (from the point of view of the triumphal narrative) presence of sports cards in many comic book and game shops.

CHAPTER ONE

1 While this image appeared around the web for some time, it went viral beginning in late 2009. I have not been able to locate the original source, of which there are several extant versions. The top Google hit is a post on *Laughing Squid* that credits *BuzzFeed* (with a hat tip to Craig Newmark of craigslist fame), but *BuzzFeed* credits no source.
2 Sacks (1992, 41) calls this the "MIR device," where "'M' stands for membership. 'I' stands for inference-rich, and 'R' stands for representative."
3 Of course, nobody considers themselves a bad nerd, though everyone knows a few.

CHAPTER TWO

1 In particular, to the anthropological version of practice theory associated with the early Bourdieu and to Lave and Wenger's (1991) concept of the community of practice.

2 One might go so far as to posit that the force of basic moral intuitions about altruism or fairness, say, derives from our experiences participating in the social institutions – which can be re-described as practices – like the nuclear family or wage labour that have served as a kind of "second nature" in the liberal capitalist west since the nineteenth century.

3 Elsewhere, MacIntyre (1988) calls them "goods of effectiveness" (as distinct from the "goods of excellence").

4 While my discussion here focuses on the former of these two potential relationships between media and collectivities, I shall return to the latter in chapter 5.

5 See Woo, Poyntz, and Rennie (2016).

CHAPTER THREE

1 Cf. Susan Pearce's (1995) typology of souvenir, fetishistic, and systematic collecting.

2 This may be attributed to both the scarcity of early comic books and the "speculator boom" of the late 1980s and early 1990s, during which the rising value of classic comics at auction and gimmicky techniques on the part of publishers fuelled "a speculator frenzy" that drove "avid consumers to purchase multiple copies of the same comic book" (Beaty 2010, 204). Although the boom (and its eventual bust) is now widely discussed as a misstep, it established a template for understanding collecting as an "investment" that is still culturally available to participants.

3 By way of contrast, Sean suggested that for his generation of fans and collectors, the artwork was considered paramount.

4 For more on collectors and readers as distinct "understandings" of comics, see Woo (2012).

5 The PAX brand is now under the aegis of ReedPOP, "a quirky offshoot of Reed Exhibitions," itself part of the multinational Elsevier family, which runs five annual PAX conventions in four different cities.

6 This, despite the prominence at the time of the "fake geek girl" discourse. See ch. 8.

CHAPTER FOUR

1 Cf. John Durham Peters's (1991) discussion of the "transmission" model of communication as a kind of telepathic communion.
2 On conventions and other forms of reason-giving, see Tilly (2006).
3 With respect to conversational performance of subcultural authenticity, see Widdicombe and Wooffitt (1995) and Locke (2012). For a more general overview, see Lindholm (2008).
4 In the SCA, the term "period" refers to "pre-17th-century Western Europe, with an emphasis on the Middle Ages and Renaissance" (Society for Creative Anachronism 2008, 2). However, some participants are interested in earlier civilizations, such as Ancient Rome, or in life outside of Europe during the same historical period.

CHAPTER FIVE

1 Barry was the exception, reporting a major split between "Knights of Columbus and church friends" and "science fiction and fantasy friends." As Grand Knight of his local chapter, he had to get to know all of the members, pushing this group into quantitative dominance, but he counted more people that he "shares recreational interests with" in fan circles, as "everybody else in Knights of Columbus wants to talk about fishing or sports."
2 In classical social theory, this "organic solidarity" of functions is usually associated with *Gesellschaften*, or "civil societies," not communities (or, *Gemeinschaften*). That informants consider it a criterion of community raises questions about their experiences and understandings of modern society. (Tönnies 2001)
3 But cf. Kunyosying and Soles (2012), who draw on Bauman to describe geek culture as a "simulated ethnicity."
4 I am drawing here on more recent translations of Max Weber's *Economy and Society* (Weber 2004). The standard translation (courtesy of Talcott Parsons) renders *Vergemeinschaftung* and *Vergesellschaftung* as simple adjectives ("communal" and "associative" relationships), reinforcing the view of community and society as concrete and mutually exclusive categories. Things look quite different if we restore Weber's verbal nouns: "communalization" and "societalization" become states or transformations of human relationships rather than objects separate from them.
5 Shiera was, however, somewhat critical of this model in practice, charging it with stifling innovation and, by quickly channelling capable new recruits into demanding service roles, leading to burnout among the membership.

CHAPTER SIX

1 Public libraries are perhaps the major exception as a cultural institution that has taken popular taste seriously and not merely out of desperation.
2 King Con, which had rented the same hall for twenty years, and the Alternate Universe Club, which had free access to space at the university for most events, were relatively fortunate in this regard.
3 Hank keeps a bottle of deodorant spray behind the counter to offer to the occasionally smelly gamer. He views it as a sign of his close relationship with his customers that no one has ever been offended by the offer.
4 Another example of negotiating the application of membership categories. See ch. 1.
5 Although some might find them nerdy in a more general sense.
6 DC Comics' *Legion of Super-Heroes*. At the time of this interview, the series had just been re-launched. It was re-launched again in September, 2011 as part of DC's *New 52* initiative and cancelled in 2013.
7 A trend that has arguably intensified in the years since I conducted this interview.

CHAPTER SEVEN

1 "Have nothing in your houses that you do not know to be useful, or believe to be beautiful" (quoted in MacKail 1899, 2:63–4).
2 Although they note that hiring a babysitter has inflated the costs of an evening at the cinema, making it prohibitively expensive for all but those films they judge as requiring the "big screen" in order fully to appreciate the spectacle.

CHAPTER EIGHT

1 I say "style" because, although it does have some infrastructure of a political movement – with, e.g., think tanks, publications, spokespeople and conferences – what makes the alt-right "alternative" is indeed its style, which fuses white nationalism and "men's rights" misogyny with an ironic sensibility born from online trolling and griefing cultures. (Romano 2016)
2 This quote comes from a television exchange with Yiannopoulos posted on YouTube by a user with the charming name "Destroy Feminism" ("NEW: Milo Yiannopoulos 'Facts V.S. Feelings'" 2016).
3 Martín Moruno (2013, 6) notes that the French term ressentiment was in widespread use among German speakers in the nineteenth century and

holds "a strong connotation with memory and a peculiar nuance of lingering hate in comparison with its English counterpart [i.e., 'resentment']."

4 Notably, Jock Young (2009) highlights the importance of ressentiment to Albert K. Cohen's (1965) sociology of deviance and, thereby, to the development of theories of moral panic (S. Cohen 1972).

5 This is, of course, not the only possible response to controversies about Internet "piracy." Stevens and Bell's (2012) study of comics fans' beliefs about intellectual property delineates a number of arguments for and against downloading pirated comic books that circulate among fans. While selection bias may influence the number of pro-downloading *comments* in their corpus, Stevens and Bell also found a greater variety of pro-downloading *arguments*: they identify six frames in favor of downloading and two opposed. Two of these (one pro and one con) are creator-oriented and four (all pro) are user-oriented, while two fall outside this framework.

6 Curiously enough, I have witnessed plenty of people in comic shops, game stores, and conventions wearing sports merchandise without hearing a single accusation of being "fake geeks."

7 However, the game as simulation is obviously a longstanding way of thinking about designing and playing games. Other players might well have welcomed this argument.

References

Abercrombie, Nicholas, and Brian Longhurst. 1998. *Audiences: A Sociological Theory of Performance and Imagination*. London: SAGE.

Adorno, Theodor W. 2001. "On the Fetish Character in Music and the Regression of Listening." In *The Culture Industry: Selected Essays on Mass Culture*, edited by Jay M. Bernstein, 29–60. London: Routledge.

Almog, Oz. 1998. "The Problem of Social Type: A Review." *Electronic Journal of Sociology* 3 (4). http://sociology.org/content/vol003.004/almog.html.

Althusser, Louis. 1971. "Ideology and Ideological State Apparatuses (Notes towards an Investigation)." In *Lenin and Philosophy and Other Essays*, 121–73. London: NLB.

Anderegg, David. 2007. *Nerds: Who They Are and Why We Need More of Them*. New York: Jeremy P. Tarcher/Penguin.

Anderson, Benedict. 2006. *Imagined Communities: Reflections on the Origin and Spread of Nationalism*. London: Verso.

Ang, Ien. 1985. *Watching Dallas: Soap Opera and the Melodramatic Imagination*. New York: Methuen.

– 1991. *Desperately Seeking the Audience*. New York: Routledge.

Antaki, Charles, and Sue Widdicombe, eds. 1998. *Identities in Talk*. London: SAGE Publications.

Appadurai, Arjun. 1986. "Introduction: Commodities and the Politics of Value." In *The Social Life of Things: Commodities in Cultural Perspective*, edited by Arjun Appadurai, 3–63. Cambridge: Cambridge University Press.

Apple, Michael W. 1990. *Ideology and Curriculum*. 2nd ed. New York: Routledge.

Arnett, Jeffrey Jensen. 2000. "Emerging Adulthood: A Theory of Development from the Late Teens through the Twenties." *American Psychologist* 55: 469–80. doi:10.1037/0003-066X.55.5.469.

Asselin, Janelle. 2014. "I Received Rape Threats after Criticizing a Comic

Book." *The Daily Dot*, 28 April. http://www.dailydot.com/opinion/received-rape-threats-comic-book/.

Bacon-Smith, Camille. 1992. *Enterprising Women: Television Fandom and the Creation of Popular Myth*. Philadelphia: University of Pennsylvania Press.

Barley, Stephen R. 1989. "Careers, Identities, and Institutions: The Legacy of the Chicago School of Sociology." In *Handbook of Career Theory*, edited by Michael B. Arthur, Douglas T. Hall, and Barbara S. Lawrence, 41–65. Cambridge: Cambridge University Press.

Barzilai-Nahon, Karine. 2008. "Gatekeeping: A Critical Review." *Annual Review of Information Science and Technology* 43: 433–78. doi:10.1002/aris.2009.1440430117.

Bauman, Zygmunt. 2000. *Liquid Modernity*. Cambridge, UK: Polity.

Baym, Nancy K. 2000. *Tune In, Log On: Soaps, Fandom, and Online Community*. Thousand Oaks, CA: SAGE.

Beadle, Ron, and Geoff Moore. 2006. "MacIntyre on Virtue and Organization." *Organization Studies* 27: 323–40. doi:10.1177/0170840606062425.

Beaty, Bart. 2010. "The Recession and the American Comic Book Industry: From Inelastic Cultural Good to Economic Integration." *Popular Communication* 8: 203–7. doi:10.1080/15405702.2010.493421.

Becker, Howard S. 2014. *What About Mozart? What About Murder?: Reasoning From Cases*. Chicago: University of Chicago Press.

Bellah, Robert N., Richard Madsen, William M. Sullivan, Ann Swidler, and Steven M. Tipton. 1986. *Habits of the Heart: Individualism and Commitment in American Life*. New York: Perennial Library.

Benedict, R.S. 2016. Twitter post, 23 October, 6:33 p.m., https://twitter.com/RS_Benedict/status/790320333580533760.

Benjamin, Walter. 1996. "Experience and Poverty." In *Selected Writings*, edited by Marcus Paul Bullock and Michael William Jennings, 731–6. Cambridge, MA: The Belknap Press of Harvard University Press.

– 1999. *The Arcades Project*. Edited by Rolf Tiedemann. Cambridge, MA: The Belknap Press of Harvard University Press.

Bennett, Andy. 1999. "Subcultures or Neo-tribes? Rethinking the Relationship between Youth, Style and Musical Taste." *Sociology* 33: 599–617. doi:10.1177/S0038038599000371.

– 2004. "Consolidating the Music Scenes Perspective." *Poetics* 32: 223–34. doi:10.1016/j.poetic.2004.05.004.

Bennett, Andy, and Richard A. Peterson, eds. 2004. *Music Scenes: Local, Translocal and Virtual*. Nashville, TN: Vanderbilt University Press.

Bishop, John H., Matthew Bishop, Michael Bishop, Lara Gelbwasser, Shanna Green, Erica Peterson, Anna Rubinsztaj, and Andrew Zuckerman. 2004.

"Why We Harass Nerds and Freaks: A Formal Theory of Student Culture and Norms." *Journal of School Health* 74: 235–51. doi:10.1111/j.1746-1561.2004.tb08280.x.

Black, Rebecca W., and Constance Steinkuehler. 2009. "Literacy in Virtual Worlds." In *Handbook of Adolescent Literacy Research*, edited by Leila Christenbury, Randy Bomer, and Peter Smagorinsky, 271–86. New York: Guildford Press.

Blum, Alan. 2001. "Scenes." *Public* 22/23: 7–35.

Boltanski, Luc. 1999. *Distant Suffering: Morality, Media and Politics*. Translated by Graham Burchell. Cambridge: Cambridge University Press.

Booth, Paul J. 2015. "Fandom: The Classroom of the Future." *Transformative Works and Cultures* 19. doi:10.3983/twc.2015.0650.

Borgmann, Albert. 1984. *Technology and the Character of Contemporary Life: A Philosophical Inquiry*. Chicago: University of Chicago Press.

Bourdieu, Pierre. 1983. "The Field of Cultural Production, Or: The Economic World Reversed." *Poetics* 12: 311–56. doi:10.1016/0304-422X(83)90012-8.

– 1985. "The Social Space and the Genesis of Groups." *Theory and Society* 14: 723–44. doi:10.1007/BF00174048.

– 1990. "The Scholastic Point of View." *Cultural Anthropology* 5: 380–91. doi:10.1525/can.1990.5.4.02a00030.

– 1996. *The Rules of Art: Genesis and Structure of the Literary Field*. Cambridge, UK: Polity.

– 2000. *Pascalian Meditations*. Stanford, CA: Stanford University Press.

– 2010. *Distinction: A Social Critique of the Judgement of Taste*. Translated by Richard Nice. Abingdon, UK: Routledge. First published in English 1984.

Bourdieu, Pierre, and Loïc J.D. Wacquant. 1992. *An Invitation to Reflexive Sociology*. Chicago: University of Chicago Press.

Brooks, David. 2008. "The Alpha Geeks." *New York Times*, 23 May. http://www.nytimes.com/2008/05/23/opinion/23brooks.html.

Brown, Jeffrey A. 1997. "Comic Book Fandom and Cultural Capital." *Journal of Popular Culture* 30 (4): 13–31. doi:10.1111/j.0022-3840.1997.3004_13.x.

Bucholtz, Mary. 1999a. "'Why Be Normal?': Language and Identity Practices in a Community of Nerd Girls." *Language in Society* 28: 203–23. http://www.jstor.org.proxy.library.carleton.ca/stable/4168925.

– 1999b. "You Da Man: Narrating the Racial Other in the Production of White Masculinity." *Journal of Sociolinguistics* 3: 443–60. doi:10.1111/1467-9481.00090.

– 2001. "The Whiteness of Nerds: Superstandard English and Racial Markedness." *Journal of Linguistic Anthropology* 11: 84–100. doi:10.1525/jlin.2001.11.1.84.

‒ 2009. "Styles and Stereotypes: Laotian American Girls' Linguistic Negotiation of Identity." In *Beyond Yellow English: Toward a Linguistic Anthropology
   of Asian Pacific America*, edited by Angela Reyes and Adrienne Lo, 21–42.
   Oxford: Oxford University Press.

Buell, Megan. n.d. "How to Superpower Your Con with New Insights into
   Fans' Spending." *Eventbrite Blog*. https://www.eventbrite.com/blog/academy
   /how-to-superpower-your-con-with-new-insights-into-fans-spending/.

Bui, Hoai-Tran. 2015. "'Star Wars' Boycott Hashtag Calls Film 'Anti-White.'"
   USA Today, 20 October. http://www.usatoday.com/story/life/movies/2015
   /10/20/star-wars-force-awakens-twitter-boycott-backlash/74260778/.

Burgess, Jean. 2006. "Hearing Ordinary Voices: Cultural Studies, Vernacular
   Creativity and Digital Storytelling." *Continuum* 20: 201–14.
   doi:10.1080/10304310600641737.

Burke, Kenneth. 1969. *A Rhetoric of Motives*. Berkeley and Los Angeles: University of California Press.

Bury, Rhiannon. 2005. *Cyberspaces of Their Own: Female Fandoms Online*. New
   York: Peter Lang.

Busse, Kristina. 2013. "Geek Hierarchies, Boundary Policing, and the Gendering of the Good Fan." *Participations: Journal of Audience & Reception Studies*
   10 (1): 73–91.

‒ 2015. "Fan Labor and Feminism: Capitalizing on the Fannish Labor of
   Love." *Cinema Journal* 54 (3): 110–15. doi:10.1353/cj.2015.0034.

Carbone, Gina. 2016. "Early 'Ghostbusters' Reviews Are Positive, Cynics Call
   Critics Paid-Off Cowards." *Moviefone*, 11 July. https://www.moviefone
   .com/2016/07/11/early-ghostbusters-reviews-positive-cynics-critics-paid-
   cowards/.

Chess, Shira, and Adrienne Shaw. 2015. "A Conspiracy of Fishes, or: How We
   Learned to Stop Worrying About #GamerGate and Embrace Hegemonic
   Masculinity." *Journal of Broadcasting & Electronic Media* 59: 208–20.
   doi:10.1080/08838151.2014.999917.

Ching, Albert. 2015. "DC Comics Cancels 'Batgirl' Joker Variant at Artist's Request." *CBR.com*, 16 March. http://www.cbr.com/dc-comics-cancels-batgirl-
   joker-variant-cover-at-artists-request/.

Clarke, John. 2006. "Style." In *Resistance through Rituals*, edited by Stuart Hall
   and Tony Jefferson, 2nd ed, 147–61.

Cohen, Albert K. 1965. "The Sociology of the Deviant Act: Anomie Theory
   and Beyond." *American Sociological Review* 30: 5–14. doi:10.2307/2091770.

Cohen, Noam. 2014. "We're All Nerds Now." *New York Times*, 13 September.
   http://www.nytimes.com/2014/09/14/sunday-review/were-all-nerds-
   now.html.

Cohen, Phil. 2005. "Subcultural Conflict and Working-Class Community." In *The Subcultures Reader*, edited by Ken Gelder, 2nd ed. New York: Routledge.

Cohen, Stanley. 1972. *Folk Devils and Moral Panics: The Creation of the Mods and Rockers*. London: MacGibbon & Kee.

Connell, R.W. 1993. "The Big Picture: Masculinities in Recent World History." *Theory and Society* 22: 597–623. doi:10.1007/BF00993538.

– 2005. *Masculinities*. 2nd ed. Cambridge, UK: Polity.

Couldry, Nick. 2006. *Listening Beyond the Echoes: Media, Ethics, and Agency in an Uncertain World*. Boulder, CO: Paradigm Publishers.

– 2012. *Media, Society, World: Social Theory and Digital Media Practice*. Cambridge, UK: Polity.

Couldry, Nick, and Andreas Hepp. 2017. *The Mediated Construction of Social Reality*. Cambridge, UK: Polity.

Couldry, Nick, and Mark Hobart. 2010. "Media as Practice: A Brief Exchange." In *Theorising Media and Practice*, edited by Birgit Bräuchler and John Postill, 77–82. New York: Berghahn Books.

Coulson, Juanita. 1994. "Why Is a Fan?" In *Science Fiction Fandom*, edited by Joe Sanders, 3–9.

Coulson, Robert. 1994. "Fandom as a Way of Life." In *Science Fiction Fandom*, edited by Joe Sanders, 11–14.

Danesi, Marcel. 1994. *Cool: The Signs and Meanings of Adolescence*. Toronto: University of Toronto Press.

de Certeau, Michel. 2011. *The Practice of Everyday Life*. Berkeley and Los Angeles: University of California Press.

de Coning, Alexis. 2016. "Recouping Masculinity: Men's Rights Activists' Responses to *Mad Max: Fury Road*." *Feminist Media Studies* 16: 174–6. doi:10.1080/14680777.2016.1120491.

Deuze, Mark. 2011. "Media Life." *Media, Culture & Society* 33: 137–48. doi:10.1177/0163443710386518.

Dmytrewycz, Paul. 2012. "*The Big Bang Theory* and Nerd Minstrelsy." *The Brown Tweed Society*, 25 July. http://thebrowntweedsociety.com/2012/07/25/the-big-bang-theory-and-nerd-minstrelsy/.

Dorkin, Evan. 2008. "Will Elder R.I.P." *Livejournal* (blog), 15 May. http://evandorkin.livejournal.com/159687.html.

– 2016. *The Eltingville Club*. Milwaukie, OR: Dark Horse Comics.

Douglas, Mary. 2003. *Purity and Danger: An Analysis of Concepts of Pollution and Taboo*. New York: Routledge. First published 1966.

du Gay, Paul, and Michael Pryke, eds. 2002. *Cultural Economy: Cultural Analysis and Commercial Life*. London: SAGE.

Duncombe, Stephen. 2007. *Dream: Re-Imagining Progressive Politics in an Age of Fantasy*. New York: The New Press.

Eglash, Ron. 2002. "Race, Sex, and Nerds: From Black Geeks to Asian American Hipsters." *Social Text* 20 (2): 49–64.

Elliott, Richard, Susan Eccles, and Michelle Hodgson. 1993. "Re-Coding Gender Representations: Women, Cleaning Products, and Advertising's 'New Man.'" *International Journal of Research in Marketing* 10: 311–24. doi:10.1016/0167-8116(93)90013-O.

"fandom, *n.*" 1933. *A Supplement to the New English Dictionary*. OED Online. http://www.oed.com/view/Entry/68041.

Farrell, Warren. 1975. *The Liberated Man: Beyond Masculinity: Freeing Men and Their Relationships with Women*. New York: Bantam Books.

Fathallah, Judith. 2014. "'Except That Joss Whedon Is God': Fannish Attitudes to Statements of Author/ity." *International Journal of Cultural Studies* 19: 459–76. doi:10.1177/1367877914537589.

Feeney, Matt. 2011. "Angry Nerds: How Nietzsche Gets Misunderstood by Jared Loughner Types." *Slate*, 14 January. http://www.slate.com/id /2281133/.

Feineman, Neil. 2005. *GeekChic: The Ultimate Guide to Geek Culture*. Corte Madera, CA: Gingko Press.

Fiske, John. 1989a. *Reading the Popular*. Boston: Unwin Hyman.

– 1989b. *Understanding Popular Culture*. Boston: Unwin Hyman.

– 1992a. "Audiencing: A Cultural Studies Approach to Watching Television." *Poetics* 21: 345–59. doi: 10.1016/0304-422X(92)90013-S.

– 1992b. "The Cultural Economy of Fandom." In *The Adoring Audience: Fan Culture and Popular Media*, edited by Lisa A. Lewis, 30–49. London: Routledge.

Ford, Sam. 2014. "Fan Studies: Grappling with an 'Undisciplined' Discipline." *The Journal of Fandom Studies* 2: 53–71. doi:10.1386/jfs.2.1.53_1.

Foucault, Michel. 1977. "What Is an Author?" In *Language, Counter-Memory, Practice: Selected Essays and Interviews*, edited by Donald F. Bouchard, 113–38. Ithaca, NY: Cornell University Press.

– 1995. *Discipline and Punish: The Birth of the Prison*. Translated by Alan Sheridan. 2nd ed. New York: Vintage.

Gans, Herbert J. 1999. *Popular Culture and High Culture: An Analysis and Evaluation of Taste*, rev. ed. New York: Basic Books.

Gardner, Jared. 2012. *Projections: Comics and the History of Twenty-First-Century Storytelling*. Stanford, CA: Stanford University Press.

Gauntlett, David. 2011. *Making Is Connecting: The Social Meaning of Creativity, from DIY and Knitting to YouTube and Web 2.0*. Cambridge, UK: Polity.

"geek, *n.*" 2012. *The Oxford English Dictionary*, 3rd ed. OED Online. http://www
.oed.com /view/Entry/77307.

Geraghty, Lincoln. 2014. *Cult Collectors: Nostalgia, Fandom and Collecting Popular Culture*. Abingdon, UK: Routledge.

Giddens, Anthony. 1984. *The Constitution of Society: Outline of the Theory of Structuration*. Cambridge, UK: Polity.

Gill, Rosalind. 2003. "Power and the Production of Subjects: A Genealogy of the New Man and the New Lad." *The Sociological Review* 51 (S1): 34–56. doi:10.1111/j.1467-954X.2003.tb03602.x.

Gitelman, Lisa. 2004. "Media, Materiality, and the Measure of the Digital; or the Case of Sheet Music and the Problem of Piano Rolls." In *Memory Bytes: History, Technology, and Digital Culture*, edited by Lauren Rabinovitz and Abraham Geil, 199–217. Durham, NC Duke University Press.

Goldberg, Herb. 1979. *The New Male: From Macho to Sensitive But Still All Male*. New York: Signet.

Goltz, Dustin Bradley. 2013. "It Gets Better: Queer Futures, Critical Frustrations, and Radical Potentials." *Critical Studies in Media Communication* 30: 135–51. doi:10.1080/15295036.2012.701012.

Gonchar, Michael. 2014. "Are You a Nerd or a Geek?" *New York Times Learning Network*, 23 September. http://learning.blogs.nytimes.com/2014/09/23 /are-you-a-nerd-or-a-geek/.

Gray, Jonathan. 2005. "Antifandom and the Moral Text." *American Behavioral Scientist* 48: 840–58. doi:10.1177/0002764204273171.

Great White Snark. 2010. "Geek, Nerd, or Dork: A Venn Diagram Explains the Differences." Great White Snark, 25 March. http://www.greatwhitesnark .com/2010/03/25/difference-between-nerd-dork-and-geek-explained-in-a-venn-diagram/.

Grimes, Sara M. 2015. "Little Big Scene: Making and Playing Culture in Media Molecule's LittleBigPlanet." *Cultural Studies* 29: 379–400. doi: 10.1080/09502386.2014.937944.

Hall, Stuart. 1985. "Signification, Representation, Ideology: Althusser and the Post-structuralist Debates." *Critical Studies in Mass Communication* 2: 91–114. doi:10.1080/15295038509360070.

Hall, Stuart, and Tony Jefferson, eds. 2006. *Resistance through Rituals: Youth Subcultures in Post-War Britain*. 2nd ed. New York: Routledge. First published 1975.

Hathaway, Jay. 2014. "What Is Gamergate, and Why? An Explainer for Non-Geeks." *Gawker*, 10 October. http://gawker.com/what-is-gamergate-and-why-an-explainer-for-non-geeks-1642909080.

Hayden, Robert A. 1996. "The Code of the Geeks v3.12." *The Geek Code*, 5 March. http://www.geekcode.com/geek.html.

Hebdige, Dick. 1979. *Subculture: The Meaning of Style*. London: Methuen.

Hellekson, Karen, and Kristina Busse, eds. 2006. *Fan Fiction and Fan Communities in the Age of the Internet: New Essays*. Jefferson, NC: McFarland.

Hester, Stephen, and Peter Eglin, eds. 1997. *Culture in Action: Studies in Membership Categorization Analysis*. Washington, DC: International Institute for Ethnomethodology and Conversation Analysis and University Press of America.

Hills, Matt. 2002. *Fan Cultures*. New York: Routledge.

– 2005. "Negative Fan Stereotypes ('Get a Life!') and Positive Fan Injunctions ('Everyone's Got to Be a Fan of Something!'): Returning to Hegemony Theory in Fan Studies." *Spectator* 25 (1): 35–47.

– 2014a. "From Dalek Half Balls to Daft Punk Helmets: Mimetic Fandom and the Crafting of Replicas." *Transformative Works and Cultures* 16. doi:10.3983/twc.2014.0531.

– 2014b. "Returning to 'Becoming-a-Fan' Stories: Theorising Transformational Objects and the Emergence/Extension of Fandom." In *The Ashgate Research Companion to Fan Cultures*, edited by Linda Duits, Koos Zwaan, and Stijn Reijnders, 9–21. Farnham, UK: Ashgate.

– 2015. "From 'Multiverse' to 'Abramsverse': *Blade Runner, Star Trek*, Multiplicity, and the Authorizing of Cult/SF Worlds." In *Science Fiction Double Feature: The Science Fiction Film as Cult Text*, edited by J.P. Telotte and Gerald Duchovnay, 21–37. Liverpool: Liverpool University Press.

Hodkinson, Paul. 2002. *Goth: Identity, Style and Subculture*. Oxford: Berg.

– 2006. "Subcultural Blogging? Online Journals and Group Involvement among UK Goths." In *Uses of Blogs*, edited by Axel Bruns and Joanne Jacobs, 187–97. New York: Peter Lang.

– 2011. "Ageing in a Spectacular 'Youth Culture': Continuity, Change and Community amongst Older Goths." *The British Journal of Sociology* 62: 262–82. doi:10.1111/j.1468-4446.2011.01364.x.

– 2012. "Family and Parenthood in an Ageing 'Youth' Culture: A Collective Embrace of Dominant Adulthood?" *Sociology* 47: 1072–87. doi:10.1177/0038038512454351.

– 2013. "Spectacular Youth Cultures and Ageing: Beyond Refusing to Grow Up." *Sociology Compass* 7: 13–22. doi:10.1111/soc4.12008.

Hofstadter, Richard. 1966. *Anti-Intellectualism in American Life*. New York: Vintage.

Holland, Dorothy. 2010. "Symbolic Worlds in Times/Spaces of Practice: Identities and Transformations." In *Symbolic Transformation: The Mind in*

Movement through Culture and Society, edited by Brady Wagoner, 269–83. London: Routledge.

Holland, Dorothy, William Lachiotte, Jr, Debra Skinner, and Carole Cain. 1998. *Identity and Agency in Cultural Worlds*. Cambridge, MA: Harvard University Press.

Holland, Dorothy, and Naomi Quinn. 1987. *Cultural Models in Language and Thought*. Cambridge: Cambridge University Press.

Holt, Douglas B. 2000. "Does Cultural Capital Structure American Consumption?" In *The Consumer Society Reader*, edited by Juliet B. Schor and Douglas B. Holt, 212–52. New York: New Press.

Huang, S.L. 2014. "A Timeline of the 2013 SFWA Controversies." *SL Huang: Speculative Fiction Writer. Mathematician. Gunslinger*, 10 April. http://www.slhuang.com/blog/2013/07/02/a-timeline-of-the-2013-sfwa-controversies/.

Hudson, Laura. 2015. "Serious Bill-Paying Skillage." *Slate*, 7 July. http://www.slate.com/articles/arts/books/2015/07/armada_by_ernest_cline_follow_up_to_ready_player_one_reviewed.single.html.

Huizinga, Johan. 1949. *Homo Ludens: A Study of the Play-Element in Culture*. London: Routledge and Kegan Paul.

Hunt, Nathan. 2003. "The Importance of Trivia: Ownership, Exclusion and Authority in Science Fiction Fandom." In *Defining Cult Movies: The Cultural Politics of Oppositional Tastes*, edited by Mark Jancovich, Antonio Lázaro Reboll, Julian Stringer, and Andy Willis, 185–201. Manchester: Manchester University Press.

Huyssen, Andreas. 1986. "Mass Culture as Woman: Modernism's Other." In *After the Great Divide: Modernism, Mass Culture and Postmodernism*, 44–62. Basingstoke, UK: Macmillan.

Ito, Mizuko, Sonja Baumer, Matteo Bittanti, danah boyd, Rachel Cody, Becky Herr-Stephenson, Heather A. Horst, et al. 2010. *Hanging Out, Messing Around, and Geeking Out: Kids Living and Learning with New Media*. Cambridge, MA: MIT Press.

Jancovich, Mark. 2002. "Cult Fictions: Cult Movies, Subcultural Capital and the Production of Cultural Distinctions." *Cultural Studies* 16: 306–22. doi:10.1080/09502380110107607.

Jemisin, N.K. 2014. "Wiscon 38 Guest of Honor Speech." *N.K. Jemisin*, 25 May. http://nkjemisin.com/2014/05/wiscon-38-guest-of-honor-speech/.

Jenkins, Henry. 1988. "Star Trek Rerun, Reread, Rewritten: Fan Writing as Textual Poaching." *Critical Studies in Mass Communication* 5: 85–107. doi:10.1080/15295038809366691.

– 1995. "'Infinite Diversity in Infinite Combinations': Genre and Authorship in *Star Trek*." In *Science Fiction Audiences: Watching* Doctor Who *and* Star Trek, by John Tulloch and Henry Jenkins, 173–93. London: Routledge.

– 2006. *Fans, Bloggers, and Gamers: Exploring Participatory Culture*. New York: New York University Press.

– 2008. *Convergence Culture: Where Old and New Media Collide*, 2nd ed. New York: New York University Press.

– 2013. *Textual Poachers: Television Fans and Participatory Culture*, 2nd ed. New York: Routledge. First published 1992.

Jenkins, Henry, Ravi Purushotma, Margaret Weigel, Katie Clinton, and Alice J. Robison. 2009. *Confronting the Challenges of Participatory Culture: Media Education for the 21st Century*. The John D. and Catherine T. MacArthur Foundation Reports on Digital Media and Learning. Cambridge, MA: MIT Press.

Jenkins, Henry, and Suzanne Scott. 2013. "Textual Poachers, Twenty Years Later: A Conversation between Henry Jenkins and Suzanne Scott." In Jenkins, *Textual Poachers*, vii–l.

Jensen, Joli. 1992. "Fandom as Pathology: The Consequences of Characterization." In *The Adoring Audience: Fan Culture and Popular Media*, edited by Lisa A. Lewis, 9–29. London: Routledge.

Johnson, Derek. 2007. "Fan-tagonism: Factions, Institutions, and Constitutive Hegemonies of Fandom." In *Fandom: Identities and Communities in a Mediated World*, edited by Jonathan Gray, Cornel Sandvoss, and C. Lee Harrington, 285–300. New York: New York University Press.

– 2013. *Media Franchising: Creative License and Collaboration in the Culture Industries*. New York: New York University Press.

– 2014. "'May the Force Be with Katie': Pink Media Franchising and the Postfeminist Politics of HerUniverse." *Feminist Media Studies* 14: 895–911. doi:10.1080/14680777.2014.882856.

Keane, Webb. 2005. "Signs Are Not the Garb of Meaning: On the Social Analysis of Material Things." In *Materiality*, edited by Daniel Miller, 182–205. Durham, NC: Duke University Press.

Keat, Russell. 2000. *Cultural Goods and the Limits of the Market*. New York: St Martin's Press.

Kelly, Kevin. 1995. "Gossip Is Philosophy." *Wired*, May. https://www.wired.com/1995/05/eno-2/.

Kendall, Lori. 1999a. "Nerd Nation: Images of Nerds in US Popular Culture." *International Journal of Cultural Studies* 2: 260–83. doi:10.1177/136787799900200206.

– 1999b. "'The Nerd Within': Mass Media and the Negotiation of Identity

Among Computer-Using Men." *The Journal of Men's Studies* 7: 353–69. doi:10.3149/jms.0703.353.

– 2011. "'White and Nerdy': Computers, Race, and the Nerd Stereotype." *Journal of Popular Culture* 44: 505–24. doi:10.1111/j.1540-5931.2011.00846.x.

Kimmel, Michael S. 1987. "Men's Responses to Feminism at the Turn of the Century." *Gender & Society* 1: 261–83. doi:10.1177/089124387001003003.

– 2010. *Misframing Men: The Politics of Contemporary Masculinities*. New Brunswick, NJ: Rutgers University Press.

Kington, Candie Syphrit. 2015. "Con Culture: A Survey of Fans and Fandom." *The Journal of Fandom Studies* 3: 211–28. doi:10.1386/jfs.3.2.211_1.

Kingwell, Mark. 2004. "Nietzsche's Styles." In *Practical Judgments: Essays in Culture, Politics, and Interpretation*, 182–93. Toronto: University of Toronto Press.

Kinkade, Patrick T., and Michael A. Katovich. 2009. "Beyond Place: On Being a Regular in an Ethereal Culture." *Journal of Contemporary Ethnography* 38: 3–24. doi:10.1177/0891241607312266.

Kline, Stephen, Nick Dyer-Witheford, and Greig de Peuter. 2003. *Digital Play: The Interaction of Technology, Culture, and Marketing*. Montreal and Kingston: McGill-Queen's University Press.

Knight, Kelvin. 2008a. "After Tradition? Heidegger or MacIntyre, Aristotle and Marx." *Analyse & Kritik* 30: 33–52. doi:10.1515/auk-2008-0103.

– 2008b. "Practices: The Aristotelian Concept." *Analyse & Kritik* 30: 317–29. doi:10.1515/auk-2008-0118.

Kohnen, Melanie. 2014. "'The Power of Geek': Fandom as Gendered Commodity at Comic-Con." *Creative Industries Journal* 7: 75–8. doi:10.1080/17510694.2014.892295.

Krahulik, Mike, and Jerry Holkins. 2004. "Green Blackboards (And Other Anomalies)." *Penny Arcade* (comic strip), 19 March. https://www.penny-arcade.com/comic/2004/03/19/.

Kunyosying, Kom, and Carter Soles. 2012. "Postmodern Geekdom as Simulated Ethnicity." *Jump Cut* 54. http://www.ejumpcut.org/archive/jc54.2012/SolesKunyoGeedom/index.html.

Laclau, Ernesto, and Chantal Mouffe. 2001. *Hegemony and Socialist Strategy: Towards a Radical Democratic Politics*. New York: Verso.

Lamont, Michèle. 1992. *Money, Morals, and Manners: The Culture of the French and American Upper-Middle Class*. Chicago: University of Chicago Press.

– 2000. *The Dignity of Working Men: Morality and the Boundaries of Race, Class, and Immigration*. New York: Russell Sage Foundation.

Lave, Jean, and Etienne Wenger. 1991. *Situated Learning: Legitimate Peripheral Participation*. Learning in Doing. Cambridge: Cambridge University Press.

Leavenworth, Maria Lindgren. 2015. "The Paratext of Fan Fiction." *Narrative* 23: 40–60. doi:10.1353/nar.2015.0004.

Leland, John. 2004. *Hip: The History*. New York: HarperCollins.

Lewin, Kurt. 1943. "Forces behind Food Habits and Methods of Change." *Bulletin of the National Research Council* 108: 35–65.

"life, *n.*" 2009. *Oxford English Dictionary*, 3rd ed. OED Online. http://www.oed .com/view/Entry/108093.

Lindholm, Charles. 2008. *Culture and Authenticity*. Malden, MA: Blackwell.

Livingstone, Sonia. 1998. "Audience Research at the Crossroads: The 'Implied Audience' in Media and Cultural Theory." *European Journal of Cultural Studies* 1: 193–217. doi:10.1177/136754949800100203.

Locke, Simon. 2012. "Fanboy as a Revolutionary Category." *Participations: Journal of Audience & Reception Studies* 9 (2): 835–54.

Losh, Elizabeth. 2016. "Hiding inside the Magic Circle: Gamergate and the End of Safe Space." *Boundary 2 Online*, 15 August. http://www.boundary2.org/2016/08/elizabeth-losh-hiding-inside-the-magic-circle-gamergate-and-the-end-of-safe-space/.

Lothian, Alexis. 2009. "Living in a Den of Thieves: Fan Video and Digital Challenges to Ownership." *Cinema Journal* 48 (4): 130–6. doi:10.1353 /cj.0.0152.

MacIntyre, Alasdair. 1988. *Whose Justice? Which Rationality?* Notre Dame, IN: University of Notre Dame Press.

– 1998. "Notes from the Moral Wilderness." In *The MacIntyre Reader*, edited by Kelvin Knight, 31–49. Notre Dame, IN: University of Notre Dame Press.

– 2007. *After Virtue: A Study in Moral Theory*. 3rd ed. Notre Dame, IN: University of Notre Dame Press. First published 1981.

Mackail, J.W. 1899. *The Life of William Morris*, 2 vols. London: Longmans, Green, & Co.

Maffesoli, Michel. 1996. *The Time of the Tribes: The Decline of Individualism in Mass Society*. Translated by Don Smith. London: SAGE.

Maguire, Jennifer Smith, and Julian Matthews. 2012. "Are We All Cultural Intermediaries Now? An Introduction to Cultural Intermediaries in Context." *European Journal of Cultural Studies* 15: 551–62. doi:10.1177/1367549412445762.

Mailer, Norman. 1959. "The White Negro: Superficial Reflections on the Hipster." In *Advertisements for Myself*, 337–58. New York: G.P. Putnam's Sons.

Majkowski, Tina. 2011. "The 'It Gets Better Campaign': An Unfortunate Use of Queer Futurity." *Women & Performance: A Journal of Feminist Theory* 21: 163–5. doi:10.1080/0740770X.2011.563048.

Majors, Richard, and Janet Mancini Billson. 1992. *Cool Pose: The Dilemma of Black Manhood in America*. New York: Lexington Books.

Marcuse, Herbert. 2002. *One-Dimensional Man: Studies in the Ideology of Advanced Industrial Society*. Abingdon, UK: Routledge. First published 1964.

Martín Moruno, Dolores. 2013. "Introduction: On Resentment: Past and Present of an Emotion." In *On Resentment: Past and Present*, edited by Bernardino Fantini, Dolores Martín Moruno, and Javier Moscoso, 1–16. Newcastle upon Tyne, UK: Cambridge Scholars Publishing.

Martin, Richard, and Harold Koda. 1989. *Jocks and Nerds: Men's Style in the Twentieth Century*. New York: Rizzoli.

McArthur, J.A. 2009. "Digital Subculture: A Geek Meaning of Style." *Journal of Communication Inquiry* 33: 58–70. doi:10.1177/0196859908325676.

McCracken, Grant. 1988. *Culture and Consumption: New Approaches to the Symbolic Character of Consumer Goods and Activities*. Bloomington: Indiana University Press.

McDonald, Landon. 2015. "The Joker, Batgirl and the Specter of Censorship in Comics." *Daily Trojan*, 26 March. http://dailytrojan.com/2015/03/26/the-joker-batgirl-and-the-specter-of-censorship-in-comics/.

McRobbie, Angela. 2016. *Be Creative: Making a Living in the New Culture Industries*. Cambridge, UK: Polity.

Meehan, Eileen R. 2000. "Leisure or Labor? Fan Ethnography and Political Economy." In *Consuming Audiences? Production and Reception in Media Research*, edited by Ingunn Hagen and Janet Wasko, 71–92. Cresskill, NJ: Hampton Press.

– 2005. *Why TV Is Not Our Fault: Television Programming, Viewers, and Who's Really in Control*. Lanham, MD: Rowman & Littlefield.

Messner, Michael A. 1998. "The Limits of 'the Male Sex Role': An Analysis of Men's Liberation and Men's Rights Movements' Discourse." *Gender & Society* 12: 255–76. doi:10.1177/0891243298012003002.

Mezrich, Ben. 2009. *The Accidental Billionaires: The Founding of Facebook: A Tale of Sex, Money, Genius and Betrayal*. New York: Doubleday.

Mikkelson, David. 2013. "Some Rules Kids Won't Learn in School." *Snopes*, 25 November. http://www.snopes.com/politics/soapbox/schoolrules.asp.

Miller, Daniel. 1998. *A Theory of Shopping*. Cambridge, UK: Polity.

– 2008. *The Comfort of Things*. Cambridge, UK: Polity.

Milner, Murray, Jr. 2004. *Freaks, Geeks, and Cool Kids: American Teenagers, Schools, and the Culture of Consumption*. New York: Routledge.

Moosa, Tauriq. 2014. "Female Journalist Gets Rape Threats Over Comic Book Criticism." *The Daily Beast*, 21 April. http://www.thedailybeast.com/articles/2014/04/21/female-journalist-gets-rape-threats-over-comic-book-criticism.html.

Morris, Michael W., Daniel R. Ames, and Eric D. Knowles. 2001. "What We Theorize When We Theorize That We Theorize: Examining the 'Implicit Theory' Construct from a Cross-Disciplinary Perspective." In *Cognitive Social Psychology: The Princeton Symposium on the Legacy and Future of Social Cognition*, edited by Gordon B. Moskowitz, 143–61. Boulder, CO: NetLibrary.

Muggleton, David. 2000. *Inside Subculture: The Postmodern Meaning of Style*. Oxford: Berg.

Muñiz, Albert M., Jr, and T.C. O'Guinn. 2001. "Brand Community." *Journal of Consumer Research* 27: 412–32. doi:10.1086/319618.

Myketiak, Chrystie. 2016. "Fragile Masculinity: Social Inequalities in the Narrative Frame and Discursive Construction of a Mass Shooter's Autobiography/manifesto." *Contemporary Social Science* 11: 289–303. doi:10.1080/21582041.2016.1213414.

"nerd, *n.*" 2012. *Oxford English Dictionary*, 3rd ed. OED Online. http://www.oed.com /view/Entry/126165.

"NEW: Milo Yiannopoulos 'Facts V.S. Feelings.'" 2016. YouTube video, 5:21, from an interview with Cathy Newman televised by Channel 4 on 17 November, 2016, posted by "Destroy Feminism," 27 November, https://www.youtube.com/watch?v=omwGXCfoMaI.

Nietzsche, Friedrich. 1989. "On the Genealogy of Morals." In *On the Genealogy of Morals and Ecce Homo*, edited by Walter Kaufmann, translated by Walter Kaufmann and R.J. Hollingdale, 3–198. New York: Vintage Books.

Nixon, Sean, and Paul du Gay. 2002. [Special Issue] *Cultural Studies* 16 (4).

Obsession_inc. 2009. "Affirmational vs. Transformational Fandom." *Dreamwidth*, 1 June. http://obsession-inc.dreamwidth.org/82589.html.

O'Guinn, Thomas C., and Albert M. Muñiz Jr. 2005. "Communal Consumption and the Brand." In *Inside Consumption: Consumer Motives, Goals, and Desires*, edited by S. Ratneshwar and David Glen Mick, 252–72. London: Routledge.

Oswalt, Patton. 2010. "Wake Up, Geek Culture. Time to Die." *Wired*, 27 December. http://www.wired.com/magazine/2010/12/ff_angrynerd _geekculture/all/1.

Park, Douglas B. 1982. "The Meanings of 'Audience.'" *College English* 44: 247–57. doi:10.2307/377012.

Pearce, Susan. 1995. *On Collecting: An Investigation into Collecting in the European Tradition*. Abingdon, UK: Routledge.

Penley, Constance. 1997. *NASA/Trek: Popular Science and Sex in America*. London: Verso.

Peters, John Durham. 1999. *Speaking into the Air: A History of the Idea of Communication*. Chicago: University of Chicago Press.

Peterson, Mark Allen. 2005. "Performing Media: Toward an Ethnography of Intertextuality." In *Media Anthropology*, edited by Eric W. Rothenbuhler and Mihai Coman, 129–38. Thousand Oaks, CA: SAGE.

Peterson, Richard A. 1992. "Understanding Audience Segmentation: From Elite and Mass to Omnivore and Univore." *Poetics* 21: 243–58. doi:10.1016/0304-422X(92)90008-Q.

Phillips, Whitney. 2015. *This Is Why We Can't Have Nice Things: Mapping the Relationship Between Online Trolling and Mainstream Culture*. Cambridge, MA: MIT Press.

Pierre, Levy. 1997. *Collective Intelligence: Mankind's Emerging World in Cyberspace*. Cambridge, MA: Perseus Books.

Pilkington, Hilary, and Elena Omel'chenko. 2013. "Regrounding Youth Cultural Theory (in Post-socialist Youth Cultural Practice)." *Sociology Compass* 7: 208–24. doi:10.1111/soc4.12023.

Postman, Neil. 1994. *The Disappearance of Childhood*. 2nd ed. New York: Vintage.

Pountain, Dick, and David Robins. 2000. *Cool Rules: Anatomy of an Attitude*. London: Reaktion Books.

Putnam, Robert D. 2000. *Bowling Alone: The Collapse and Revival of American Community*. New York: Simon and Schuster.

Quail, Christine. 2011. "Nerds, Geeks, and the Hip/Square Dialectic in Contemporary Television." *Television & New Media* 12: 460–82. doi:10.1177/1527476410385476.

Radway, Janice. 1984. *Reading the Romance: Women, Patriarchy, and Popular Literature*. Chapel Hill: The University of North Carolina Press.

Reagle, Joseph. 2015. "Geek Policing: Fake Geek Girls and Contested Attention." *International Journal of Communication* 9: 2862–80.

Reckwitz, Andreas. 2002. "Toward a Theory of Social Practices: A Development in Culturalist Theorizing." *European Journal of Social Theory* 5: 243–63. doi: 10.1177/13684310222225432.

Redhead, Steve. 1997. *Subculture to Clubcultures: An Introduction to Popular Cultural Studies*. Oxford: Blackwell Publishers.

Reginster, Bernard. 1997. "Nietzsche on Ressentiment and Valuation." *Philosophy and Phenomenological Research* 57: 281–305. doi:10.2307/2953719.

Rhodes, Megan. 2014. *Nerd Classification Index*. http://portfolios.moore.edu/gallery/16500621/Nerd-Classification-Index.

Robbins, Alexandra. 2011. *The Geeks Shall Inherit the Earth: Popularity, Quirk Theory, and Why Outsiders Thrive after High School*. New York: Hyperion.

Rogers, Adam. 2008. "Geek Love." *New York Times*, 9 March. http://www.ny-times.com/2008/03/09/opinion/09rogers.html?_r=2&pagewanted=all.

Romano, Aja. 2016. "How the Alt-right Uses Internet Trolling to Confuse You into Dismissing Its Ideology." *Vox*, 23 November. http://www.vox.com/2016/11/23/13659634/alt-right-trolling.

Rosenberg, Alyssa. 2013. "Fake Geek Girls Are Not Coming to Destroy You." *Slate*, 15 January. http://www.slate.com/blogs/xx_factor/2013/01/15/fake_geek_girls_no_they_are_not_coming_to_destroy_you.html.

Rüling, Charles-Clemens, and Jesper Strandgaard Pedersen. 2010. "Film Festival Research from an Organizational Studies Perspective." *Scandinavian Journal of Management* 26: 318–23. doi:10.1016/j.scaman.2010.06.006.

Ryle, Gilbert. 2009. *The Concept of Mind*. London: Routledge. First published 1949.

Sacks, Harvey. 1972. "On the Analysability of Stories by Children." In *Ethnomethodology: Selected Readings*, edited by Roy Turner, 216–32. Harmondsworth, UK: Penguin Education.

– 1979. "Hotrodder: A Revolutionary Category." In *Everyday Language: Studies in Ethnomethodology*, edited by George Psathas, 7–14. New York: Irvington Publishers.

– 1984. "On Doing 'Being Ordinary.'" In *Structures of Social Action: Studies in Conversation Analysis*, edited by J. Maxwell Atkinson and John Heritage, 413–29. Cambridge and Paris: Cambridge University Press and Editions de la Maison des Sciences de l'Homme.

– 1992. *Lectures on Conversation*. Edited by Gail Jefferson. 2 vols. Oxford: Blackwell.

Safire, William. 1980. "Words for Nerds." On Language. *New York Times Magazine*, 20 July. https://timesmachine.nytimes.com/timesmachine/1980/07/20/111797335.html?pageNumber=282.

Saler, Michael. 2004. "Modernity, Disenchantment, and the Ironic Imagination." *Philosophy and Literature* 28: 137–49. doi:10.1353/phl.2004.0012.

Salkowitz, Rob. 2012. *Comic Con and the Business of Pop Culture: What the World's Wildest Trade Show Can Tell Us about the Future of Entertainment*. New York: McGraw-Hill.

Sandel, Michael. 1984. "The Procedural Republic and the Unencumbered Self." *Political Theory* 12: 81–96. doi:10.1177/0090591784012001005.

Sanders, Joe, ed. 1994. *Science Fiction Fandom*. Westport, CT: Greenwood Press.

Sanders, Joe, and rich brown. 1994. "Glossary of Fanspeak." In Sanders, *Science Fiction Fandom*, 265–9.

Sandvoss, Cornel. 2005. *Fans: The Mirror of Consumption*. Cambridge, UK: Polity.

Sayer, Andrew. 2000. "Moral Economy and Political Economy." *Studies in Political Economy* 61: 79–103. doi:10.1080/19187033.2000.11675254.

– 2005. *The Moral Significance of Class*. Cambridge: Cambridge University Press.

– 2011. *Why Things Matter to People: Social Science, Values and Ethical Life*. Cambridge: Cambridge University Press.

Schatzki, Theodore R. 1996. *Social Practices: A Wittgensteinian Approach to Human Activity and the Social*. Cambridge: Cambridge University Press.

– 2001. "Introduction: Practice Theory." In *The Practice Turn in Contemporary Theory*, edited by Theodore R. Schatzki, Karin Knorr Cetina, and Eike von Savigny, 1–14. London: Routledge.

Schatzki, Theodore R., Karin Knorr Cetina, and Eike von Savigny, eds. 2001. *The Practice Turn in Contemporary Theory*. New York: Routledge.

Schroeder, Karl. 2011. "Science Fiction as Foresight." *Charlie's Diary* (blog), 22 September. http://www.antipope.org/charlie/blog-static/2011/09/science-fiction-as-foresight.html.

Schutz, Alfred. 1967. *The Phenomenology of the Social World*. Evanston, IL: Northwestern University Press.

Scott, Suzanne. 2013a. "Dawn of the Undead Author: Fanboy Auteurism and Zach Snyder's 'Vision.'" In *A Companion to Media Authorship*, edited by Jonathan Gray and Derek Johnson, 440–62. Malden, MA: Wiley-Blackwell.

– 2013b. "Fangirls in Refrigerators: The Politics of (In)visibility in Comic Book Culture." *Transformative Works and Cultures* 13. doi:10.3983/twc.2013.0460.

– 2017. "#Wheresrey?: Toys, Spoilers, and the Gender Politics of Franchise Paratexts." *Critical Studies in Media Communication* 34: 138–47. doi:10.1080/15295036.2017.1286023.

Shank, Barry. 1994. *Dissonant Identities: The Rock'n'Roll Scene in Austin, Texas*. Hanover, NH: Wesleyan University Press.

Shirky, Clay. 2010. *Cognitive Surplus: How Technology Makes Consumers into Collaborators*. New York: Penguin.

Shoemaker, Pamela J. 1991. *Gatekeeping*. Newbury Park, CA: SAGE Publications.

Silverstone, Roger. 2007. *Media and Morality: On the Rise of the Mediapolis*. Cambridge, UK: Polity.

Sjöberg, Lore. [2002?] "The Geek Hierarchy." *Brunching Shuttlecocks*. http://brunching.com/geekhierarchy.html.

Smith, Russell. 2007. "We're Apologizing to Cleveland for Being Square?"

Globe and Mail, 1 February. http://www.theglobeandmail.com/arts/were-apologizing-to-cleveland-for-being-square/article721432/.

Society for Creative Anachronism. 2008. "New Member's Guide to the SCA." http://www.sca.org/officers/chatelain/pdf/NewcomersGuidePages-hi.pdf.

Stanfill, Mel. 2011. "Doing Fandom, (Mis)Doing Whiteness: Heteronormativity, Racialization, and the Discursive Construction of Fandom." *Transformative Works and Cultures* 8. doi:10.3983/twc.2011.0256.

Statistics Canada. 2017. "Daily Average Time Spent in Hours on Various Activities by Age Group and Sex, 15 Years and Over, Canada and Provinces, Occasional (Hours unless Otherwise Noted)." CANSIM database, Table 113-0004. Ottawa. http://www5.statcan.gc.ca/cansim/a26?lang=eng&retrLang=eng&id=1130004.

Stebbins, Robert A. 1982. "Serious Leisure: A Conceptual Statement." *The Pacific Sociological Review* 25: 251–72. doi:10.2307/1388726.

– 1992. *Amateurs, Professionals and Serious Leisure*. Kingston and Montreal: McGill-Queen's University Press.

– 2007. *Serious Leisure: A Perspective for Our Time*. Piscataway, NJ: Transaction Publishers.

Stevens, J. Richard, and Christopher Edward Bell. 2012. "Piracy Cultures | Do Fans Own Digital Comic Books? Examining the Copyright and Intellectual Property Attitudes of Comic Book Fans." *International Journal of Communication* 6: 751–72.

Straw, Will. 1991. "Systems of Articulation, Logics of Change: Communities and Scenes in Popular Music." *Cultural Studies* 5: 368–88. doi:10.1080/09502389100490311.

– 2004. "Cultural Scenes." *Loisir et société / Society and Leisure* 27: 411–22. doi:10.1080/07053436.2004.10707657.

Suler, John. 2004. "The Online Disinhibition Effect." *CyberPsychology & Behavior* 7: 321–6. doi:10.1089/1094931041291295.

Sykes, Charles J. 2007. *50 Rules Your Kids Won't Learn in School*. New York: St Martin's Press.

Taylor, Charles. 1989. *Sources of the Self: The Making of the Modern Identity*. Cambridge, MA: Harvard University Press.

Thornton, Sarah. 1996. *Club Cultures: Music, Media, and Subcultural Capital*. Middletown, CT: Wesleyan University Press.

Tilly, Charles. 2006. *Why?* Princeton, NJ: Princeton University Press.

Tokumitsu, Miya. 2014. "In the Name of Love." *Jacobin*. https://www.jacobinmag.com/2014/01/in-the-name-of-love/.

Tönnies, Ferdinand. 2001. *Community and Civil Society*. Edited by Jose Harris.

Translated by Jose Harris and Margaret Hollis. Cambridge: Cambridge University Press. First published in German 1887.

Turkle, Sherry. 1984. *The Second Self: Computers and the Human Spirit*. New York: Simon and Schuster.

Valenti, Jessica. 2015. "Anita Sarkeesian Interview: 'The Word "Troll" Feels Too Childish. This Is Abuse.'" *Guardian*, 29 August. http://www.theguardian.com/technology/2015/aug/29/anita-sarkeesian-gamergate-interview-jessica-valenti.

Veblen, Thorstein. 1948. "The Theory of the Leisure Class." In *The Portable Veblen*, edited by Max Lerner, 53–214. New York: Viking. First published 1899.

Walter, Damien. 2016. "How the Alt-right Invaded Geek Culture." *Independent*, 29 August. http://www.independent.co.uk/voices/how-the-alt-right-invaded-geek-culture-a7214906.html.

Wanzo, Rebecca. 2015. "African American Acafandom and Other Strangers: New Genealogies of Fan Studies." *Transformative Works and Cultures* 20. doi:10.3983/twc.2015.0699.

Warde, Alan. 2005. "Consumption and Theories of Practice." *Journal of Consumer Culture* 5: 131–53. doi:10.1177/1469540505053090.

Warner, Michael. 2002. "Publics and Counterpublics." *Public Culture* 14: 49–90. doi:10.1215/08992363-14-1-49.

Weber, Max. 1997. *The Theory of Social and Economic Organization*. Edited by Talcott Parsons. New York: The Free Press.

– 2004. *The Essential Weber: A Reader*. Edited by Sam Whimster. London: Routledge.

Wenger, Etienne. 1998. *Communities of Practice: Learning, Meaning, and Identity*. Cambridge: Cambridge University Press.

Widdicombe, Sue, and Robin Wooffitt. 1995. *The Language of Youth Subcultures: Social Identity in Action*. New York: Harvester Wheatsheaf.

Wilkinson, Abi. 2016. "We Need to Talk about the Online Radicalisation of Young, White Men." *Guardian*, 15 November. https://www.theguardian.com/commentisfree/2016/nov/15/alt-right-manosphere-mainstream-politics-breitbart.

Williams, Raymond. 1989. *Resources of Hope: Culture, Democracy, Socialism*. London: Verso.

– 2001. "Base and Superstructure in Marxist Cultural Theory." In *Media and Cultural Studies: KeyWorks*, edited by Meenakshi Gigi Durham and Douglas M. Kellner, 152–65. Malden, MA: Blackwell.

Willis, Paul. 1977. *Learning to Labour: How Working Class Kids Get Working Class Jobs*. Aldershot, UK: Gower.

– 1990. *Common Culture: Symbolic Work at Play in the Everyday Cultures of the Young*. Milton Keynes, UK: Open University Press.

Wolf, Mark J.P. 2012. *Building Imaginary Worlds: The Theory and History of Subcreation*. New York: Routledge.

Woo, Benjamin. 2012a. "Alpha Nerds: Cultural Intermediaries in a Subcultural Scene." *European Journal of Cultural Studies* 15: 659–76. doi:10.1177/1367549412445758.

– 2012b. "Understanding Understandings of Comics: Reading and Collecting as Media-Oriented Practices." *Participations: Journal of Audience & Reception Studies* 9 (2): 180–99.

– 2014. "A Pragmatics of Things: Materiality and Constraint in Fan Practices." *Transformative Works and Cultures* 16. doi:10.3983/twc.2014.0495.

– 2015. "Nerds, Geeks, Gamers, and Fans: Doing Subculture on the Edge of the Mainstream." In *The Borders of Subculture: Resistance and the Mainstream*, edited by Alexander Dhoest, Steven Malliet, Barbara Segaert, and Jacques Haers, 17–36. London: Routledge.

Woo, Benjamin, Stuart R. Poyntz, and Jamie Rennie, eds. 2016. *Scene Thinking: Cultural Studies from the Scenes Perspective*. New York: Routledge.

Woo, Benjamin, Jamie Rennie, and Stuart R. Poyntz. 2015. "Introduction: Scene Thinking." *Cultural Studies* 29: 285–97. doi:10.1080/09502386.2014.937950.

Wright, Erik Olin. 2010. *Envisioning Real Utopias*. London: Verso.

Young, Cathy. 2015. "Comics Like Batgirl Shouldn't Require a 'Good Feminist' Seal of Approval." *Time*, 24 March. http://time.com/3755285/batgirl-joker-cover-controversy-feminism/.

Young, Jock. 2009. "Moral Panic: Its Origins in Resistance, Ressentiment and the Translation of Fantasy into Reality." *British Journal of Criminology* 49: 4–16. doi:10.1093/bjc/azn074.

Zhao, Shanyang. 2004. "Consociated Contemporaries as an Emergent Realm of the Lifeworld: Extending Schutz's Phenomenological Analysis to Cyberspace." *Human Studies* 27: 91–105. doi:10.1023/B:HUMA .0000012246.33089.68.

Index

Abercrombie, Nicholas, 17

"actually," 70–1

Adorno, Theodor W., 199

African American Vernacular English, 8

After Virtue. *See* MacIntyre, Alasdair; MacIntyre's theory of practice

aggrieved entitlement. *See* ressentiment

Almog, Oz. *See* social types

Alternate Universe Club (fan club), 19, 21, 73–4, 79, 142, 148, 149, 162, 201, 205–6, 234ch6n2. *See also* Bobby

alt-right, 173, 178, 189, 190, 234ch8n1. *See also* masculinity, toxic; ressentiment

amateur press associations (APAs). *See* fanzines

Anderegg, Dave, 9, 15, 123

Anderson, Benedict, 115, 152. *See also* community, imagined

Ang, Ien, 16, 50–1, 52

anime, 62, 73, 147, 148, 149, 162, 197, 205, 206, 216, 217

Anime Con (convention), 79, 206, 217

anonymity, 186–7

Anonymous, 123

anti-intellectualism, 14

Appadurai, Arjun, 88

Aristotle, 52, 56, 57, 58–9; and virtue ethics, 24, 55, 179

Armada, 199

articulation, 19, 66, 107, 144, 147, 151, 204

Asimov, Isaac, 106, 198

Asselin, Janelle, 176

audience, 16, 50–2, 182, 194; active audience theory, 16, 63–4, 95, 195–6; empirical-abstract distinction, 51–2; as social practice, 52, 55, 64

authenticity, 99, 106, 109, 141, 154, 177, 233ch4n3

authorship, 85, 180–3, 196. *See also* creator-orientation and user-orientation (under consumption; cultural production)

autism spectrum, 15

Babylon 5, 30

Barley, Stephen J., 89, 90

Barry (research participant), 23, 31–2, 33, 39, 71, 92–3, 95, 96, 97, 98, 100,

101, 102–3, 110, 111, 116, 117, 119–
    20, 124, 125, 153, 158–9, 160, 166,
    167, 170, 184, 201, 217–19, 223,
    233n1; as aspiring novelist, 96, 182,
    218; and conflict, 45, 103, 126, 163,
    177; definition of community,
    112–14; at home, 162–4, 217–18
Barthes, Roland, 180
Batman, 71, 227. See also DC Comics
Bauman, Zygmunt, 112, 114, 115,
    126, 233n3
Beadle, Ron, 87
Beaty, Bart, 232n2
Bell, Christopher Edward, 235n5
Benedict, R.S., 189
Benjamin, Walter, 75, 108–9
The Big Bang Theory, 3, 13
Billson, Janet Mancini, 7–8
Black Lives Matter, 178, 189
Blood Bowl (miniatures game), 23, 96,
    166, 169, 228–9
Bobby (president, Alternate Universe
    Club), 21, 140, 147, 148, 205–6
Boltanski, Luc, 62
Booth, Paul J., 65
Borgmann, Albert, 24, 54–5, 66. See
    also practices, focal
boundary work, 38–9, 40–5, 46, 99,
    125, 144, 164, 176, 182, 196; "geek"
    and "nerd" as, 189–90, 231ch1n3.
    See also symbolic boundaries
Bourdieu, Pierre, 10, 17, 46, 53, 78,
    81–2, 85, 96, 138, 144, 190; as prac-
    tice theorist, 53, 232n1; and taste
    distinctions 69, 71, 181; on value,
    68. See also capital; cultural inter-
    mediaries; field; habitus; scholastic
    disposition
Bowling Alone, 127–30
Bradbury, Ray, 218

Brooks, David, 11
Brown, Jeffrey A., 69
brown, rich, 167, 231n3
Bucholtz, Mary, 8, 11
Buffy the Vampire Slayer, 109, 115,
    124, 160–1, 226, 227
bullying. See school, peer cultures
Burke, Kenneth. See consubstantiality
Busse, Kristina, 10, 15–16, 172–3
Byrne, David, 11

capital, 68–9, 71, 78, 87, 118, 177;
    Bourdieu's theory of, 68, 78; cul-
    tural, 25, 68–9, 70, 71, 72, 74, 77,
    78, 87, 138, 149, 185; economic, 68,
    77, 154; field-specific, 25; linguis-
    tic, 41 (see also scholastic disposi-
    tion; superstandard English);
    social, 68, 73, 118, 127, 128, 129–
    30, 138, 158, 204; subcultural, 25,
    68, 69, 70, 74, 78, 138, 154, 199
career scripts, 90. See also identity,
    narrative conception of
careers (leisure), 18, 25, 55, 84, 88,
    89–90, 95, 96, 100, 105, 139, 150,
    152; deepening engagement, 95–9;
    durable attachments, 104, 105,
    116; post-fandom, 96, 101–3, 104–
    5, 125, 192–3, 227; recruitment
    into, 91–5, 105, 116, 207
careers (occupational), 89–90, 128,
    139–40, 141, 145, 150; as cultural
    producers, 96, 139, 182–3
Certified Guaranty Company (CGC),
    76–7
Cheetos, 34, 45, 111
Chicago School, 53, 89–90
"chicken fat" cartooning, 191
childishness, 9, 90, 92, 192, 199
City Gaming Network, 19, 21, 77,

116, 127, 134, 135, 142, 148–9, 169, 208–9, 210, 228. *See also* Kurt

class (role-playing games), 14

class (social), 12, 16, 20, 40, 47, 62, 82, 138, 156–7, 172, 224, 226

classification. *See* boundary work; membership categorization analysis

Cohen, Albert K., 235n4

Cohen, Noam, 10–11, 12

Cohen, Phil, 139, 200

collecting, collections, 74–8, 115, 135–6, 155, 162, 164, 166, 196, 211; as capital, 74–5, 77, 78; as fan practice, 77–8; hoarding, 162–3; purging, 162, 164–5

collectors: denial of, 223; speculators, 207; typology of, 75, 76

comic books, 9, 26, 39, 41, 43, 50, 71, 87, 91, 96, 97, 98, 115, 123, 131, 133, 144, 147, 155, 162, 165, 181, 183, 185, 187, 191, 207, 212, 219; and continuity, 70 (*see also* scholastic disposition; trivia); fan culture, 18, 19, 49, 69, 70, 74–5, 78, 85, 94, 109, 115, 118–19, 124–5, 142, 176, 193, 195, 201, 212, 215, 235n5; "floppies," 91, 92, 215; graphic novels and trade paperbacks, 43, 91, 102, 207, 215, 227; indie-main-stream divide, 148, 208; reading, 76, 77, 93, 155, 212, 223, 226, 227, 232ch3n4; slabbing (*see* Certified Guaranty Company); and status, 81, 86, 122, 194. *See also* collecting; DC Comics; Marvel Comics

comic-cons. *See* conventions

comic shops, 3, 20, 38, 61, 62, 64, 75, 79, 98, 102, 111, 115, 133, 134, 135, 136, 141–2, 145, 163, 164, 185, 190,

204, 206, 208, 214, 221, 224, 227, 235n6. *See also* retailers; and specific stores

communalization, 109, 113, 116, 117, 119, 120, 130, 152, 200–1, 233ch5n4

communitarianism, 114, 115, 127–30

community, 108, 110–12, 115–16, 126–30; commitment and, 100, 114–15, 117; communities of practice, 15, 60, 104, 107, 232ch2n1; ersatz, 108, 112, 199; imagined, 115, 152; sense of, 113–14, 117–18; tensions within, 103–4, 147. *See also* communalization; MacIntyre's theory of practice

community-making. *See* communalization

Conan the Barbarian, 67, 228

Connell, Raewyn, 11, 174. *See also* masculinity, hegemonic

consubstantiality, 44–5, 47, 78, 115, 136, 152, 189. *See also* boundary work; communalization

consumption, 55, 93, 109, 129, 134, 150, 195, 196–7; and creativity, 153, 181–2, 199; creator-orientation and user-orientation, 85, 181–3, 235n5

conventions, 16, 19, 20, 33, 89, 91, 95, 141, 147–8, 153, 169, 185, 195, 197, 203, 206, 208, 209, 219, 225, 232ch3n5; business of, 207–8; as communities, 113, 116–7; as institutions, 61, 88, 98, 120, 132, 137, 204; as spectacle, 99, 49–50. *See also* individual conventions

Convivium (fan club), 102–3, 112, 113

cool, 6–10, 126; and gender, 10; hip/square dialectic, 11–12 (*see also* triumphal narrative); as practical consciousness, 9; racialization of, 7–8. *See also* capital, subcultural

co-ordination, 159–60, 168

cosplay, 21, 40, 49, 50, 73, 99, 126, 194, 195, 197, 200, 205

Couldry, Nick, 24, 57, 58, 62–3, 64, 65

Coulson, Juanita, 65

Coulson, Robert, 101

cultural intermediaries, 138–40, 150–1; amateur and professionalism, 141–2, 204; curation, 145–7; diversification, 148–9; education, 147–8; as institutions, 61; introversion and extroversion, 142–4; and power, 133–4, 146–7

cultural models, 46–8, 66. *See also* figured worlds; lay theories; social types

cultural omnivore thesis, 129

Day, Felicia, 182

DC Comics, 91, 94, 147–8, 183, 214, 227, 234ch6n6

de Certeau, Michel, 171

determination, 96, 153

Deuze, Mark, 26, 150

Dewey, John, 53, 137

Diana (research participant), 23, 32, 33–5, 41–2, 43–4, 45, 90, 96, 99, 101–2, 109, 111, 119, 124, 125–6, 155–7, 159, 162, 181–2, 184, 201, 219–21; as member of a "nerd family," 92, 93, 94, 164, 167–8, 169–70, 219

digital media, 16, 110, 118–20, 161, 194–5, 197–8, 204, 208; and disinhibition, 186–8; and materiality, 165–6; as substitute for subcultural institutions, 119, 166; as virtual communities, 129

diversity: appealing to, 216; erasure of, 124, 177, 190; in geek culture, 10, 12, 176, 184

Doctor Who, 98, 137, 161, 223, 225

Dr Seuss, 6

Dorkin, Evan. *See* The Eltingville Comic Book, Science-Fiction, Fantasy, Horror, and Role-Playing Club

Douglas, Mary, 163

Downtown Comics & Collectibles (comic shop), 20, 21, 73, 137, 141, 142, 146, 149, 212, 215–16, 221. *See also* Sean

Duncan, Louise, 3

Duncombe, Stephen, 27

Dune, 92, 228

Dungeons & Dragons, 11, 13, 23, 32, 34, 71, 94, 96–7, 99, 106, 111, 156, 160, 161, 189, 164, 166, 168, 199, 219, 220–1, 223, 226, 229; Dungeons & Dragons Insider, 156, 166; *Dungeons & Dragons Miniatures*, 135. *See also* games, role-playing

Eastside Games & Comics (combination game and comic book store), 20, 21, 76, 77, 92, 134, 140, 146, 147, 149, 185–6, 213–15. *See also* Scott

Eglash, Ron, 10, 12, 176, 185, 197

Elephant, 189

Elias, Norbert, 53

The Eltingville Comic Book, Science-Fiction, Fantasy, Horror, and Role-Playing Club, 26, 191–4, 201

Emo Kylo Ren, 175

emotion: fandom and, 64, 81, 95, 153; masculinity and, 7, 9, 173–4,

177–8 (*see also* cool; ressentiment); versus reason, 84–5, 177–8 (*see also* scholastic disposition)

Eno, Brian, 8

equipment-goods, 132–3, 153, 154, 159, 161–2, 165

ethereal cultures, 73, 89, 200

Everything That Ever Was, Available Forever (ETEWAF), 194–5. *See also* digital media

fake geek girls, 184–5, 232n6, 235n6

fanboys, 18, 43, 99, 148, 190; as "auteurs," 194

fan clubs, 92–3, 98, 103, 112, 102–3, 112, 119–20, 218. *See also* individual groups

fandom, fans, 8, 15–19, 20, 23, 32, 41, 49–50, 55, 61, 62, 64, 66, 69, 70, 73, 77–8, 79, 81, 85–6, 91, 92–3, 95, 99, 103, 110–11, 118–19, 124–6, 131, 139, 147, 162–4, 165–6, 173, 175–6, 177, 182, 184–6, 192, 193–4, 197, 204, 205, 220, 231n4, 231n5; affirmational-transformational distinction, 17, 78, 172–3, 195–6; and cultural industries, 194, 196, 198–9; and geek culture, 15–16, 7, 18–19, 24, 41; as identity, 46, 55, 65, 80, 107, 115; new hegemonic, 12, 37, 196; as practice, 65, 66, 101. *See also* fan culture *under* comic books *and* science fiction & fantasy

Fan Fellowship (fan club), 102–3, 112, 113

fan fiction, 16, 29, 78, 182, 222, 224

fan studies, 16, 63–4, 66, 69, 80–1, 105–6, 182, 201

fantasy (genre). *See* science fiction and fantasy

fanzines, 16, 50, 65, 120, 137

Farrell, Warren. *See* men's movements (under masculinity)

Fathallah, Judith, 182

feminism, 16, 123, 173–4

field, 87, 96, 142, 145; of cultural production, 144; of practices (*see* practice theory); relationship to capital, 68

figured worlds, 47–8, 53, 66, 232ch2n1

Fiske, John, 16, 17, 51, 52, 55, 69, 182, 195–6

Ford, Sam, 17

Foucault, Michel, 53, 82, 144, 180

Freaks and Geeks, 4

Funko Pops, 78

GAFIA, gafiation, 100, 167

game stores, 3, 20, 61, 70, 76, 124, 184–5, 204, 220, 231n5; as event spaces, 89, 135–7, 138, 140, 190, 208, 211–12, 214. *See also* retailers; and specific stores

gamers, 19, 34, 45, 46, 38–9, 64, 80, 98, 99, 116, 124, 133, 136, 140, 142, 159, 176, 185, 201, 209, 221, 234ch6n3; Gamergate, 123, 176–7, 178, 186, 187, 190; as identity, 18, 64, 99, 110, 176–7, 224, 228

games, board, 21, 57–8, 68, 70, 72, 75, 134, 143, 146, 147, 149, 158, 161, 164, 169, 194, 210, 211, 214, 216, 228

games, collectible card (CCG), 21, 70, 76, 85, 140, 144, 149, 153–4, 155, 209, 210, 211, 214. *See also* specific titles

games, massively multiplayer online role-playing (MMORPG), 110, 157–8,

193, 198; as social space, 117–18, 221. *See also* games, video; and specific titles

games, miniatures, 76, 77, 96, 155, 186, 187, 193, 197, 222; collectible, 74, 76, 77, 211. *See also* specific titles

games, role-playing (RPGs), 21, 23, 32, 43–4, 62, 96, 127, 134, 143, 148, 149, 156, 169, 185, 193, 197, 201, 208, 210, 211, 214, 216, 217, 219, 220–1, 223, 228, 229; gaming groups, 43–4, 100, 101, 102, 105, 159, 169, 220, 222–3. *See also* specific titles

games, video, 32, 39, 64, 72, 98, 123, 124, 131, 157, 159–60, 165, 181, 183, 187, 188, 194, 217, 221, 227; digital games industry, 11, 50, 176, 204, 221

Gans, Herbert J., 87, 81

Garfinkel, Harold, 53

gatekeeping, 25, 126, 144–9, 185, 197

Gates, Bill, 11, 12, 14, 197

geek. *See* nerd

"geek chic," 7, 11, 12, 13, 15, 42, 99, 122, 123, 126, 200. *See also* geek culture, mainstreaming of; triumphal narrative

Geek Code, 29

geek culture, 15, 129, 194; critique as materialistic, 77, 127, 134, 143, 211; mainstreaming of, 12–13, 34–5, 50, 86, 106, 120, 121–6, 133, 142–3, 148, 195 (*see also* subcultures, incorporation; triumphal narrative); media representations of, 3, 10–12, 13, 14, 15–16, 40, 45–6, 49–50, 124, 174, 175, 184, 189 (*see also* diversity; "get a life"); and technology, 14, 196–7, 198

Geek Hierarchy, 29

geeking out, 9, 81

gender, 167–70, 184, 185–6, 188; gender-based harassment, 173, 176, 183, 186, 187–8, 192; gendered participation in geek culture, 124, 170, 175, 183, 184, 185, 205–6, 214–15, 220. *See also* diversity; fake geek girls; masculinity

Geraghty, Lincoln, 74, 75, 77–8, 196

"get a life," 27, 28, 49, 201–2

Ghostbusters, 3, 21, 175, 176, 180, 187, 203

Gibson, William, 125

Giddens, Anthony, 53, 160

Giffords, Gabrielle, 172

Gitelman, Lisa, 165

gleaning, 134, 158–9

Goldberg, Herb. *See* men's movements (under masculinity)

Gray, Jonathan, 62

Green Lantern, 115. *See also* DC Comics

Gygax, E. Gary, 11. *See also Dungeons & Dragons*

habitus, 82, 84, 85

Hall, Stuart, 107, 121

Hamill, Mark, 4

Hank (owner, Plaza Games), 21, 45, 69, 70, 75, 92, 137, 140, 143, 146, 147, 185, 199, 211–12, 234ch6n3

Harry Potter, 3, 11, 92, 182, 183, 226–7

Harry Potter Alliance, 123, 198

Hebdige, Dick, 8, 12, 121

Hills, Matt 12, 17, 18, 25, 37, 80–1, 105–6, 177, 182, 196. *See also* fandom, new hegemonic

hip. *See* cool

hipsters, 10

The Hobbit. See Tolkien, J.R.R.

Hodkinson, Paul, 20, 39, 68, 104, 132, 138, 170

Holland, Dorothy. *See* cultural models; figured worlds

Hoppenstand, Gary, 13

Hudson, Laura, 199

Huizinga, Johan, 187

Hunt, Nathan, 69–70

identity, 37, 44, 47, 93, 107, 151, 175, 176, 187, 188; narrative conception of, 56, 90, 92, 96–8, 105, 106, 109; and politics, 13, 172–3, 176, 178, 192; and value, 67

individualism, 8, 39, 68, 126, 127

intertextuality, 72–4, 191, 199. *See also* capital

"it gets better," 124

Ito, Mizuko, 52, 60, 197

Jemisin, N.K., 176

Jenkins, Henry, 16, 18, 27, 63–4, 81, 85–6, 119, 182, 195–6, 197–8, 201

Jensen, Joli, 8, 86

jocks, 4, 9, 11, 12, 14, 17, 19, 45, 55, 64, 106, 179, 189, 204, 231n4, 233ch5n1, 235n6

John (owner, Westside Board Games), 21, 136–7, 139, 145–6, 209–10

Johnson, Derek, 175

Katovich, Michael A. *See* ethereal cultures

Keat, Russell, 25, 59, 132–3, 153

Kendall, Lori, 12, 30, 35, 37, 41

Kimmel, Michael, 172, 173, 177, 179

King Con (convention), 19, 21, 141, 206–8, 227, 234ch6n2. *See also* Peter

King St Comics (comic shop), 20, 21, 71, 136, 148, 163, 201, 212–13. *See also* Warren

Kington, Candie Syphrit, 95, 100

Kingwell, Mark, 178

Kinkade, Patrick T. *See* ethereal cultures

Knight, Kelvin, 52, 56, 61, 180

knowledge. *See* capital, cultural; intertextuality; scholastic disposition; trivia

Koda, Harold, 4, 14

Kurt (president, City Gaming Network), 21, 34, 45, 77, 127, 134, 140, 142, 143, 148, 208–9

Laclau, Ernesto, 107. *See also* articulation

Lamont, Michèle, 24, 40–1. *See also* boundary work; symbolic boundaries

Lave, Jean. *See* communities of practice (under community; situated learning)

lay theories, 31, 40, 46, 47, 67, 180; of education, 83–4; of geek culture, 13–4, 47–8, 98–9

Legend of the Five Rings (*L5R*), 76, 214, 229

legitimate peripheral participation. *See* situated learning

LEGO, 105, 122, 226

leisure: careers (*see* careers, leisure); casual, 55, 64; and community, 128 (*see also* communalization; community; MacIntyre's theory of practice); and freedom, 101–2, 167, 170, 186; and media, 14, 15, 18, 55; serious, 17–18, 55, 63, 64, 82, 104, 126, 200–1

Lewin, Kurt, 144
libraries, 158, 159, 234ch6n1
Livingstone, Sonia, 51–2
Locke, Simon, 39, 233ch4n3
Logan (president, Screens & Sorcery), 21, 34, 75, 133, 141, 142, 203–4; and City Gaming Network, 127, 208; as networker, 23, 127, 140, 220, 228.
Longhurst, Brian, 17
The Lord of the Rings. See Tolkien, J.R.R.
Losh, Elizabeth, 187
Loughner, Jared Lee, 172, 173, 178
Lucas, George. *See Star Wars*

MacIntyre, Alasdair, 56–7, 179, 200. *See also* MacIntyre's theory of practices; morality; practices, practice theory
MacIntyre's theory of practice, 55–63, 64, 86, 87–8, 105, 106–7, 179–80, 190; communities, 59–60, 61, 62, 64, 151; goods, external, 57–8, 60, 61, 62, 132, 232ch2n3; goods, internal, 57–9, 60, 62, 64, 102, 105; institutions, 60–1, 62, 64, 98, 116, 126, 131–2, 138–9, 142, 170–1; tradition, 59; virtues, 59–60, 62, 85, 129, 180
Mad Max: Fury Road, 175, 181
Maffesoli, Michel, 63, 108, 117
Magic: The Gathering (CCG), 70, 89, 147, 155, 162, 221–2, 229
Mailer, Norman, 10
Majors, Richard, 7–8
Marcuse, Herbert, 86
Martín Moruno, Dolores, 234ch8n3
Martin, Richard, 4, 14
Marvel Comics, 50, 147, 148, 165, 193, 214

masculinity, 7, 9, 191, 192; hegemonic, 10, 174, 179; men's movements, 173–4; "new man," 173–4; toxic, 172, 173, 175, 178, 179. *See also* cool; gender; ressentiment
Massachusetts Institute of Technology (MIT), 4, 6, 14
mass shootings, 172, 179, 188–9
media literacy, 176, 197–8
Meehan, Eileen, 13, 146
membership categorization analysis (MCA), 15, 31, 36–8, 39, 40–1, 45, 46, 99, 234ch6n4
memes, 73, 149, 184–5, 195, 197, 206
messiness. *See* hoarding (under collecting); at home (under Barry)
Messner, Michael A., 73, 74
Mezrich, Ben, 197
Miller, Daniel, 93, 163–4, 165, 166
Moore, Geoff, 87
morality, 172, 178, 182–3; absence in communication, media, and cultural studies, 57, 62–3; moral economy, 63, 73, 117, 134, 158, 182; relationship to practice, 56, 179, 232ch2n2
Morley, David, 60
Morris, William, 165, 197, 234ch7n1
Mouffe, Chantal, 107. *See also* articulation
Mr Fox (research participant), 23, 38–9, 40, 41–3, 46, 79–80, 94, 96, 97, 98, 99, 102, 109, 111, 114, 115, 122–4, 155, 157, 159–60, 164, 165, 170, 182–3, 185, 201, 221–3
"MSTing," 73–4
Muggleton, David, 40, 189
mundanes, 15, 41, 45, 73, 91, 167, 200
Munroe, Randall. See *xkcd*
Mystery Science Theatre 3000, 73

nerd. *See* geek
The Nerd (Broadway play), 4
Nerdity Test, 30
Nerds (candy), 4
Newsweek, 6
New York Times, 6, 10–11, 50
Nietzsche, Friedrich, 172, 178–9. *See also* ressentiment
nostalgia, 9, 127–8, 139, 164, 166, 198–9, 204
Nugent, Benjamin, 15

Obsession_inc, 17, 78, 172, 195
ordinariness, 38–9, 45
Oswalt, Patton, 106–7, 126, 194
otaku, 19. *See also* anime; fandom
Oxford English Dictionary, 4, 6, 201

Park, Douglas B., 51
participatory culture, 129, 143, 195; fandom as model for, 197–8; vernacular creativity, 129, 197 (*see also* creator-orientation and user-orientation [under consumption]; fan fiction)
Pearce, Susan, 232ch3n1. *See also* collecting
Pedersen, Jesper Strandgard, 49
Penny Arcade, 98, 187
Penny Arcade Expo (PAX), 79, 232ch3n5
Peter (organizer, King Con), 21, 91, 140, 141, 206–8, 226
Peters, John Durham, 233ch4n1
Peterson, Mark Allen, 72
Phillips, Whitney, 188
piracy, 161, 183, 235n5. *See also* gleaning
play, 47, 50, 72, 75–6, 81–2, 84–5, 154, 180, 181, 186–8, 190, 194, 218

Plaza Games, 20, 21, 72, 74, 135, 140, 147, 149, 201, 210, 211–12. *See also* Hank
Pokémon, 111, 225
politics, 45, 187, 189
Postman, Neil, 199
Pountain, Dick, 7, 8
practices, 15, 16, 91–2, 102, 127, 133, 150, 152; dispersed, 54, 55, 74, 116; evil, 179–80; focal, 24, 54–5, 56, 57, 60, 63, 65, 66, 72, 75, 84, 87, 116, 133; integrative, 54, 55; media-oriented, 55, 57, 63, 64, 80, 128–9, 130
practice theory, 52–5, 150, 190; practical consciousness, 9, 74, 150–1; *See also* MacIntyre's theory of practice
Putnam, Robert, 127–30

Quail, Christine, 10, 11–12
Quinn, Zoë, 176

race, 36, 47, 124, 177, 184. *See also* diversity; identity; whiteness
Radloff, Toby, 14
Reagle, Joseph, 185, 190
real utopias, 27–8, 85–6, 170–1, 172, 179–80
referencing. *See* intertextuality
regime of value, 80, 85
Reginster, Bernard, 178–9
religion, 45, 58, 62, 103, 233n1
ressentiment, 177, 178–9, 180, 190, 192, 234ch8n3, 235n4
retailers, 19–20, 132, 135, 137, 146, 188; conflicts of interest, 134, 140; relationships with customers, 136, 147
revenge of the nerds. *See* triumphal narrative

Revenge of the Nerds (film), 4, 11–12, 14, 45, 179

"The Revenge of the Nerds" (Hoppenstand), 13

Robbins, Alexandra, 11, 37, 231n2

Robins, David, 7, 8

Roddenberry, Gene. *See Star Trek*

Rosenberg, Alyssa, 184–5

Rowling, J.K. *See Harry Potter*

Rüling, Charles-Clemens, 49

Sacks, Harvey, 24, 36–7, 38, 46, 87, 231ch1n2. *See also* membership categorization analysis

Safire, William, 6

Saler, Michael, 81, 187

Salkowitz, Rob, 50

San Diego Comic-Con, 49, 50, 124–5, 192

Sandel, Michael, 114–15

Sanders, Joe, 167, 231n3

Sandvoss, Cornell, 18, 66

Sarkeesian, Anita, 176, 198

Saturday Night Live, 49, 201

Sayer, Andrew, 31, 65, 134

scenes, 98, 149, 200; in popular music studies, 19; geek culture scene, 15, 19, 66, 99, 109, 138, 190

Schatzki, Theodore, 52–3, 54, 72. *See also* practice theory

scholastic disposition, 81–2, 107, 131, 154, 181–2, 183, 187, 207, 235n7; geek infographics, 29–31; reason as normative frame, 84–5, 177; *See also* Bourdieu; emotion; play; school

school, 8–9, 10, 52, 82–4, 106, 109, 140, 172, 188–9, 215, 222, 224; bullying, 11, 123, 172, 198; peer cultures, 11, 37, 84, 105, 136; shootings (*see* mass shootings)

science fiction and fantasy (SF&F), 9, 26, 31–2, 64, 71, 81, 84, 86, 90, 92–3, 96–7, 106, 110, 131, 159, 163, 167–8, 170, 185, 191, 194, 195, 198, 203, 213, 217, 218, 220, 221, 222, 227, 228–9, 233ch5n1; fan culture, 15, 16, 48, 61, 64, 98, 100, 101, 112, 116, 131, 153, 167, 181, 184, 201, 231n3; in film and television, 3, 11, 16, 21, 97, 126, 218, 219, 227, 228–9; and futurity, 198, 219–20; and gender, 220; Science Fiction Writers of America, 176. *See also* individual titles

Scott (manager, Eastside Games & Comics), 21, 70, 134, 136, 143, 153–4, 185–6, 213–15

Scott, Suzanne, 175, 176, 184–5, 194

Screens & Sorcery (fan club), 19, 21, 34, 73, 127, 133, 142, 146, 149, 201, 203–4. *See also* Logan

Sean (owner, Downtown Comics & Collectibles), 21, 84–5, 136, 140, 141–2, 146, 215–16, 223, 232ch3n3

sexuality, 20, 35, 226. *See also* diversity; identity

SF&F Con (convention), 73, 103, 112, 217, 218

Shank, Barry, 66, 139, 149, 200

Shatner, William, 49, 201. *See also* *Star Trek*

Shiera (research participant), 23, 33, 35, 41, 42, 43, 71, 83–4, 96, 99, 103, 105, 110, 111, 113, 114, 116, 117–18, 119, 122, 154, 157–8, 162–3, 164, 165, 170, 177, 182, 201, 223–5

Shirky, Clay, 197, 198

Shoemaker, Pamela, 144

Silverstone, Roger, 62–3

Simmel, Georg, 14

situated learning, 89–90, 104
Smith, Russell, 12, 196
social action, 18, 24, 47, 56, 64–5, 66
social awkwardness, 43, 73, 106, 120, 136, 140, 163, 191
social types, 3–4, 10, 11, 14–15, 18, 46, 200
Society for Creative Anachronism (SCA), 19, 23, 93, 96, 97, 100, 103, 112–13, 117, 119, 154, 160, 163, 167, 217, 218–19, 223, 225, 228, 233ch4n4, 233ch5n5
Solo (research participant), 23, 32, 39, 40, 70–1, 83, 91, 92, 94, 96, 102, 109–10, 111–12, 113–15, 121–2, 124, 155, 158, 160–1, 164, 170, 183, 201, 226–7, 228
Stanfill, Mel, 10, 12, 176
Star Trek, 18, 21, 29, 43, 49, 81, 86, 95, 98, 99, 126, 147, 161, 180, 182, 187, 193, 194, 198, 201, 203, 219
Star Wars, 4, 43, 50, 70, 73, 81, 106, 110, 122, 147, 165, 180, 182, 190, 199, 224, 226, 227, 228; 501st Legion, 73; expanded universe, 70, 122; The Force Awakens (2015), 174–5; Rogue One: A Star Wars Story (2016), 174; Star Wars Galaxies (MMORPG), 23, 96, 110, 111, 116, 117–18, 119, 224–5
Stebbins, Robert. See leisure, serious
Stevens, J. Richard, 235n5
stigma, 13, 99, 121–3, 192–3. See also geek culture, mainstreaming of
stranger-relationality, 73
strategic foresight, 198
Straw, Will, 19, 66, 200
subcultures, 15, 36, 47, 189–90, 196, 233ch4n3, 235n4; and aging, 20, 104, 124, 168, 170; Birmingham

School subculture theory, 12, 36, 121, 139, 177; casual-hardcore distinction, 99, 140, 159, 167, 213; geek culture as subculture, 37, 190; incorporation, 12, 121, 123, 177. See also capital, subcultural; community; subcultural infrastructures
subcultural infrastructures, 98, 132, 138, 149, 150–1; commodities and markets, 132–4, 140 (see also equipment-goods); communication and networks, 132, 137–9 (see also digital communication); interaction and venues, 132, 135–7. See also cultural intermediaries; institutions (under MacIntyre's theory of practices)
Suler, John, 187–8
superstandard English, 8
Sykes, Charles J., 12, 173
symbolic boundaries, 22, 38–40, 40–1, 44, 45, 112, 125, 189–90, 196; enthusiasm, 42–3, 84, 99, 104, 136; etiquette, 44, 183; interestingness, 41, 42, 44, 218–19 (see also trivia); taste, 31–2, 41–2, 71–2, 75, 79–80, 92, 93, 96, 109, 123, 145–6, 147–8, 164. See also boundary work

taste. See taste distinctions (under Bourdieu); taste (under symbolic boundaries)
taste cultures, 87, 122
television, 16, 18, 23, 55, 70, 95, 115, 156, 160–1, 194, 219, 227
Thornton, Sarah, 66, 68, 108, 189–90. See also capital, subcultural; subcultures
Tolkien, J.R.R., 11, 13, 92, 93, 97, 119, 163, 217, 218

Tönnies, Ferdinand, 60, 233ch5n2
trading card games. *See* collectible card games
trading cards, 144, 211, 216, 231n5
triumphal narrative, 10–14, 15, 22, 27, 37, 121, 125, 173, 177, 189, 194–5, 200, 231n5. *See also* geek culture, mainstreaming of
trivia, 69–71, 191, 196, 199. *See also* capital; scholastic disposition
t-shirts, 73, 110, 149, 194, 212, 213, 216, 236
Twilight, 50, 124
Turkle, Sherry, 4, 14
Twitter, 173, 175, 189

value, valuation, 67–8, 80, 85, 132, 178–9, 181

Wanzo, Rebecca, 17, 176
Warde, Alan, 55
Warhammer (miniatures game), 23, 39, 86, 99, 155, 162, 166, 222–3, 229
Warmachine (miniatures game), 77, 187
Warner, Michael, 63, 73
Warren (owner, King St Comics), 21, 71, 76, 136, 139, 142, 145, 148, 163, 164, 212–13
Weber, Max, 18, 233ch5n4
webcomics, 98
Wedge (research participant), 23, 33, 34, 41, 82–3, 84, 96–7, 109, 110–11, 116, 117, 120, 158, 159, 161, 162, 164–5, 166, 167, 169–70, 201, 228–9
Wenger, Etienne. *See* communities of practice (under community; situated learning)
Westernesse (fan club), 93, 119, 163, 217. *See also* Tolkien, J.R.R.
Westside Board Games (game store), 20, 21, 136–7, 184, 209–10. *See also* John
whiteness, 8, 20, 224, 234ch8n1; and cultural appropriation, 7–8, 9–10. *See also* race
Widdicombe, Sue, 36, 38, 39, 68, 233ch4n3
Williams, Raymond, 14, 96, 108
Willis, Paul, 11, 16, 108
Wittgenstein, Ludwig, 46, 53, 72, 188
Wizards of the Coast. *See Dungeons & Dragons*; *Magic: The Gathering*; *Pokémon*
Wolf, Mark J.P., 131
Wollheim, Donald A., 61, 131
Wooffitt, Robin, 36, 38, 39, 68, 233ch4n3
World of Warcraft (MMORPG), 23, 46, 96, 101–2, 155–6, 164, 166, 168, 219, 220, 221, 226
world-building, 131, 182; and ironic imagination, 81, 187
WoW. See *World of Warcraft*
Wright, Erik Olin. *See* real utopias

xkcd, 6, 7 (figure), 30

Yiannopolous, Milo, 178, 234ch8n2. *See also* alt-right
Young, Jock, 235n4

zoning, 164–5